101 Ethical Dilemmas

Second Edition

Reviews of the first edition

'a chatty, jokey journey through philosophical dilemmas, ancient and modern ... but the philosophy is the real thing.' **New Scientist**

'... Cohen does a good job in weaving some intriguing stories and classic philosophical ideas.' **Times Higher Education Supplement**

'The logical positivists might have called ethics gobbledegook, but it's well and truly on the menu here in 101 courses.' **The Age**

'always thought-provoking, funny and iconoclastic about the whole business of doing philosophy ... the most perfect toilet reading I know.' **http://www.fish.co.uk/**

'[A] hugely entertaining gallop through philosophy's thorniest questions. Saving philosophy from dry abstractions Cohen's enlightening, irreverent style dismisses any set rules. Instead he balances the arguments and highlights the flaws of ancient and modern philosophers ...The debates are real enough to create passion and provoke thought ...The book starts with the warning that it is not a guidebook for ethical living. What it does do is plant hundreds of more ethical questions in your mind, fulfilling its role as a light-hearted, lively introduction to the subject of ethical philosophy. It may not make you a better person or resolve all your problems, but it's a great work out for your brain!' **The Big Issue/ Red Pepper**

'This book is great fun. Many of the dilemmas are obviously profound, others appear to be entertaining, trivial diversions, but because they are all short and easily digestible the temptation is to read the whole of the first part quickly and without regard for the fact that each one captures a real and difficult ethical dilemma worth mulling over. The best way to use the book is to take the dilemmas slowly, one by one (or at most, group by group) and to try to resolve them for yourself. Cohen tells us that the discussion section can be read or left alone according to our discretion, but reading it should reveal why the seemingly trivial "little things" are, in Sherlock Holmes' words, "infinitely the most important".' **Larry Brown, Amazon, UK**

101 Ethical Dilemmas

Second edition

MARTIN COHEN

LONDON AND NEW YORK

First published 2003
by Routledge
2 Park Square, Milton Park, Abingdon, Oxon OX14 4RN

Simultaneously published in the USA and Canada
by Routledge
711 Third Avenue, New York, NY 10017

Second edition published 2007

Routledge is an imprint of the Taylor & Francis Group, an informa business

© 2003, 2007 Martin Cohen

Typeset in Helvetica Light by
Taylor & Francis Books Ltd

British Library Cataloguing in Publication Data
A catalogue record for this book is available from the British Library

Library of Congress Cataloging in Publication Data
A catalog record for this book has been requested

ISBN10: 0-415-40399-5 (hbk)
ISBN10: 0-415-40400-2 (pbk)
ISBN10: 0-203-96317-2 (ebk)

ISBN13: 978-0-415-40399-3 (hbk)
ISBN13: 978-0-415-40400-6 (pbk)
ISBN13: 978-0-203-96317-3 (ebk)

To Tessa too

'It isn't that they can't see the solution. It is that they can't see the problem.'

G. K. Chesterton, *Scandal of Father Brown*

Contents

Anti-social dilemmas

A dose of medical ethics

The censor's dilemma

Business week: dilemmas from business ethics . . .

And another dilemma for business ethics (with the emphasis on ethics)

A pentad of moral stories: searching for divine justice

Some monkey business

Searching for the good life

Three more trolley dilemmas (that no one really cares about anyway)

Watching brief

Animals too: the vegetarian's dilemma

Ethically suspect fairy tales

Stories of Relatavia

War ethics

Environmental ethics

Money matters

Legal dilemmas

Island ethics

Some really rather implausible ethical dilemmas that could only happen in the movies . . .

Nearly at the ends if not the means

Discussions 180

Forward!

Ethics is about choices which matter, and choices which matter are dilemmas. The Greek word means 'two horns'. *The horns of the dilemma* – only two choices: is or is not, to be or not to be, true or false. Or, indeed, only one choice, to find the way between the horns of the dilemma. That is nearer to the original sense of the term.

Now one hundred *and one* certainly seems like a lot of ethical dilemmas. Enough to cover the main issues you would have thought. And there are a lot of issues covered here. But ethics is a deep well, and once you start to lower the bucket, there comes no obvious jolt to tell you that at last it has reached the bottom. Instead, we find we are plumbing the depths of the human psyche, and no, it is not a pretty sight. In fact, if each dilemma were a bucketful of water, and we took our 101 Dilemmas and sprinkled them over the Sahara, we would have the same sort of impact on that environmentally challenged landscape as this book can be expected to have in tackling the myriad issues of our ethically challenged world.

What of the old question of the fundamental nature of human beings – whether we are basically good, or basically evil? *Not known.* When is the beginning of life, when the end? *Maybe.* Depends. Are there any ethical absolutes? We'd like to think so. Well, does the bucket at least dredge up the key issues? In fact, no. It does not even provide proper questions. Because, at the end of it, despite the 'epic' quality of the survey, whole swathes of ethical life have not been dealt with at all.

Put that way, it could be rather depressing. But that is not the point and not the way to put it. For the aim of ethics, much less a book, like this, is not to be a rule book, or even an uplifting sermon. Rather the aim of ethics is to improve our navigational skills, to help us find what the ancient Chinese called the '*Tao*', but we would call 'the way'. It is no coincidence that Plato's most detailed description of the nature of 'justice' describes the person who has discovered the answer as like a traveller who knows the path to their destination, as opposed to those, like the rest of us, who are strangers in an unknown land, reliant on the odd landmark and half-understood instruction.

But if ethics is a journey, it is not one where it is enough for the individual to find their private destination alone, even if many have set off with that delusion in mind.

The Ancient philosophers realised a quite different approach was necessary. Ethics for them was the study of how to organise the world to make it most harmonious, seeing it as an organism, how to ensure its 'correct ordering' – its health and well-being. It was in this sense an entirely practical study, indeed a political study, and the various philosophical variants that have been conjured up since are merely misnamed, because misunderstood. Ethics was centred on the search for justice – *dikaiosyne* in the Greek – justice in a moral rather than a legal sense, closely linked to the idea of wisdom.

Marxists ought to like all that, yet Marx and Engels dismissed ethics as the myth making of the superstructure, the lies of the bourgeoisie. They exclaimed in disgust: 'Philosophers have just interpreted the world – the point is to change it!' And we find echoes of this contempt all the time today, from right as much as left. But Marx was wrong about this, as in other things. Ethics is not just an effect in the world. Ethics is a fundamental cause.

Not that they were the first or only ones to complain. Socrates ridiculed the efforts of the 'ethical' experts of his time. Thomas Hobbes said, in the seventeenth century, that there was no 'nonsense so absurd' that one or other of the great philosophers had not steadfastly maintained it. In the early decades of the twentieth century the logical positivists ruled the whole notion of ethics 'inadmissible'. Indeed, such an effective hatchet job have philosophers done to their own subject one way or another, that nowadays ethics is generally considered an obstacle to serious attempts at making private and public policy.

Of course there are many other sources of policy insight apart from the dubious guide of philosophy. There is religion – not to mention divination, which is in fact the oldest form of ethics. (The *I Ching* is the world's oldest guide to 'the virtuous life'.) There are the infinite frozen ethical worlds of narrative, there is the quasi-scientific analysis of the social construction of values, there are even the materialistic techniques favoured by economics as the supreme arbiters of right and wrong. *But none of these can delve as deeply as philosophy can.*

And if too many philosophers have tried to take the politics out of ethics, they still belong together, two sides of the same coin. As Aristotle put it: 'the science that studies the supreme Good for man is politics'. If some find 'this study', in Susan George's phrase, 'unduly controversial, tendentious and partisan', the only response is, as she put it, *I should certainly hope so.* For ethics is not about platitudes, let alone tautologies, logic or mathematics, but about difficult choices – dilemmas. There are already plenty of people who will take a firm stand on the need to be completely impartial between right and wrong. Many are ready to turn ethics into a purely technical analysis of concepts, even attempting to create a new 'layer' of ethical issues, of so-called meta-ethics. But how can they create an 'after ethics' when they cannot offer an ethics first? The abstraction of questions of 'right and wrong' from the world is in any case a futile exercise. There are real dilemmas out there, and real decisions to be taken.

How real? What sort of decisions? Big ones or little ones? But the big ones are often made up of little ones. 'It has long been an axiom of mine that the little things are infinitely the most important' remarked Sherlock Holmes, in the *Case of Identity*. Certainly, the man who loaded the atomic bomb into *Enola Gay* in August 1945 was taking a little decision, following on from a long series of little decisions, which killed hundreds of thousands of innocent people later that day. Yet that was a little decision, with no clear 'right or wrong' about it. (Every day he loaded things into planes!) Too often ethics misses the real questions completely.

Let's pause a moment and look at that great issue again. Perhaps the greatest single decision ever taken – whether to drop the atom bomb – or not? Whether to drop it on a city of men, women and children? On big children, middling children and little ones too? Old people and handicapped people and sick people? The lot? Or not.

In the spring of 1945 the US Air Force had almost a free run at all the Japanese cities, sprinkling incendiary bombs of napalm in their thousands into seas of fire that swept through the wooden houses of Tokyo and a score of lesser cities. The Japanese were a cruel and merciless foe, and had shown no concern or pity for their many victims – civilian more often than military – whom they treated, mark this, *as animals*. As Minoru Matsui's film *Japanese Devils* (2002) records, using the voices of Japanese soldiers themselves, the troops massacred men, women, children, and, yes, babies. But now it almost seemed the victors of the Second World War were reaping the morals of the vanquished.

So with the Japanese people themselves at their feet, now was the time for the victors to show their superior values, their mercy, and their humanity. An early kind of military ethics committee, chaired by the Secretary of Defence, met to consider instead the use of the new atom bomb. The nameless members of the committee had in front of them a report of the scientists on the Manhattan Project, who warned against using the weapon lest the USA thereby open a Pandora's box it would never be able to close. The committee (unlike the American public) knew that Japan was militarily defeated and, far from digging in for last-ditch resistance to the last kamikaze,[1] was already seeking surrender terms. *And they recommended that the bomb be dropped.*

Not just anywhere, of course. *That* would be unethical. But not wasted on a mountain either, say. Better, they decided, ' . . . on a vital war plant employing a large number of workers and closely surrounded by workers' houses'.

That was their decision. Ralph Bards, an under-secretary to the US Navy, was to resign in protest. He thought they should at least warn the Japanese of the catastrophic power of the new weapon. On 17 July 1945, the day after a successful test of the bomb in the deserts of New Mexico, the decision of the atom scientists was to petition the President against using it. (Maybe Truman never saw their letter – it went first to their military intermediaries. More decisions there . . .) In due course, as part of the Potsdam Declaration, the USA and Great Britain gave a grand warning that Japan faced 'prompt and utter destruction' if it did not surrender 'unconditionally' – a windy-sounding ultimatum that was refused.

And on 6 August 1945, at the peak of the morning rush hour, approximately 600 metres above the Shima Hospital at the centre of Japan's fifth city, the first atom bomb exploded. Within sixty seconds a giant fireball had destroyed 100,000 people.

President Truman announced that the new bomb had been dropped on 'an important military base' chosen in order to avoid civilian deaths. A month later, with Japan now under Allied occupation, a smuggled report gave a different picture.

> patients just wasted away and died. Then people . . . not even here when the bomb exploded, fell sick and died. For no apparent reason their health began to fail. They lost their appetite, head hair began to fall out, bluish spots

---

[1] The official US Strategic Bombing Survey of July 1946 confirms that 'Japan would have surrendered even if atomic bombs had not been dropped' – see for example, Robert Lifton, *Hiroshima in America: Fifty Years of Denial* (New York, 1995). This and other facts are from Sven Lindqvist's appalling account *A History of Bombing* (Granta, 2001). The reader can find footnotes and sources like this for the dilemmas in the Notes and Cuttings section at the end of the book.

appeared on their bodies, and bleeding started from the nose, mouth and eyes. We started giving vitamin injections, but the flesh rotted away from the puncture caused by the needle. But in every case the patient dies.

The USA issued its own reports though. A government reporter wrote of having watched the bomb being 'fashioned into a living thing so exquisitely shaped that any sculptor would be proud to have created it': one with a strange power that made him feel himself somehow to be 'in the presence of the supernatural'. A general assured Congress that a team of scientists had found no traces whatsoever of radiation in Hiroshima and that, in any case, radiation poisoning was 'a very pleasant way to die'. Facts are often contested. No one should let facts drag values along behind them. Yet values too seem to be elusive at the most critical times, hard to identify and equally difficult to agree on.

So instead consider the story about a famous American golfer, Bobby Jones, who found himself facing a dilemma. He was being hailed as the winner of a tournament even though he had accidentally knocked his ball at one hole while lining it up, a small detail which no one else had noticed. *But he knew.* He insisted on adding another two strokes to his total, making himself lose instead. In handing him second prize, the tournament officials praised him for his ethical stance. But his reply? 'Nonsense! You may as well praise someone for not robbing a bank!'

Forward!

Did Bobby make the right choice? Yes – huzzah! But no, his point was that it makes no sense to praise people for not doing the wrong thing. Most people, most of the time, are doing the right thing, for the right reasons, and just quietly get on with it. In that sense, it is a shame that ethics often concentrates on 'doing the wrong thing' – why people do it, what it is, whether it exists really. It is a consequence of a focus on 'ethical reasoning' at the expense of practical ethics, real ethics, ethics in action. Which involves all sorts of skills: listening, responding, empathising, compromising.

The ethics of rigid rule following, on the other hand, so much favoured by philosophers over the centuries, is not so much a recipe for human flourishing, as a recipe for bigotry, intolerance and suffering. 'The infliction of cruelty with a good conscience is a delight to moralists', Bertrand Russell once wrote. And so, if this book does not offer the reader any firm rules to follow, or deal authoritatively on a 'case by case' basis with problems, finishing with an impressive and lofty sounding summary, they will, I hope be grateful for that.

How to use this book

Philosophy is an activity. It might even be thought of as a kind of thought experiment. (And there's an example of one itself, a sort of logical loop or paradox straight away.) So the dilemmas posed here should not be accepted passively, far less the discussions. It would be possible by simply rote-learning these to obtain a solid grounding in philosophical techniques, and a good base in philosophical and ethical facts – but not to philosophise. For that you will need to read the book critically, questioning the assumptions, disputing the arguments. That is the mark of a philosopher. But it is also that of the sophist and the pedant (those who like to baffle people with fancy language, or nit-pick over trivia). So some words of caution are perhaps advisable here.

1   Resist any temptation to read the whole book in some kind of strange ethical intuitionist frenzy. Take the dilemmas instead at a more leisurely pace, one by one, or at most group by group.
2   Never try to break the issues down into their 'logical' form, as a friend of mine tried to do. He went quite mad of course, and is now reduced to teaching 'corporate governance', poor fellow.
3   Finally, don't overuse the problems with students, children or your dog, far less throw the entire book to them as tiresome exercises. For philosophy is better approached with an eager mind than with a tired and unwilling one.

101 Ethical Dilemmas is a mixture of true stories and made-up ones, a mixture of philosophical theory and philosophical musings. It is not a book of logical puzzles with solutions at the back – because that is not what ethics is about. It is really 101 ideas, or thought experiments even. Each can be read on its own – and thought about. So, to make sense of this book, take it slowly, and don't hesitate to ignore completely the discussions at the back. They are there not as solutions, though they inevitably may also appear to serve that purpose, but as a contribution to a dialogue, in which the reader is the other voice. So if there is a 'political' or factual claim that 'they cannot accept' (perhaps sneaked in as parenthetical asides), the reader need not throw the book at the cat in disgust about it. After all, that would be unethical, and anyway, there is nothing more useless, or more self-defeating than for ethics to descend into a sanctimonious exchange of pleasantries that no one has any practical use for, and equally, no one uses in practice. Helping people may be good, and harming people may be bad, but saying 'good is good' and 'bad is bad', although a fine sounding thing, would not satisfy anyone outside philosophy, and must not satisfy us either. We must move beyond those kinds of 'analytic' truth to the real ground of ethical debate.

So the best way to use the book is to take the dilemmas as the first course, and the discussions as the desserts and accept the main activity, that of resolving the dilemmas, as one for yourself. For that is when the most important – and the most interesting – part begins.

Note on the philosophical pictures

In this edition, a new picture introducing each section has been added. Drawn especially to illustrate the philosophical texts by the French artist, Judit, each one provides proof that there are verily two parts to the brain, if not the mind, one to process images, one to process words, and the one that processes images is much more powerful. In this way, we add a new layer to the dilemmas.

Four dodgy dilemmas to get started with

Dilemma 1
The lifeboat

The battleship *Northern Spirit* was torpedoed in the engine room, and began to sink rapidly. 'Abandon Ship!' shouts Captain Flintheart. But few of the lifeboats are intact. One boat, desperately overloaded, manages to struggle away from the sinking vessel, Flintheart at the prow. The cold, grey waters of the Atlantic around it are filled with screaming, desperate voices, begging to be saved.

But faced with the grim knowledge of the danger of capsizing the little boat, endangering the lives of those already on board, *should any more sailors be picked up and rescued*?

Dilemma 2
Sinking further

Flintheart mutters unpronounceably under his breath (in Latin), and then, in a bark, orders 'no stopping'. Some of the others in the boat mutter too, in Anglo-Saxon – about 'bleedin' murder', 'pitiless bastards' and even about 'Captains wot oughter go down with their ships', but all are accustomed to obeying. Until that is, one of the sailors in the water struggles up to the side of the boat, revealing himself to be Tom, the young cabin boy, who manages to get two frozen hands onto the ship's gunnels (whatever they are), and with a last desperate, heroic effort begins to haul himself in, tipping the boat alarmingly as he does so.

'Knock him back in!' shouts Flintheart, from the rear of the boat, to Bert, the cook, who is nearest.

Should Bert obey?

Dilemma 3
The psychologists' tale

The psychologist Dr Philip Zimbardo of Stanford University, conducted an experiment (in 1971) which started by taking ordinary groups of volunteer college students (one an 'all female' group), and dividing them into two. One half was then 'depersonalised' – names were replaced by numbers, their clothes were concealed with laboratory smocks, and they had to wear hoods with eyeholes. They became the 'prisoners' for the experiment. They were housed in a specially mocked up prison. The other half was similarly depersonalised, but this time with laboratory coats and numbers. They became the 'guards'.

The guards were given control over their 'prisoners', control which they abused, secretly, they thought, late at night. They imposed strip searches in the small hours, and made up additional punishments for their prisoners, such as to clean toilet bowls with their hands. During the days, they shouted abuse at them, tripped them up for laughs as they went past: the jokers!

In fact, videotapes made exposed the fact that within six days their behaviour had become so sadistic and indeed violent that the experiment had to be hurriedly aborted. Zimbardo himself was compromised by the excesses of the student volunteers. 'These guys were all peaceniks', he later said apologetically, but 'they became like Nazis'.

It's an easy mistake to make, but *is the difference really so small*?

Dilemma 4
Custom is king

It was Herodotus who originally decided not only that 'custom is king', but also that custom should be king, respected over other considerations. Today, further anthropological research has uncovered a few more constants. We can draw up a sort of 'customary guide to living', to trump things like the UN Declaration of Human Rights.

After all, ethics is bound up with the network of rights and duties each member of the community owes to each other. What better way, then, than to distil from the long history of human society a few basic ethical tenets – and to start from these in our search for the good life?

The customary guide to human rights

1   We assert the fundamental right to torture and kill other people in all sorts of ingenious and cruel ways.
2   We assert the inalienable right to own slaves and declare now that some people are fit only to be slaves.
3   We claim the natural right to kill babies for any reason we care to think of.
4   And demand the right to kill the old and infirm and eat their bodies afterwards.

Of course, as declarations go, it's not very long yet – but it's certainly a step in the right direction. Or is it a step backwards?

And three personal dilemmas which maybe a business ethics course could help with . . . well, maybe

Dilemma 5
The internet bargain

You have bought a new computer from a particularly inefficient internet store, and when it arrives, you notice that the invoice says 'paid', although in fact you have not paid for it. You clicked the 'sending money by post' option instead, and then forgot to. Now do you:

Hope they don't notice, and keep mum . . . or ring up straight away to advise a cheque is being sent in the post?

Dilemma 6
The toaster

Sam's live-in partner has a taste in expensive nick-nacks – things like toasters which burn an icon of the day's weather on the toast, or solar-powered fountains for the garden pond. The toaster is in the cupboard as it always burnt the middle of the toast and under-did the rest, whilst the garden fountain clogged up after a day and sank to the bottom of the pond.

Unsolicited, a catalogue drops through the letterbox from a very fancy – and expensive – postal store, computer-addressed to the partner.

Should Sam quietly get rid of it before they can be misled – or give it to them when they get home and wait for the next disastrous mistake?

Dilemma 7
The liar

Poor Zjamel. Her boyfriend seems to spend more time with Ethel than with her these days. 'Are you two having an affair?' she asks him, more by way of a reminder that she exists, than out of any real concern.

But Bernard is having an affair with Ethel. On the other hand, he doesn't look on it as a 'serious' affair. Ethel is married, and he is basically quite committed to Zjamel, who has been through a rough patch recently. He doesn't want to upset her, even though he doesn't like lying either. Gritting his teeth then, and remembering Nietzsche's dictum that 'lying is a necessity of life', just part of the 'terrifying and problematic character of existence', he says: '*Of course* not, darling,' and gives her a big kiss.

Zjamel's heart picks up, and she feels much better. And anyway, in a few months Bernard and Ethel have got bored of the affair and no one ever thinks about the matter again.

Did Bernard do the right thing?

Three tricky trolley dilemmas (that need to be solved together)

Dilemma 8
The dodgy donor clinic

Doctor Dedicated of the Backstreet OrganShop has five patients with life-threatening disorders arising from various failing bodily organs. One needs a heart, another a stomach, another lungs, another something else. You get the picture. Because they all need organs, and there are tragically none available, at least not in time, the patients are all going to die unless . . . Dr Dedicated has another patient that he has just cured, and who is now dozing quietly in the recovery ward. One way, indeed, the only way the good doctor can save his five patients is to use the sixth patient as an emergency organ supply. (Of course, in doing this, the patient will die.)

Dr Dedicated is very troubled at the fate of the five patients, all of whom are very fine people, but worries that it might be 'inappropriate' to use another patient like this.

It's obviously a bargain at five for the price of one, but is it ethical?

Dilemma 9

The famous footbridge dilemma

On the way home, Fred always walks across a little footbridge over a railway line. And one day, as he looks over the parapet, he sees a runaway 'trolley', that is a small rail wagon, has somehow loosed its brake and begun to roll at alarming speed down the track. In just a few seconds it will pass under the bridge and crash into a group of railway workers who (owing to government privatisation policies – and is that ethical?) have been poorly trained and are eating their lunchtime sandwiches out of plastic boxes, and not keeping proper watch. In seconds the wagon will whoosh past under the bridge and plough into them!

Now, from where he is, Fred can easily see the signalman in the signal box, quietly oblivious to the drama as it unfolds. Fred realises that if he alerts the signalman to quickly change the points, the trolley will be diverted onto a different track just in time. Complicating factor is, Fred also sees, there is someone on the other track too. An old lady not paying attention to anything but collecting butterflies in a jar.

Should Fred tell the signalman to switch the runaway trolley onto the track where it will run over 'just the old lady' – or do nothing and watch the five picnicking railway workers die?

Dilemma 10
The human cannonball

Yes! Yes! Yes! Fred thinks it's a no-brainer. He shouts and gesticulates to the signalman in his box, but – rats! – the man, not surprisingly really, cannot understand him and does not do anything. Nor is there time to get to the box and move the signal himself. If only he had something large, like a big rock to drop onto the track! Then he could derail the trolley and save everybody. But there are of course no rocks. Only a large youth with a 'Walkman' sitting on the rail of the footbridge, coincidentally just over the centre of the track, and rolling a cigarette. Now, seeing Fred, the youth asks for a light, thus providing Fred with the perfect opportunity, should he wish to, to push the youth off the bridge and onto the track.

It's a terrifying and terrible dilemma for Fred.

But would he really be justified in pushing someone off the bridge and down onto the tracks, killing him – in order to save all the workmen?

The descent begins

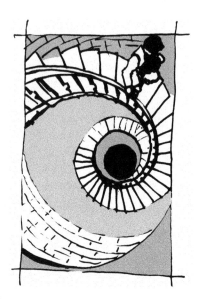

Dilemma 11

The first stage of cruelty

William Hogarth, *The First Stage of Cruelty* (1751)

© Archiv für Kunst und Geschichte, Berlin; photo: AKG London.

But what are the second, third and fourth stages?

'Animals are Just Machines' is the title of today's lecture . . .

Dr Descartes dons a white coat and proceeds to sharpen a large knife. A large African monkey (actually a chimpanzee) is on the table in front of him.

'I wish here to set forth the explanation of the movement of heart and arteries which, being the first and most general movement that is observed in animals, will give us the means of easily judging as to what we ought to think about all the rest. And so that there may be less difficulty in understanding what I shall say on this matter, *I should like that those not versed in anatomy should take the trouble . . . of having cut up before their eyes the heart of some large animal which has lungs (for it is in all respects sufficiently similar to the heart of a man)*, and cause that there be demonstrated to them the two chambers or cavities which are within it . . . '

So saying Dr Descartes plunges the knife into the beast which squeals horribly, before triumphantly pulling out the still beating heart.

'In order that those who do not know the force of mathematical demonstration [panting slightly] and are unaccustomed to distinguish true reasons from merely probable reasons, should not venture to deny what has been said without examination, I wish to acquaint them with the fact that this movement which I have just explained follows as necessarily from the very disposition of the organs, as can be seen by looking at the heart, and from *the heat which can be felt with the fingers* . . . '

Descartes passes the organ around the class now, ' . . . and from the nature of the blood of which we can learn by experience, as does that of a clock from the power, the situation, and the form, of its counterpoise and of its wheels'. Descartes, pausing only to wipe his hands on his coat-front, moves over to the blackboard, starts scribbling energetically on it and enters lecture mode.

'I had explained all these matters in some detail in the *Treatise* which I formerly intended to publish. And afterwards I had shown there, what must be the fabric of the nerves and muscles of the human body in order that *the animal spirits* therein contained should have the power to move the members, just as the heads of animals, a little while after decapitation . . . '

Descartes moves towards the monkey as though to demonstrate again, but then seems to change his mind.

' . . . are still observed to move and bite the earth, notwithstanding that they are no longer animate; what changes are necessary in the brain to cause wakefulness, sleep and dreams; how light, sounds, smells, tastes, heat and all other qualities pertaining to external objects are able to imprint on it various ideas by the intervention of the senses; how hunger, thirst and other internal affections can also convey their impressions upon it; what should be regarded as the "common sense" by which these ideas are received, and what is meant by the memory which retains them, by the fancy which can change them in diverse ways and out of them constitute new ideas, and which, by the same means, distributing *the animal spirits* through the muscles, can cause the members of such a body to move in as many diverse ways, and in a manner as suitable to the objects which present themselves to its senses and to its internal passions, as can happen in our own case . . . '

This is all good stuff, especially the idea of having a poke around the animal's heart to see how it breathes. But a student's hand is up:

Surely Dr Descartes, your arguments must apply just as much to people too?

Dilemma 12

Stage 2: free to do otherwise

Dr Descartes looks annoyed. 'If I might continue', he says caustically, ' . . . can cause the members of such a body to move in as many diverse ways, and in a manner as suitable to the objects which present themselves to its senses and to its internal passions, as can happen in our own case . . . *apart from the direction of our free will*'.

The class relaxes. They are all familiar with that elusive concept, 'free will', which nonetheless seems to be the bedrock of moralising. Descartes is now firmly on his preferred theme, scratching up on the board, under the title 'Man as Machine', an elaborate diagram of the circulatory system, puffing enthusiastically all the while like a not-yet-invented steam engine.

'And this will not seem strange to those, who, knowing how many different *automata* or moving machines can be made by the industry of man, without employing in so doing more than a very few parts in comparison with the great multitude of bones, muscles, nerves, arteries, veins, or other parts that are found in the body of each animal. From this aspect *the body is regarded as a machine* which, having been made by the hands of God, is incomparably better arranged, and possesses in itself movements which are much more admirable, than any of those which can be invented by man.'

Not that anyone dares to say, but if there really was no such thing as 'free will', *what then would be that difference between people and animals?*

Dilemma 13
Penultimate stage: the two tests

But Dr Descartes is only part way through his lecture. He has more tests to distinguish human from non-human than just that invisible concept of freedom. Jabbing at his notes on the board and wheezing intermittently, he continues:

'Here I specially stopped to show that if there had been such machines, possessing the organs and outward form of *a monkey or some other animal without reason*, we should not have had any means of ascertaining that they were not of the same nature as those animals. On the other hand, if there were machines [puff puff!] which bore a resemblance to our body and imitated our actions as far as it was morally possible to do so, we should always have two very certain tests by which to recognise that, for all that, they were *not real men*. The first is:

- that they could never use speech or other signs as we do when placing our thoughts on record for the benefit of others.

'For we can easily understand a machine's being constituted so that it can utter words, and even emit some responses to action on it of a corporeal kind, which brings about a change in its organs; for instance, if it is touched in a particular part it may ask what we wish to say to it; if in another part, it may exclaim that it is being hurt, and so on. But it never happens that it arranges its speech in various ways, in order to reply appropriately to everything that may be said in its presence, as even the lowest type of man can do. And the second difference is:

- that although machines can perform certain things as well as or perhaps better than any of us can do, they infallibly fall short in others, by which means we may discover that they did not act from knowledge, but only from the disposition of their organs.

'For while reason is a universal instrument which can serve for all contingencies, these organs have need of some special adaptation for every particular action. From this it follows that *it is morally impossible* that there should be sufficient diversity in any machine to allow it to act in all the events of life in the same way as our reason causes us to act.'

Dr Descartes surveys his earnest audience with satisfaction.

'By these two methods we may also recognise the difference that exists between men and brutes. For it is a very remarkable fact that there are none so depraved and stupid, without even excepting idiots, that they cannot arrange different words together, forming of them a statement by which they make known their thoughts; while, on the other hand, there is no other animal, however perfect and fortunately circumstanced it may be, which can do the same. *It is not the want of organs that brings this to pass, for it is evident that magpies and parrots are able to utter words just like ourselves, and yet they cannot speak as we do, that is, so as to give evidence that they think of what they say.'*

Descartes leans forward.

'On the other hand, men who, being born deaf and dumb, are in the same degree, or even more than the brutes, destitute of the organs which serve the others for talking, are in the habit of themselves investing certain signs by which they make themselves understood by those who, being usually in their company, have leisure to learn their language. *And this does not merely show that the brutes have less reason than men, but that they have none at all, since it is clear that very little is required in order to be able to talk.'*

'Any questions?' snaps Descartes. Silence. But still, some amongst the student brutes have doubts. They think that animals do communicate with each other. Descartes' second point about animals having specific adaptations and humans general skills, seems rather feeble too.

Is the gulf between humanity and the animal kingdom reduced to these dubious assumptions?

Dilemma 14
Final stage: the immortal member

Descartes has one more card up his sleeve – and it is his ace.

'And when we notice the inequality that exists between animals of the same species, as well as between men, and observe that some are more capable of receiving instruction than others, it is not credible that a monkey or a parrot, selected as the most perfect of its species, should not in these matters equal the stupidest child to be found, or at least a child whose mind is clouded, *unless in the case of the brute the soul were of an entirely different nature from ours . . .*'

Descartes returns to the blackboard, wipes it clean with an odd piece of fur, and then sums up.

'I had described after this the rational soul and shown that it could not be in any way derived from the power of matter, like the other things of which I had spoken, but that it must be expressly created. I showed, too, that it is not sufficient that it should be *lodged in the human body like a pilot in his ship*, unless perhaps for the moving of its members, but that it is necessary that it should also be joined and united more closely to the body in order to have sensations and appetites similar to our own, and thus to form a true man. In conclusion, I have here enlarged a little on the subject of the soul, because it is one of the greatest importance.

'For next to the error of those who deny God, which I think I have already sufficiently refuted, *there is none which is more effectual in leading feeble spirits from the straight path of virtue, than to imagine that the soul of the brute is of the same nature as our own*, and that in consequence, after this life we have nothing to fear or to hope for, any more than the flies and ants. As a matter of fact, when one comes to know how greatly they differ, we understand much better the reasons which go to prove that our soul is in its nature entirely independent of body, and in consequence *that it is not liable to die with it*. And then, inasmuch as we observe no other causes capable of destroying it, we are naturally inclined to judge that it is immortal.'

But whoa! Has Dr Descartes thrown away his advantage? Now the human is reduced once more to a machine, controlled by a soul which can exist quite happily independently.

In that case, *what possible objection can there be to killing people as freely as people kill animals?*

Some pretty ancient dilemmas

Dilemma 15
Gyges' ring

Gyges was a shepherd. A simple, decent fellow, he liked nothing better than to tend his flock in the service of the King of Lydia. Life was hard, but straightforward. Until, one day, there was a great rumble and the earth itself trembled in a powerful earthquake. When the terrifying noise stopped, and the dust cleared and Gyges had picked himself up, he found that a gaping chasm had opened before him. Just near where his flock a moment before had been so peacefully grazing. Indeed, after a quick count, he finds now one of the King's sheep is missing!

Peering fearfully over the edge of the chasm, he sees deep down below the missing lamb, plaintively bleating. Screwing up his courage, Gyges carefully descends into the earth but as he does so the terrified sheep runs further away into the newly opened underground passage. Gritting his teeth, Gyges follows and sees to his astonishment, in the half gloom, a massive shape, like a horse – apparently released by the earthquake from its subterranean prison. Forgetting his sheep now, and investigating further, Gyges discovers that it is indeed a horse, with long fleet limbs, but a horse made entirely of bronze whose eyes stare sightlessly through the gloom. And set into one side of the motionless steed, some doors. Prising one open, to his horror, a corpse of something falls out. Something that looks very like it was a man, only larger. And on its finger, an equally massive ring.

Terrified by now, but determined to seize something as a record of his discovery, he prises the ring off the man's finger, and half-scrambles, half-runs back to the surface. Even as he gets there, the earth begins to heave again and the chasm closes. Now Gyges regrets abandoning the sheep to the chasm, and worries about what to say to the King when he has to report with all the other shepherds on the well-being of the flocks.

When the day comes, he is still worrying and so waiting to see the King with the other shepherds, starts nervously playing with the ring, twisting the bezel. And then he notices a curious thing. On twisting it a particular way, he discovers that it appears no one in the room can see him – they begin to talk about him as if he had left them. Astonished, he tries to attract their attention, waving his arms, but it is in vain. It is as though, he realises, *he has become invisible*.

Emboldened by this new power of twisting the ring's bezel and becoming invisible, the shepherd who had arrived at the palace so humble and contrite, embarks instead on a spree of self-indulgence. He steals a banquet from the King's kitchens, and raids the Palace treasury for jewels. Growing bolder, he even sneaks into the royal bedchamber and seduces the Queen. He finds in her a willing ally, and the two conspire to overthrow the King, who had been so honest a master to a poor shepherd. The next day, using his cloak of invisibility, Gyges commits the final crime of murder to ensure himself of the ultimate reward and vanity – the throne itself.

Magic rings don't exist, which is a weakness even in a thought experiment like this. But if they did, would people continue be hard-working and honest, *or would they behave disgracefully like Gyges*?

Dilemma 16
The woeful tale of St Augustine

Augustine (AD 354–430) it was, who wrote so movingly over many thousands of pages, alternately apologising for and blaming himself, for stealing pears as a boy: *knowing* it was wicked and worst of all, as he solemnly recounts, *enjoying* it. Woe! We mortals have but limited time on earth, but here is some of Augustine's tale.

'I wish now to review in memory my past *wickedness* and the *carnal corruptions* of my soul. Not because I still love them, but that I may love thee, *O my God*. For love of thy love I do this, recalling in the bitterness of self-examination my wicked ways, that thou mayest grow sweet to me, thou sweetness without deception! Thou sweetness happy and assured!

'There was a pear tree close to our own vineyard, heavily laden with fruit, which was not tempting either for its colour or for its flavour. Late one night, having prolonged our games in the streets until then, as our bad habit was, a group of young scoundrels, and I among them, went to shake and rob this tree. We carried off a huge load of pears, not to eat ourselves, but to dump out to the hogs, after barely tasting some of them ourselves. Doing this pleased us all the more *because it was forbidden.*

'Such was my heart, O God, such was my heart – which thou didst pity *even in that bottomless pit*. Behold, now let my heart confess to thee what it was seeking there, when I was being gratuitously wanton, having no inducement to evil *but the evil itself*. It was foul, and I loved it. I loved my own undoing. I loved my error – not that for which I erred *but the error itself*. A depraved soul, falling away from security in thee to destruction in itself, seeking nothing from the shameful deed but shame itself!

'Those pears that we stole were fair to the sight because they were thy creation, O Beauty beyond compare, O Creator of all, O thou good God – God the highest good and my true good! Those pears were truly pleasant to the sight, but it was not for them that *my miserable soul lusted*, for I had an abundance of better pears. I stole those simply that I might steal, for, having stolen them, I threw them away. My sole gratification in them was my own sin, which I was pleased to enjoy; for, if any one of these pears entered my mouth, the only good flavour it had was my sin in eating it. And now, O Lord my God, I ask what it was in that theft of mine that caused me such delight?

'Who can unravel such a twisted and tangled knottiness? It is unclean. I hate to reflect upon it. I hate to look on it. But I do long for thee, O Righteousness and Innocence, so beautiful and comely to all virtuous eyes – *I long for thee* with an insatiable satiety. With thee is perfect rest, and life unchanging. He who enters into thee enters into the joy of his Lord, and shall have no fear and shall achieve excellence in the Excellent. I fell away from thee, O my God, and in my youth I wandered too far from thee, my true support. *And I became to myself a wasteland.*'

It's pretty grim stuff. But is Augustine right to say he knowingly chose evil – *when he plucked the forbidden fruit*?

Dilemma 17
A balanced tale for the Yellow Emperor

When the Yellow Emperor, Shih Huang Ti, asked his Chief Minister, the very learned Qi Bo, why it was that people 'nowadays' (that was in 2700 BC) did not live as long as they used to, and what could be done about it? The venerable grey beard replied that it was because in the past, people practised the *Tao*, which is the way of life. They appreciated the principle of balance in all things, of the flow of *yin* and *yang*, of the ceaseless, eternal transformation of the energies of the universe.

But 'these days', Qi Bo, advised the Yellow Emperor, in one of the earliest pieces of medical advice recorded, 'people have changed their way of life. They drink wine as though it were water, indulge in destructive activities, drain their *jing* [the body's essence, centred on the kidneys] and deplete their *qi* [life energy]. They do not know the secret of conserving their *qi* or their vitality. Seeking emotional excitement and monetary pleasures, people disregard the natural rhythm and order of the universe. They fail to regulate their lifestyle and diet, and sleep improperly. So it is not surprising that instead of living well for over 100 years they look old at fifty and die soon after.'

Should the Yellow Emperor swallow the advice?

Dilemma 18

The ascetic tale of Chrysippus the Stoic

Some say 'pleasure' is good. But this is a nonsense. *Pleasure is not good.*

For if they want to maintain that it is, then they must also say that there are disgraceful pleasures, and forget that nothing disgraceful can be good.

Can it?

Dilemma 19
The sensible tale of Epicurus

'The beginning and the root of all good is the pleasure of the stomach; even wisdom and culture must be referred to this. . . . Beauty and virtue and the like are to be honoured, if they give pleasure; but if they do not give pleasure, we must bid them farewell.

'Me? I spit upon the beautiful and those who vainly admire it, when it does not produce any pleasure.'

After all, the only constant thing in life is the pursuit of constant pleasure. And the only way to ensure that your supply of pleasure is constant, is to achieve that underrated state of mind congenitally known as satisfaction. Stimulation can be fun, but it is rather transitory. Whereas satisfaction can be stretched out long-term.

'Hey! Send me a pot of cheese, so that I may have a feast when I care to.'

Ain't that right?

Dilemma 20
Magnanimous Man

'Our reading today' (the Vicar intones, his voice slow and serious) 'is from Book IV, passages 1,120–35.

'"Now the man is thought to be proud who thinks himself worthy of great things, being worthy of them; for he who does so beyond his deserts is a fool, but no virtuous man is foolish or silly. The proud man, then, is the man we have described. For he who is worthy of little and thinks himself worthy of little is temperate, but not proud; for pride implies greatness, as beauty implies a good-sized body, and little people may be neat and well-proportioned but cannot be beautiful . . .

'" . . . it is hard to be truly proud; for it is impossible without nobility and goodness of character. It is chiefly with honours and dishonours, then, that the proud man is concerned; and at honours that are great and conferred by good men he will be moderately pleased, thinking that he is coming by his own or even less than his own; for there can be no honour that is worthy of perfect virtue, yet he will at any rate accept it since they have nothing greater to bestow on him; but honour from casual people and on trifling grounds he will utterly despise, since it is not this that he deserves . . . "'

Now just where is that reading from? It doesn't sound very 'virtuous' to me.

Dilemma 21
The Magnanimous Man in heaven

Up above the clouds on the slopes of Mount Olympia, where the Greek Gods and some of the philosophers too now live, the story goes that, one day, little Immanuel Kant was walking along the lakeside with his handsome friend, Aristotle, and (let us say) the swaggering Jean-Jacques Rousseau. Aristotle will be enjoying all the plants and animals, and speculating on their origins, purposes and 'causes'. Rousseau will be running hither and thither sniffing all the flowers and recalling scornfully the words of Socrates loftily maintaining that there is nothing in nature to learn from. It is a pleasant scene. Until, suddenly, amongst all this harmless philosophical banter, comes a terrified scream. 'Zeus, Zeus!' comes the fearful sound.

Rousseau points a flabby white finger excitedly at a small figure swirling helplessly round and round in some hidden current. 'Look, look! A slave boy in a whirlpool in the lake – how terrible!' Then adds in shocked tones, 'But, my friends, they do say the waters there run very fast and deep!' It is clear he has no intention of finding out the truth of the matter.

But Kant has already plunged in to the water, and is swimming ineffectually towards the slave boy. The current is strong, and Kant's black gown becomes waterlogged and extremely heavy. After a few yards, caught up in deceptive currents and eddies, Kant himself is in trouble, sinking under the surface of the water with a despairing wave to his philosophical colleagues, now in earnest debate over the best course of action.

Aristotle is nodding wisely. In a deep resonant voice he replies to his agitated friend, 'Yes, little man, you are right. It looks as though our companion is finding out for himself why no one swims in that stretch of water!' But he strides determinedly towards an old rotten tree and with a swift powerful motion breaks one of the largest branches clean off. 'What are you doing?' cries Rousseau, torn between watching the desperate struggles of Kant and the boy, still whirling round and round screaming all the time, and the actions of the great philosopher. Aristotle ignores him, but returns to the bank with the branch and in best Olympian fashion hurls it into the water just by Kant who grabs it, and then paddles over towards the slave boy.

In a few moments the two are safe, back on the bank and congratulating Aristotle both on his action and his presence of mind. 'I not only have the strength of an Atlas', explains Aristotle, laughing hugely at his own cleverness, 'but my throwing accuracy, as you see, is second only to Titan!' But he, in turn, magnanimously congratulates Kant for his good intentions, whilst chastising him for letting his irrational side overrule his normal good sense. 'Yes, you are right, my young friend', says a bedraggled Kant, much chastened and abandoning one of his fundamental philosophical tenets: 'Good intentions are not enough'.

No one says anything to Rousseau, who busies himself with wrapping clothes around the slave boy to hide his embarrassment at his own lack of moral fibre and (as Aristotle guffaws later over a huge dinner) his 'feminine courage'.

Who is the hero?

Anti-social dilemmas

Dilemma 22
Against e-Ville

Lawrence and Lina hated the e-Ville Corporation in all its many commercial forms: e-Ville Food, e-Ville Wood and, of course, e-Ville Cars. In fact, they hated them so much that they had joined a shadowy organisation called STUMP, whose aim was to organise resistance to big business in general and e-Ville Corps in particular.

As part of a special training weekend for the STUMP activists, they learnt about the enemy: e-Ville Corps. was *huge*. The name stood for the original de Ville family, with the 'e' a recent addition to make the business sound more 'internet ready'. (STUMP itself, stood for something, but no one seemed sure what. Stop Transnationals Uprooting something or other, was Lawrence's impression; Save Trees, Unite against Market Power, was Lina's best guess.) Anyway, operating out of the USA as it did (other than for tax purposes, when it was based on a remote Pacific island), e-Ville had a world turnover greater than any country in Africa or South America, with the exception of Brazil and South Africa, although it was rapidly overtaking the latter. It had many different tentacles. One of its world beating brands was *RealWood*, which marketed its top-end products as 'genuine rainforest' with the seductive slogan – 'buy today, it might not be there tomorrow!' Its construction arm, e-Ville Dam-Roads was involved in a number of really massive projects involving large-scale 'managed ecological changes', as e-Ville put it in its brochures – re-routing whole rivers, bisecting vast undisturbed forests with the latest in tarmac technology. Then there was *GMFood*, its food products store, whose packets generally carried a splashline promising they were 'the very latest in scientifically improved food'; and whose megamarkets included, most controversially of all for Lawrence, a range of 'rare and exotic bushmeats' including monkeys, kangaroos, tiger paws and (occasionally) koala bears. Its jokey 'tuna friendly' tins of dolphin offended some too.

An earnest youth with a straggly beard explained at the activists' weekend that the Third World subsidiaries of e-Ville were also involved in a number of child 'workplace training' schemes, where adults with debts signed agreements committing their offspring to unpaid labour in e-Ville's factories until the debt was paid off. All of this was public knowledge, Lawrence found out – but no one seemed to mind. It was STUMP's job to change that through its campaigns of non-violent civil disobedience.

First of all, STUMP organised a mass 'world justice' march to coincide with a meeting of the e-Ville shareholders in New York. Lina and others dressed up as flowers to symbolise the loss of habitats and species involved in various e-Ville projects, thinking especially of the *GMFood* ones. It was a massive success, in marching terms, and the New York Police Department even congratulated the organisers for managing to do it with so little disruption. But the leaders of STUMP were disappointed at the newspaper coverage, which consisted not of photos of their long march, or even of the flower parades' sit-down protest opposite e-Ville Towers, but a paragraph in which e-Ville announced loftily that the protesters were 'politically motivated' and would not be allowed to restrict consumer choice, or hold back 'progress'.

Next time, everyone in STUMP agreed, they would have to do better. They would go beyond mere marches and civil disobedience to civil disorder.

The dilemma for Lawrence and Lina was whether this conflicted with their deeply held non-violent beliefs. But as fellow activists pointed out, there was a greater violence going on all the time carried out by e-Ville forces.

But is setting one evil against another in itself 'unethical'?

Dilemma 23
Stumped

The next meeting of e-Ville shareholders was in London, and after this one the British police were definitely not praising the organisers. During a day of running battles with the forces of law and order, teams of balaclava-clad STUMP activists split off from the marchers and sprayed slogans on the monuments of the e-Ville business interests, and even managed to smash a few windows. Lina herself saw terrified employees (or passers-by anyway, she can't be sure which) in e-Ville House cowering as the protesters rampaged and she couldn't help feeling sorry for some of them. Lawrence was worried about the marbles thrown at the police horses, and upset when he learnt that the action against e-Ville Wood's central store had resulted in the death of the manager, who had suffered a heart attack. But as their fellow activists said later, no one was hurt deliberately (they could not be held responsible for those who got in the way).

But, it still seemed to Lawrence at least, that the protest could not be justified if it itself involved hurting people or animals. He thought that the non-violence and avoidance of harm principle must apply equally to STUMP as to e-Ville. 'If you are a believer in non-violence then whatever other "greater" violence is going on – you only add to it by being violent yourself! You lose your own moral ground, don't you? Isn't that what Gandhi believed? You must be the change you wish to see in the world', says Lawrence to Lina later.

Surely the way forward is through peaceful campaigns and waiting for the weight of mass opinion to change e-Ville, which after all depends on consumers for its existence, he pleads. But Lina doesn't agree. Eventually, Lina and Lawrence split up over the issue.

'Whose side are you on anyway?' she screams, tipping a box of Lawrence's old leaflets out of the window over him.

Dilemma 24
Cracked?

But then it turns out that e-Ville are clearly rattled. On the one hand, they demand a crackdown by the security apparatus on STUMP, and that the public be cleared en masse from areas where the Corporation holds its international meetings. But they also announce that they are considering closing the 'bushmeat' sections of stores in areas 'where communities feel for moral reasons it is not appropriate', and stopping completely certain lines. (Although some say these are lines which are now so rare as to be commercially non-viable anyway, and were therefore about ready to be dropped.) With a flourish, e-Ville introduce 'environmental auditing' of some of their other enterprises.

It seems to Lina like a great triumph. She sees now that non-violence is a kind of con trick played by those in power on those that are being oppressed. It is a bogus morality – after all, governments wage wars when it suits their interests to do so. One evening, she knelt in front of her copy of the famous poster of Che Guevara, 'the heroic guerrilla', taken by the fashion photographer Alberto Diaz Gutierrez, in 1960. (Despite its wide 'merchandising', Che refused to take any fee from it.) Later, the CIA had the revolutionary leader shot and his body buried under a runway, all in a far away corner of Bolivia where he had been fighting for peasants' rights, which seemed terribly sad to her, but now it seemed to make sense. She seemed to hear Che's address to the UN against 'imperialism' in her head, and his words, as the poster said: 'Other hands will take up the weapons.'

She endorses the new approach of 'civil disobedience plus', as some of the others put it. Lawrence drops out.

Is the new policy a success?

Dilemma 25
Getting hotter

Still, some of the others are not so sure. Mad Dog, the group's *de facto* leader, is furious that people are talking of successes. She insists that the reforms announced so far are mere window-dressing. The e-Ville organisation is still there, and still carrying on largely the same way. Mad Dog enunciates the new doctrine with the air of a someone who has discovered the political equivalent of the 'philosophers' stone': IT-IS-ONLY-THROUGH-VIOLENCE-THAT-THE-SYSTEM-CAN-BE-CHANGED. After vigorous debate, STUMP activists are split on the next step. Surprised by herself, Lina sees the logic of the radicals' argument (and anyway, there is something about 'Mad Dog', when she's angry) and joins with an offshoot fearsomely called 'Death Stump' and committed to 'direct action' against leading figures in e-Ville Corps. So Lina becomes 'quartermaster' to Death Stump, manufacturing little firebombs made out of cigarette boxes (a pleasing irony, Lina thinks) for planting in the megastores or executive homes of e-Ville's staff.

The bombs use a battery to start a small smouldering blaze. Most of the time, the 'damage' is caused by the automatic fire sprinklers in the stores targeted. Within a few months some twenty-two targets have been 'hit'. The tally is a huge bill in repairs for the corporation, but six prominent STUMP campaigners are in prison. (Fortunately no Death Stump yet.) Then, one night, an e-Ville director and his family are caught up in a fire at their home which goes up faster than expected, and suffer serious burns. A week later, a fire-fighter is killed at another STUMP fire when a roof collapses.

Lina is sorry about the other people, not really the e-Ville director, and helps draft a press release saying so, but consoles herself with the utilitarian argument that she is saving many more people in the Third World.

And anyway, she can't be held responsible for the unintended consequences of the campaign, can she?

Dilemma 26
Feeling drained

e-Ville's cronies in government react with typical viciousness, and many STUMP members, as well as, this time, a few Death Stump members are put in prison. With (she fears) secret police everywhere, Lina herself loses the ability to leave her bomb factory, in a small tatty bedsit in suburbia, in case of being seen. Instead she works away on her biggest project to date, a bio-warfare package which she intends to threaten to release into the water supply. The clever thing is that it mutates very rapidly, and Lina thinks it is so deadly that e-Ville will have to come to terms with Death Stump, once and for all. In fact, it seems to be so powerful that she thinks it could wipe out all human life on the planet, leaving only the animals. Which in a way would be a nice touch. (However, whatever Mad Dog seems to think, Lina is determined to only make the weapon as a bargaining counter – a kind of poor people's nuke.)

Unfortunately, one day, when she is experimenting with making car bombs, her assistant takes the phials and pours them down the sink, thereby releasing the virus into the environment anyway.

Now whose fault was that?

A dose of medical ethics

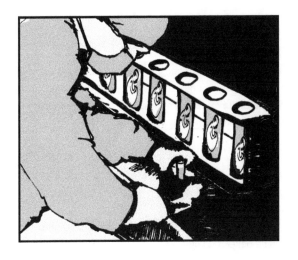

Dilemma 27
Breeding experiments

It's not widely known, but Plato's idealised republic was influenced by hunting dogs. A visit by Socrates to his friend Glaucon's hunting lodge, and the sight of his dogs, trained to run after the pheasants and retrieve them after they had been shot, provided Plato with material for one of his most controversial ideas. Plato records the occasion like this:

SOCRATES: I see in your house dogs for hunting, and of the nobler sort of birds not a few. Now, I beseech you, do tell me, have you ever attended to their pairing and breeding?

GLAUCON: In what particulars?

SOCRATES: Why, in the first place, although they are all of a good sort, are not some better than others?

GLAUCON: True.

SOCRATES: And do you breed from them all indifferently, or do you take care to breed from the best only?

GLAUCON: From the best.

SOCRATES: And do you take the oldest or the youngest, or only those of ripe age?

GLAUCON: I choose only those of ripe age.

SOCRATES: And if care was not taken in the breeding, your dogs and birds would greatly deteriorate?

GLAUCON: Certainly.

SOCRATES: And the same of horses and animals in general?

GLAUCON: Undoubtedly.

SOCRATES: Good heavens! My dear friend, what consummate skill will our rulers need if the same principle holds of the human species!

Good heavens! The principle established, Socrates then continues:

the best of either sex should be united with the best as often, and the inferior with the inferior, as seldom as possible; and that they should rear the offspring of the one sort of union, but not of the other, if the flock is to be maintained in first-rate condition. Now these goings on must be a secret which the rulers only know, or there will be a further danger of our herd breaking out into rebellion!

Why, what are they worried about? Surely it is right to bring science to bear on the important matter of breeding?

Dilemma 28
Designer babies

Dr Eleanor Frankenstein is an expert on genetic engineering. She has been given the job of identifying desirable and less desirable genes for the government of Diktatias' health care screening programme for new babies.

Dr Frankenstein has an ambitious programme. First of all, she plans to eliminate all the serious illnesses and handicaps – sickly people are no longer necessary in a modern society. No one need be brought into today's world with any kind of physical handicap. In place will come enhancements for life expectancy, genes for strength and virility and so on – even intelligence. From the menu of 'designer genes', parents can choose eye or even skin colour, height, type of bone structure, and so on, using a set of popular celebrity 'template' babies as a guide. To meet the Interior Ministry's requirements, there are some socially useful characteristics, such as honesty, consideration for others, and good temper (placidity). And to meet the Minster for Minorities' concerns there's even a fault retaining service where couples will be able to opt to remove those enhancements they don't want – for example, choosing to have an asthmatic, bad tempered baby. Or a deaf one. As long as those were the characteristics of the original embryo – you can't just choose them.

It will all be done very democratically. But still, the Vicar of Diktatiaville is concerned. Whilst some flaws in embryos are treatable, many others result in potential babies being terminated. 'Picking and choosing between babies is God's task – not the government's', he rages angrily, from the pulpit.

Or is it?

Dilemma 29
KwikBaby

KwikBaby has opened a branch in Diktatiaville's posh shopping street, offering a new fertility service to the ever more busy professionals of that fine city. On day one, the queues stretch down the street for the embryology and fertilisation service. A couple can pop in, supply some gametes in the morning, and *KwikBaby* does the rest, producing a genetically perfect little embryo in a test tube which the lady can have implanted, at her convenience, or have stored until a more opportune time. Now how could anything be wrong with that?

Another service offered by *KwikBaby* and marketed under the slogan 'Too Posh to Push', is full grown babies. Couples can opt to have the embryos implanted in one of *KwikBaby*'s experienced 'surrogate Mums' (usually abroad) who will take over the task of carrying the child for nine months. In some clinics, indeed, a new ectogenesis technique is available in which the embryos are implanted in an artificial placenta and fed a special *KwikBabyFood* diet of the correct nutrients until ready.

The technique has great health advantages. *KwikBaby*'s publicity advertisements points them out:

- STRONG HEALTHY babies
- REDUCED allergies
- LOW cancer risk

Or, as the less scrupulous advertisers put it:

Mums!

- KEEP smoking
- KEEP drinking
- *No exercise needed*

For healthy-looking customers there is another leaflet headed: *Keep up those dangerous water sports!* which runs:

For just 1,000 Diktatia Dollars a month, you can continue to live the way you like, secure in the knowledge that your baby is getting the best start in life. *Remember, it's your body, not your baby's.*

Some people (men particularly) think something has been lost by not going through the traditional motherhood procedure, and pine for old-fashioned pregnancies. But no one is really sure quite what has been lost, or given that something has, whether it matters.

The campaign for real babies is short-lived, and the health advantages of the new techniques become clearer. As *KwikBaby's* consultants are keen to point out: it may not be natural, but *isn't it really just another example of how modern life is improving on nature?*

Dilemma 30
The downmarket rival

Walking down the street one day, idly window-shopping, Sharon's eye was caught by the board outside one of the local branches of *DIYBabies*. As a result of changes in the laws regarding sex workers, new types of licensed City sex clinics, what some fuddy duddies called derogatively, 'brothels', had become possible. But one of the most popular services was for women who wanted to – how extraordinary! – have a baby, rather than visit for the lustful pleasures of the activity, as in more conventional brothels. In fact, the special *DIYBabies* package made a virtue of the fact that (for those wishing to start a family) the most Catholic standards of passionless anonymity would be ensured. Famously, the lady customers donned the sort of robes of heavy cloth with strategic holes in them, as worn by God-fearing folk in years long gone by. Thereby ensuring that there was no physical contact other than the most, ahem, essential one, during the transmission of the all-important gametes from the male sex worker to the female client. Additionally, almost non-existent lighting levels guaranteed that the anonymity of both the woman and the man were fully protected.

DIY *SEX* $100

SPEED: Within five minutes, a baby, or your money back.

proclaimed the poster outside the doors of DIYBabies.com. Meaning, of course, the start of the process that leads inexorably to a baby, rather than the infant itself.

QUALITY: Don't have your baby with any old man – have your baby with a fully tested and approved professional.

Although wags said it was exactly indeed 'any old man' off the street, rather than the 'university educated Adonis' of the adverts, that made up the duty rota at *DIYBabies*, safe behind their cloak of anonymity. Nonetheless, undaunted, the advertising board finished in a flourish of sanctimony:

ETHICS: Mums – have your baby the natural way!

This last claim seemed to rest on the superiority of the service to *DIYBabies*' rivals up the street at the local *in vitro* fertilisation clinic, who were famously dogged by problems of multiple conceptions and the destruction of 'unwanted' embryos. Yet somehow the *DIYBabies* offer seems a bit downmarket, a bit 'déclassé'.

Sharon's dilemma is: *which baby service to use?*

Dilemma 31
TGN1412

In 2006, an American company called Parexcel called for 'healthy males' to take part in a drug trial exploring treatments for arthritis. The volunteers, some of whom were students, some of whom were unemployed, were offered £2,000 for just a few days of their time. Parexcel's information for potential volunteers included pictures of videogames, pool tables, and most appealing of all, signed cheques. The drug was the, with hindsight, rather sinister-sounding, TGN1412.

One bioethicist, Dr Ezekiel Emanuel, of the US National Institutes of Health, defended such procedures in the press afterwards, saying 'Research is a social good – we need better treatments for arthritis and leukaemia – but there are risks. Being a construction worker is risky and we pay people to do that.'

'So why not this?' he asks, provocatively.

Dilemma 32

The Nobodie Rules: a drama in three acts

Act I: Felix and the eye problem

Mr and Mrs Nobodie have a little boy called Felix. Unfortunately, Felix has a problem with his eyes which makes it increasingly hard to see. The doctors warn that unless he has a transplant of optic nerve he will lose his sight altogether within four years.

The Nobodies go to see Dr Blur at the Clinic for Obscure Diseases. Dr Blur is a world expert in eye problems. He explains that the problem is that Felix requires not just any old optic nerve cells, but that they must come from someone with a very similar genetic code (otherwise the new cells will be rejected by Felix's own immune defence system).

The trouble is, no one else does have exactly the right DNA. Not Mr Nobodie, not Mrs Nobodie – not nobody, one might say. However, Dr Blur thinks that it is possible that were the couple to have another child, that child *might*, and he stresses it is only might, *might* be compatible and could become a donor of the much-needed optic nerve cells.

Mr and Mrs Nobodie are delighted with this idea. 'Then that, Doc., is what we must do,' says Mr Nobodie firmly, before turning to Mrs Nobodie to add: 'More little Nobodies!'

At this Dr Blur looks uncomfortable. 'Of course,' he says quickly, 'the size of your family is a matter for you, but you must remember that there is only a possibility that the new baby will be a suitable match for Felix – and if he is not, he will still need to be loved!'

'Don't worry, doctor,' said Mrs Nobodie earnestly, 'It sounds like a wonderful chance for Felix, and even if it doesn't work out, why, we always wanted a family of four.'

Mr Nobodie nods in agreement, and as the couple leave Dr Blur's surgery adds, 'You can leave the "loving" to us, Doctor!'

Has Dr Blur provided good guidance?

Act II: The Nobodie Rules memo

Alas, one year later the couple are back in Dr B's surgery very disappointed. They explain that 'following his advice', they had another child, George, and he is not a match! To make matters worse, he has his own health problems. 'He's just another big worry to us, Doctor Blur – and a big expense we can ill afford.'

Then Mr Nobodie leans forward to explain why they have come back to the clinic. 'Mrs Nobodie and I have decided to give your idea one more try. But this time,' and he taps the table firmly, 'this time, we want to make sure the baby is right for Felix!'

And he explains that they would like the experts of the clinic to help make this happen by using special genetic techniques.

'They can scan to make sure that the baby will be suitable, can't they doctor?' adds Mrs Nobodie, who has read about such things in the papers.

Dr Blur says he is very sorry to hear that their second baby is not a suitable donor after all, and that yes, in theory, the clinic could identify a suitable embryo that could then be 'implanted' in Mrs Nobodie's womb, but that the procedure was far from automatic and in any case, he would have to refer it to the Hospital Ethics Committee. 'They might not agree,' and here he coughs politely, 'as to some people it might look like we were creating a, ahem, a baby for "spare parts"'.

'Well, it would save us a lot of bother, wouldn't it, Doctor?' says Mrs Nobodie, folding her arms defiantly, as Mr Nobodie nods his head in vigorous agreement.

As Dr Blur feels responsible for them, he promises to make as strong a case for them as he can.

He writes a memo requesting that the Nobodies be allowed to select their next baby on the basis of a need to ensure tissue compatibility with an existing sibling with a serious disorder. He adds that in simple 'utilitarian' terms, everyone gains:

- Mr and Mrs 'N' gain as they have not only a third child but their first child is restored to good health.
- The first child gains, as they can receive treatment.
- The new child gains as, even if they are initially used for what is, in effect, an involuntary medical procedure on behalf of their sibling, and even indeed if they are obliged in their future life to repeat the donations, or even if they feel a 'second best' child, created not entirely for their own selves . . . even if all this is true, they still gain as as the alternative is that they will simply not exist.

'And clearly,' scribbles Dr Blur, 'a baby that does not exist has no value, no happiness or interests. So the new baby must always be better off.'

The Hospital Ethics Committee is so impressed by this that not only does it raise no objections to the particular case, but the memo is enshrined in official hospital policy. 'The N Rules' becomes the basis for its new policy in similar cases.

Are the 'N Rules' correct?

Act III: The Nobodie Rules!

But just a few days after the Nobodies' first visit to the clinic to have a new 'test tube baby', Dr Blur finds out that new research has identified the number of optic nerve cells needed to save Felix's eyesight. And, unfortunately, it turns out that Felix will need more or less ALL of his younger sibling's optic nerve to be transplanted, not just a few cells.

That would leave the new baby with a visual handicap. Actually, more or less blind.

Dr Blur doesn't like having to do it, but calls the Nobodies to explain that the procedure must be abandoned as future transplants will be quite impossible. Of course, the Nobodies are furious! They say that the baby is already 'on the way' and they won't take 'no' for an answer. After all, they point out, referring to their copy of the celebrated memo, the situation has not changed. As long as they can have a new 'donor baby':

- They will gain as they have not only a third child but their first child is restored to good health.
- Felix will gain, as he will receive treatment.
- The new child gains since, even if they do go blind, the only alternative (if the Nobodies are denied the procedure) is that the new baby will simply not exist.

'And clearly,' says Mr Nobodie to Dr Blur, 'a baby that does not exist is worse off than one that does!'

Who's following the rules?

Dilemma 33
Witheringspoon-X disease

Mr Purplepatch has some bad news for his patient. The test results have been received from the lab and show that Mrs Blank has the potentially fatal Witheringspoon-X disease. Witheringspoon-X is so rare that it affects only one in 100,000 people. But according to the tests, which have a pretty final 95 per cent accuracy, Mrs Blank has got it. (Probably.)

Purplepatch explains the situation carefully: the disease is progressive and needs speedy treatment if there is to be any chance of success. However, it is a hazardous course of treatment, very intrusive as it includes surgically removing the kidneys and the liver too sometimes. Even if successful, she will require constant medical support and treatment.

Mrs Blank looks . . . blank. Should she undertake the risky course of treatment – or the risky course of non-treatment in the hope that the test was wrong? She asks her consultant for his opinion. He nods gravely. 'I'm afraid, Mrs Blank, I think there is only one course we can take.'

What should Purplepatch advise?

Dilemma 34
The hospital's dilemma

Dr Doe shakes her head sadly. A very sad case! John Brown had his whole life ahead of him, but now lies in the hospital bed connected to a life-support machine, apparently in a deep, deep sleep.

John has been terribly injured after a motorcycle accident, and his parents, Mr and Mrs Brown, are waiting for Dr Doe's report. It will be a delicate matter. Going through to the next room, where the Browns are waiting, Dr Doe sits strategically behind the table and begins by clearing her throat:

'I'm afraid, Mr and Mrs Brown, your son, has, ah, no chance of recovering any further function,' says Dr Doe, and shuffles and squares the case study notes on the table decisively. Mr and Mrs Brown nod encouragingly. There is a long pause and Dr Doe, seeing some doubt on their countenances, adds 'It is not possible to hold out any hope for recovery.'

'But doctor, he might do, mightn't he? There is always hope.' Poor Mrs Brown, she looks dreadfully tired, pale and pinched.

'Now I don't want to increase your grief at a time like this, Mr and Mrs Brown, and if I thought there was any small hope I would certainly say so, but *in my clinical judgement*, there is effectively *no chance* of your son recovering. We can keep him on the life-support machine for longer, but at some point soon we have to make the decision about the effective allocation of resources.'

Mrs Brown gasps and sobs, and Mr Brown hugs her.

'I'll leave you a while to think about it,' says Doe, getting up. 'We understand Doctor,' they say.

Some time later the hospital philosopher is brought in to talk to the Browns. Dr Gnatt is a cheery fellow, who claps his hands brightly and says: 'Well now, what do we know about this young John – was he a utilitarian – or a Kantian?'

'Oh no, Doctor,' says Mrs Brown, 'our John never went to church. I'm sorry.' And she makes a little sobbing noise. 'I wish he had now!'

'Ah! I'm sure,' says the philosopher, a little less brightly perhaps. 'But what I really want to know is whether we think Johnny would have had a view on the optimisation of resources, you know, QALYS and so on, or perhaps would have stuck rigidly, as it were, to a few simple principles.' Seeing the spreading bafflement on the Browns' faces, he adds 'It's his philosophical position and beliefs I'm trying to get at here.'

'Oh no, doctor, John never had any of those at all, I'm sure.' There is another long pause. Then Dr Gnatt smiles kindly. 'Right then,' says the good doctor, 'in that case I think there are really no issues that need detain us here. We simply have a decision to make: to keep the machine on for the time being – or to turn it off? And I think this little chap will help us answer that.'

And so saying, the good Dr Gnatt produces a coin from his pocket.

'Right now, Mr Brown, heads or tails?'

What should the Browns reply?

The censor's dilemma

Dilemma 35
Foul things

Maurice the Censor has been given the unpleasant duty of assessing just what can and cannot be allowed to be read by the general public. His first job is to look at some tattily printed magazines. One reads:

> In the centre of the cell lay the body of the servant girl in her night dress, and gloating over this agony stand two ruffians with the cowardly masks of their dark trade on. She was nearly naked in fact, for much of her scanty covering had been torn off in the struggle. A vile contraption of iron weights squatted over her bosom, as it heaved and fought for every breath.

It is accompanied by a line drawing. Undaunted, Maurice reads on.

> Firstly, they fastened the poor terrified creature securely round the ankles and wrists with some stout cords. Then they passed two more ropes through these thongs, and dextrously enough stretched her out on the floor of that ghastly cell. In this unpleasant predicament they put her through such a course of novel tortures that a tribe of North American Indians might have picked up a wrinkle there. And how they made merry while she was in the greatest agony! The more she shrieked with pain, the louder grew their shrieks of laughter. They piled weights upon the plank, and threatened to burn the tip of her nose with a red-hot poker, until finally, while one of these torturers smoked a foul tobacco, the other brought a huge, square block of stone and placed it atop. Surely no rack ever known could create such awful torture as this!

The question for Maurice is whether this is encouraging all sorts of nasty things – *or is it just a bit of fun?*

Prison-tortures

© MhCons, MSU 2002.

After a while, however, they released their victim from the weight of the stone.

Dilemma 36
The criminal connection

Maurice lets it go; it is after all just fiction. But now a new publication depicts the activities of criminals who are actually at large, and actually carrying out crimes! The latest glorification of the hoodlums includes a description of how a ruthless government squad of special police have killed one of the gang's family, driving him to curse, in a gripping illustrated passage:

> 'Now I swear, by all I hold to be sacred, to be avenged! This indignity shall be wiped out with blood!'

Maurice is inclined to let this one go too, but he comes under pressure to stop being so liberal. His political masters insist he read up on what they say is the growing body of evidence showing the link between actual immoral behaviour, and the representation of it in the media.

One file they give him records an actual crime at an office in Gray's Inn, the imposing and eminently respectable centre for lawyers in London. The arresting officer described what he found:

> About 4 o'clock, I went to 7 Bedford Row. I saw Mr Wyatt in the office. Mr Wyatt asked me to look at the drawer in the table. Constable [the accused office boy] was present. I asked Constable for the key. He said, 'I have it; I took it home with me'. Amongst the papers [in the desk] were some numbers of a weekly publication called *Tales of Highwaymen*, or *Life on the the Road*, with coloured and other illustrations. I said, 'That looks bad to read such things as these'. He touched me on the arm and said, 'Come outside, I want to speak to you'. I went on the landing and he said, 'I have been tempted to do this by reading *the tales* . . . '

Although it is rather an old case (1872) Maurice gives it careful consideration. He recalls the words of the Chief Constable of Birkenhead in his annual report for 1936: 'Any film that prompts a child to commit crime, teaches him to conceal stolen goods, or to evade the Police of the truth, should never be allowed to circulate'.

If there is evidence of a link – surely that makes censorship essential for the well-being of everyone, *not least the young people*?

LIVES OF THE MOST

NOTORIOUS HIGHWAYMEN
FOOTPADS AND MURDERERS.

No. 5.　　　　SATURDAY, MAY 28, 1836.　　　　Price 1d.

LIFE OF THE GERMAN PRINCESS,—A SWINDLER.

ADVENTURES OF J. M. HOBART, A NOTORIOUS SWINDLER.

LIFE OF WILLIAM DUNCAN.

BENJAMIN TAPNER, JOHN COBBY, AND OTHERS.

LIFE OF OLD MOB, THE HIGHWAYMAN.

OLD MOB ROBBING JUDGE JEFFERIES.

Unsuitable reading

Dilemma 37
A matter of standards

In the late 1940s, public burnings of comic books took place outside schools in New York State. By June 1953, things had got to such a pretty pass, that a special subcommittee of the House of Representatives was set up to investigate. Put in front of it was the publisher Bill Gaines, of EC comics, responsible for many of the low points of the new 'dreadfuls', such as a story entitled 'Foul Play' which involved a man's intestines being used to mark out a baseball pitch. Here is part of the official house transcript of the interview:

SENATOR:	Here is your May 22 issue [of *Crime SuspenStories*]. This seems to be a man with a bloody axe holding a woman's head up which has been severed from her body. Do you think that is in good taste?
PUBLISHER:	Yessir, I do – for the cover of a horror comic. A cover in bad taste, for example, might be defined as holding the head a little higher so that the neck could be seen dripping blood from it and moving the body over a little further so that the neck of the body could be seen to be bloody.
SENATOR:	You have blood coming out of her mouth.
PUBLISHER:	A little.
SENATOR:	Here is blood on the axe. I think most adults are shocked by that.
COMMITTEE CHAIRMAN: *(earnestly, leaning over)*	Here is another one I want to show him . . .
SENATOR:	This is the July one. It seems to be a man with a woman in a boat and he is choking her to death with a crowbar. Is that in good taste?
PUBLISHER:	I think so.
SENATOR'S AIDE:	*How could it be worse?*

Maurice looks at the dreadful stuff in front of him, and then at the publisher's defence. It seems a bit feeble. Surely, on grounds of simple good taste, *the public should be protected from the depravities of the unreformed*?

Dilemma 38
The exploitative pictures

Now at last, hands shaking slightly, Maurice opens the final black case of obscene publications and pulls out a sealed envelope marked in big letters 'SEX'. His hands hesitate a moment with the paper cutter, then he almost seems to hear the voice of James Greenwood speaking to him across the years from a century ago in London.

> It is always better, if possible, to show what a thing is in its own shape and colour than to endeavour to describe it. Half the abuses and miseries that, as a civilised nation, disgrace us, might be cured if the public could be brought to view them with its own eyes instead of trusting to the evidence of those of other folk. Undoubtedly it is very convenient to rely on hearsay, but there can be no question that it fosters dilatoriness and a neglect of individual duty, and should therefore be discouraged as far as possible. People believe only half what they hear, and, though it may concern never so grave a grievance, are content to do no more than join in the general lukewarm cry of condemnation, leaving the vigorous application of a remedy to those who have inquired into what is amiss, and who are therefore in a position to know all about it. It is so with this iniquitous boy literature and the sudden outcry against it. Everybody believes it to be odious and abominable because everybody says so: and so the dog, and most deservedly, gets a bad name, but he is not hanged; he is simply avoided. Because he is such a mangy, ill-looking cur, offensive alike to the nose and to the touch, all decent people shrink away from him. But he would much rather have their room than their company, and grins to himself as they give him the path, and permit him to continue his career of ravening and rending. He must be discovered in the act of mauling one of our little ones before we are moved to take hold of the brute and strangle him.

Out falls a sheaf of lurid pictures including two graphic images of naked women. In one, 'Meluisine', Meluisine's bosom is exposed (she is apparently bathing), and there is a hint of auto-eroticism in the position of her hands. This one, at least, is in black and white. Another, in full colour, shows a naked woman standing apparently in a seashell, again with hands suggestively placed. A third shows several naked men and women in some sort of wall painting.

These last pictures, he notes, are based on originals on public display in Italy *in churches*! These foreigners! Maurice has a private collection of images garnered from previous consideration of the so-called satirical prints of London's underclasses engaged in sexy escapades by a man called Thomas Rowlandson (1756–1827), and is as unshockable as the next, *but it looks to him like pornography.*

But where do you draw the line?

Dilemma 39

The nasty pop group

In October 2001, German police swooped (as is their wont) on one of the best-known, if not most popular, pop groups. Called *Landser*, which is the old-fashioned word for a German soldier, the group had already had to change its name, after being outlawed once already when it called itself 'Final Solution'. Its first CD was called *The Reich Will Rise*, and called for attacks on foreigners, Jews, Gypsies and political opponents (just like old times). Its new CD contained the (non-ironical) ditty:

Someone told the niggers they are free to vote here
Well, that's true,
They can vote
Either for a rope round the neck
Or a bullet in the stomach

Would you buy it?

Business week:

Dilemmas from business ethics (with the emphasis on business)

Dilemma 40
The short memos by the pirate

Monday

For several months, Sandra, one of the three secretaries in the invoices and memos section, has been slacking, regularly typing up fewer, shorter memos for the senior management than either Jackie or Bob. But this morning, Jackie is fed up with it. She asks Bob whether he will come with her to take it up with Mustafa, their boss, or with the company human resources department. But Bob, while agreeing with Jackie that 'Sandy' is not doing her fair share, wonders whether, in a way, because the section has been coping alright, that would be going over the top about it?

Not according to business ethics departments, though. Bob's approach does nothing, while Jackie's brings 'attention to the poor work ethic' (as the Lockheed ethics experts put it) of the employee. Sandra's boss may want to remind her of John Stuart Mill's words: 'Duty is a thing that may be exacted from a person, as one exacts a debt.'

Then, on *Tuesday*, Jackie discovers that Sandra has been copying company software and taking it home. She is particularly irked as she herself had been saving up for the same program, and it costs a lot! She wonders whether to say nothing and copy the program herself, as clearly nothing has happened to Sandra. But she also wonders whether she ought to make a report either to Mustafa, or to the ethics office. At the very least, she thinks that perhaps the next time she has a quiet moment with Sandra, maybe over coffee, she should remind her about the fact that it is illegal to copy software.

It's straight after the other offence, but what should Jackie do *as a responsible and ethical employee*?

Dilemma 41

The blaring radio

Wednesday: all is quiet in the office. But on Thursday . . .

Thursday

Tony in the print room objects to the pop music that is played on the radio all day long. He himself is a violinist of some distinction, and has a very sensitive ear, he explains. But the supervisor informally polls all the employees in the print room, and the majority favour the type of music currently played. The aggrieved Tony appeals to Mustafa, as the division manager, for help.

What should the boss do?

A   Since the majority like pop music, do nothing.
B   Suggest to the print room supervisor that he consider playing different music periodically, e.g. classical string quartets, Monday; jazz funk, Wednesday; techno, Friday . . .

Or perhaps, if he does not think much of the current music either, order the supervisor to play something else.

Or indeed, if he is getting tired of hearing complaints about music, unplug the radio and *have done with it*?

Dilemma 42
The infectious disease

Friday

It's the end of the week, at last, and back in the memos and invoices section Jackie has written a memo of her own to Mustafa, reporting that she has heard that Bob is HIV positive (although he doesn't like people to know). She is particularly upset as she used to share the same coffee mug with Bob in the staff tea-room. Poor Mustafa. What to do now?

A   Move the AIDS-infected employee to a job where he has little contact with Jackie – or indeed, the other employees.

B   Hold a meeting with Jackie to discuss her perception of the situation, and at the next staff meeting remind the staff that the law prohibits discrimination against those infected with AIDS.

Or reach for the phone and contact the legal department to set in process redundancy procedures – as generous as he can get *for poor Bob*.

Should he reach for the phone?

Dilemma 43
The witness

Working overtime

Saturday, the machines are stilled but Mustafa has asked the team to come in and shred memos as one of the clients has gone bust 'and they won't be needed now'. To make matters worse, at lunchtime, Bob is badly cut when the shredder malfunctions. Sandra recalls how she was told to put the machine in the cupboard the last time the Health and Safety check was carried out, as there was thought to be some sort of problem with it. Bob doesn't know that though, he thinks he must have pressed the wrong button. Should she:

A   Report what she knows to the company in order to make sure that the safety hazard is corrected this time, and contact her injured co-worker to offer to speak on his behalf?

B   Or try to protect the company by keeping mum?

And if Bob does mention it, make it clear that she is not prepared to appear as a witness?

And another dilemma for business ethics (with the emphasis on ethics)

Dilemma 44
The Devil's chemists

One of the great business success stories of the twentieth century was that of the German chemical industry. It was also the story of how a mighty industrial colossus called I. G. Farben came close to dominating the world.

Originally 'IG' just made dyes. Until the middle of the nineteenth century dyes all came from crushed up berries, insects, flowers, tree bark. Then someone discovered how to make dyes out of coal. Soon, Germany had six huge companies all based on this new chemical technology: BASF, Bayer, Hoescht, Agfa, Casella and Kalle. A certain kind of corporate single-mindedness and determination led to innovative research, and the discovery of the elusive 'synthetic blue' dye, so characteristic of oriental 'China'. It also led to marketing devices such as ruthless price cutting, 'loss leaders', aggressive litigation over patents, industrial spying and even bribery.

All such methods helped build the companies up. Bayer even had enough money to develop an important new process to make nitrates, which had previously only been available from Chile after a long and expensive sea journey. Initially the nitrates were mainly for fertiliser. A few years later, these were the nitrates that became the 'nitro-glycerine' in all the high explosives of the Second World War.

Under Bayer's lead, the six companies dispensed with wasteful competition between themselves, and combined to form one large 'friendly group', what they called an *Interessen Gemeinschaft* – what we would call a monopoly, or maybe a cartel. (Similar *zaibatsu* cartels operated in Japan at this time.) Anyway, now the six were free to pursue new markets, whilst safe from attack by rivals on their home ground. And IG was so large it was even able to persuade the rest of the world's giant companies, such as Imperial Chemicals and Standard Oil, to also join in their 'community', and play by their rules.

But it was the war that made IG richest. The Nazis needed fuel and synthetic rubber to create their *Blitzkrieg* war machine. Only a massive corporation like IG could possibly have provided it. A giant complex to produce these patriotic essentials was constructed at Auschwitz, located so as to draw on the supply of prisoner labour from the nearby concentration camp. So huge was the plant that it is said it used more electricity than the whole of Berlin. Building it cost the lives of 25,000 prisoners alone!

At the end of the war some twenty-four of IG's directors were charged at the Nüremberg war trials. The indictment accused them of 'major responsibility for visiting upon mankind the most searing and catastrophic war in human history', of 'wholesale enslavement, plunder and murder'. The executives were asked to justify their policies during the war. They were asked to explain memoranda which read:

> In contemplation of experiments with a new soporific drug, we would appreciate your procuring for us a number of women . . .

> We received your answer but consider the price of 200 marks a woman excessive. We propose to pay not more than 170 marks a head. If agreeable, we will take possession of the women. We need approximately 150 . . .

> RECEIVED: the order of 150 women. Despite their emaciated condition, they were found satisfactory. We shall keep you posted on developments concerning this experiment . . .

> The tests were made. All subjects died.

> We shall contact you shortly on the subject of a new load.

These twenty-four directors were the ones dubbed 'the Devil's chemists'. Yet the accused were not Nazis, nor even extremists. They were sober businessmen, engineers and scientists of great intellect and distinction. When their government called upon them to help the war effort, they responded – just as they had to calls for help from operas and art galleries, even charities in happier times.

They had not broken any laws, they had just tried to do what they were best at – making money. *Unless there was some moral law?*

A pentad of moral stories:

Searching for divine justice

Dilemma 45
The unfruitful tree

A successful merchant was called away to a far country on a business trip he knew would last several tax years. But before he left, he called his staff together, and charged them with the care of his investments, giving each one some gold coins, worked out on the basis of each person's likely ability to use them productively. To his most reliable assistant he gave five coins; to another, two; and to the last, just the one. And then he immediately set off on his journey.

The one who had been given five coins immediately went and traded with them, and did so well that in time they had doubled in value. The employee who had received two coins also traded with his, and also doubled their value, by way of profit. But the assistant who had been given only the one went away, wrapped it up, and hid it in a sock under his bed.

Anyway, eventually, the merchant comes back and calls his staff together for a meeting, the first item on the agenda being to account for what he had entrusted to them. The first proudly presents him with the ten gold coins, saying, 'Behold, I have doubled your investment!' And the delighted merchant says: 'Well done, my good and faithful assistant; you have done well with a few things, I will put you in charge of many things.' And to the one that had had two coins, but brought back four, he says the same. But when the last one pulls out the old sock and empties it over the table, with just the one gold coin to roll leisurely out, he is not so pleased.

The merchant roars: 'Thou wicked and slothful servant! Thou knewest that I reaped where I had not sown; thou oughtest therefore to have put my money in the bank, that I might have received mine own with interest for its use!'

And then, turning to the others: 'Take the share from him, and give it to him that had ten; and then take this unprofitable servant and *cast him into the outer darkness*!'

How's that for business ethics?

Dilemma 46
Job's lot

Job is a very good, very devout fellow, and is living a very quiet, inoffensive (but successful) life. Until one day that is, when God and the Devil decide to have a wager.

The Devil says he bets Job is only good because things are so easy – if things were to go a little against him, why, he would lose his faith and soon become like everyone else and do evil!

God rises to the challenge and agrees to test Job. First of all, Satan is allowed to send down a plague of spiders, who eat all Job's crops. No matter: Job merely shrugs and prays for better times. Then Satan arranges for Job to lose his sons and daughters in freak weather conditions, of the type these days associated with global warming. Shocked at this, poor Job shaves his head and falls to his knees – but still, to Satan's fury, only says: 'The Lord hath given and the Lord hath taken away. (Blessed be the name of the Lord.)' So, reluctantly, God allows Satan to cover Job in boils from head to toe.

At which point, Job *does* lose his faith.

Where's the divine justice there?

Dilemma 47
The sacrificial lamb

Abraham takes the lamb to the chop

Abraham and Sarah are very pleased when, very late in life, they manage to have a child. A fine, bouncing boy, Isaac. Of course, they realise it is all only due to God, and God in fact contacts Abraham to say so. He also mentions that one day Abraham's descendants will be 'as numerous as the stars in the sky, and the grains of sand in the desert'.

Unfortunately, much later, when Isaac is a fine lad, God contacts Abraham again. This time it is to say he has a little thing to ask of Abraham: he wants him to make him a sacrifice on the top of the mountain. The catch? The sacrifice must be his own son.

Of course Abraham is rather downcast at this, and he hardly likes even to explain to Isaac the reason for their trip up the mountain together, carrying firewood. Even when Isaac asks 'I see the fire and the wood, but father, where is the lamb?' Abraham merely replies enigmatically that 'God will provide the lamb.' (And is that a lie? Certainly likely to be misinterpreted.) Abraham then ties Isaac to the sacrificial stone (at which point you would have thought that he might as well say something to the lad) and his hand is poised in the air ready to strike with the dagger when God's voice booms out: 'Stay your hand, Abraham!' *For it was only a test.* Now God is sure Abraham is the right man for him, and he provides a sheep to sacrifice instead.

And the moral is?

Dilemma 48

The modern day Good Samaritan

A man is travelling along the road between Jerusalem and Jericho, when suddenly, from out of the bushes spring some robbers, who beat him savagely, steal his money, even his clothes, and leave him lying injured by the side of the road. Half-dead and in great pain, he can barely manage to whisper 'help' to anyone who might pass by. But not many people are travelling that way in any case. It is some hours later before, by good chance, a priest rides past and sees the figure lying there. As a priest, of course he should have felt a special responsibility, but in fact he averts his gaze, speeds up his pace, and scuttles by on the opposite side of the road. The hot sun burns down on the injured man, who groans and then at last falls into unconsciousness. More hours drag by, and then – mercy! – along comes another official of the church. But he too merely stares at the injured man before hurrying on by.

It is almost dark when a Samaritan, a social outcast, comes by, leading his donkey, and sees the pitiful wretch lying in the dust. He immediately rushes over, and examines him to see what he can do to bind up and soothe the injuries. He then carefully lifts the man onto his donkey and takes him to the nearest inn, where he cleans the wounds properly and tends them all through the night. The next morning, the man is much better, but still in a deep sleep.

So the Samaritan sets off on his journey, but before he goes he gives the inn keeper some extra money saying: 'Take care of my poor friend until he is well, and if it should cost more than this, I will pay you when I come again.'

That is the famous Biblical tale. Now skip forward to a *real* case in the USA in January 1992. It is late at night and a man is driving along an urban motorway when he sees a car ahead which has broken down. Several other people have seen the car but they have all just driven on by. It is a frightening sort of place to stop – but then it is a frightening sort of place to be in a car which has broken down.

What should he do? Stop, *or hurry on*?

Dilemma 49

Lazarus the beggar

Once upon a time there was a rich man who dressed in rich silks and fine linen, and feasted on fattening food like pâté de foie gras and chocolate brownies with whipped cream (together) every meal. The only blot on the landscape was that every day, as he went to his office, he would pass a disgusting looking beggar, who was ragged and lumpy, and covered with sores. The beggar's name was Lazarus, and as he sat outside the rich man's gate, he hoped, so to speak, to be fed with the crumbs which might fall from the well-supplied table. ('Spare some pâté for a poor brother!') And truly, even the dogs had pity on him, for they came and licked his sores. But the rich man hated the sight of Lazarus. He gave him *nothing*.

So it was that one day, the rich man died, and reawoke to find himself, to his great surprise, being roasted in the flames of hell. And even more to his surprise, when he lifted up his eyes, who should he see there, in the distance, but his old enemy Lazarus now sitting on Holy Father Abraham's lap. The rich man cried out 'Abraham, have mercy on me! Send Lazarus, that he may dip the tip of his finger in water, and cool my tongue; for I am tormented in these flames!' But Old Abraham only frowned and said, 'Son, remember. In your lifetime you received all good things, whilst Lazarus received only evil things. Now he is comforted, and you are to be tormented.'

Now *that's* justice. But what about 'meta-heaven'? (The heaven 'after' heaven?)

Will Abraham later have to be punished too for not helping the tormented rich man?

Some monkey business

Dilemma 50
Monkey business

Albert and Samuel the Talking Chimps were a sensation. Their proud trainer, Felicity, had taught them to use sign language, and the little fellows were now able to use as many signs as a five-year-old human child might know words. It was debatable, though, to what extent they really understood concepts. Conversations typically went something like:

> Hello Albert
> Hello Felicity
> Do you want some bananas?
> Yes please!
> They are in the blue box, Albert.

Albert would then obediently pad over to the blue box, find it locked, and return looking perplexed. Then Albert might sign:

> Not like box!
> That's because it's locked. Do you want the key?

At this, Felicity often thought Albert's understanding gave out because he would often throw things at her. However, if she then volunteered 'in the second drawer of the red box', Albert would immediately go over to the red box and retrieve the key. So she concluded that the chimps certainly had a grasp of simple language. And so things went on like this until, one day, as part of a big research project, Samuel is taken away from Albert.

The next day, to Felicity's amazement, Albert signs quite differently.

> No Samuel, no eat!
> He's gone away, Albert
> No Samuel, no eat!

Albert repeats. And then, after that – nothing. Felicity is most concerned.

Over the days to come, Albert gets thinner and thinner and begins to look very ill. 'It's almost as if he was on hunger strike,' she remarks to her boss. 'Can't we bring Sam back?' Her boss, Dr Vivian Section, says no, the plan is to use Sam in an experiment which results in Sam's brain being chopped up. 'But we can get Albert another companion later,' she offers helpfully. That was when Felicity got the idea of bringing a court case against Dr Section. And that was when Albert really had his chance to use his human language in court.

JUDGE: *(sceptically)*   Are you Albert, a chimpanzee currently the property of Primate Research Labs?

ALBERT: No!

> (*Laughter in court. The judge looks smugly at Felicity and her counsel, vindicated in his scepticism. Counsel for Albert hastily confers with Felicity.*)

COUNSEL FOR ALBERT: M'Lud, my client does not accept that he is the 'property' of the laboratory. Can we avoid implying that in the question?

JUDGE: *(sighing)*   Very well. (*To Albert, with broad wink to the jury*) Are you, Albert, currently a chimpanzee in captivity at Primate Research Labs?

ALBERT: Yes

JUDGE: Do you want your companion Samuel returned?

ALBERT: Yes

COUNSEL FOR THE LABS: Objection! This proves nothing! The monkey is just saying 'yes' randomly!

JUDGE: Silence, I shall interrogate the plaintiff my own way! (*To Albert*) Albert, now this is very important. Can you explain to the Court why you want Samuel back?

ALBERT: (*Albert is looking very intently at the Judge. Then, in a flurry of gestures he gives his longest ever speech.*) Samuel and I used to live in the same forest for as long as I can remember. When we were captured by the humans, we were still kept together, and it was only that which has kept me going all these long years in captivity. Now, I fear for Samuel – what have they done to him? Why can't we at least be together? (*And then Albert thumps his head on the table in frustration.*)

The whole Court is in turns astonished, moved and shocked. But counsel for the labs is more determined.

COUNSEL FOR THE LABS: 'M'lud. Although sentimentality may incline people to reunite these two monkeys, it is quite inappropriate to ascribe to an animal emotions or rational understandings that correctly belong only to humans. The monkey known as Samuel is needed for medical research of great importance to the well-being of people. The monkey known as Albert is asking for rights which belong to people, not monkeys. (*Turning to face the Jury, grandly*) If this Court were to allow all his preferences to enter into the equation, it would potentially lead to a situation in which we allow animals to have rights over and above human ones! I insist we take a clear stand on this and reject the monkey's application!'

And with that he sits down, leaving a definitely tricky dilemma for the court. Certainly Albert looks pathetic there, now having stopped signing after his longest ever speech, just staring at the Jury with big brown eyes. But it remains clearly the case, remarkable though his achievement was, that the gaze is not human . . .

What should the Court rule?

Dilemma 51
More monkey business

Having Albert there staring at them, the Jury naturally find for him. There is a great celebration. But equally naturally, being scientists, the laboratory appeal. This time, their counsel rests their case on chimpanzees having no responsibilities. 'No responsibilities, no rights,' he says. 'It's as simple as that,' and wags his finger reprovingly.

Although Albert is in court, and proceedings are carried out using sign language as well for his benefit, he takes no part in the appeal. But he looks disgusted. (After all, what is there to say?)

Counsel for Albert counter-argues that the law allows certain human groups rights – even though they too have no responsibilities. They may be too young, too old, too handicapped to be considered responsible for anything, but they are nonetheless consulted where they are able to give an opinion. For example, a chronically handicapped person will be allowed to express a view on most matters affecting them – and it would be considered quite incredible for someone to attempt to treat them as Samuel is being treated – taken away from their friends and family, experimented upon, and then killed. Incredible, but that of course is what did happen to human beings in the research centres of the Third Reich's concentration camps, so it is not, unfortunately, unthinkable at all.

Again the Court finds for Albert and against the lab, who again appeal the decision, this time to the highest court of the land. A new, more expensive counsel, produces a new, more expensive argument. After a few preliminary remarks about magpies and crows also being able to recognise themselves in mirrors, and find hidden objects, a pig is then led out blinking confusedly into the centre of the courtroom.

'This,' says counsel rather unnecessarily, 'is a pig.'

'And what is the point of bringing this, er . . . animal here?' asks the senior judge, leaning forward and lowering his horn-rimmed glasses ominously.

'Well, m'Lud,' replies the counsel with a flourish, 'Pigs are said to be the most intelligent of all land animals – and no one would think to attribute to this creature any rights.' At this the pig makes a sort of snuffling noise and deposits something rather smelly on the floor. The judges do not seem very impressed, but as the demonstration seems to have been intended to appeal more to the watching media than to them, counsel continues to smile confidently, and explains that the origins of rights are in social conventions and the workings of communities. Chimpanzees and bonobos play no part in human society, therefore they cannot meaningfully be extended rights.

At this Albert gets up from the witness bench where he is sitting, and walks over to Felicity and slowly extends a long hairy arm around her.

Is that any sort of an answer to a legal point?

Dilemma 52
Life's not fair

Thomas is in a sulk. He's just been told off for scribbling on his notebook. Some of the children get more pocket money than him. Samantha says he's not pretty enough to go out with her. James is better at football than him. And (whisper it) 'Brains' is better at maths. That's so *unfair* – it's not even Brains' favourite subject!

Then there are *events*. He's just not lucky any more. Sometimes, he writes in his diary, it seems as if there is a curse attached to him. Like when his remote control boat malfunctioned and got run over. And then at school he is told that he must do what is 'right'. Well, why should he? The world's not right, and he's got to live in it! he explains earnestly to Mrs Heffalump, his class teacher.

Mrs Heffalump takes the recalcitrant to the school library and pulls a well-thumbed copy of Plato's *Meno* from out of the blue bookcase. Mrs Heffalump explains that this is the dialogue in which Socrates asks Meno to describe to him the nature of 'virtue', that desirable and 'advantageous' characteristic which 'makes us good'. And Socrates obtains this confident response from his friend. Clearing her throat slightly self-consciously, she reads aloud:

> There is no difficulty about it. First of all, if it's a manly kind of virtue you are after, it is easy to see that the virtue consists in managing the city's affairs competently, and so that a man helps his friends and injures his enemies, all whilst of course ensuring no disadvantage to himself. Or, if you want to know what is virtuous for a woman, that too is easily described. She must be a good housewife, careful with her housekeeping, and obedient to her husband. . . . For every act, and every time of life, for every function, there is a virtue for each one, as well as, I should say, a vice.

'No, no, no!' exclaims Thomas. 'Mrs Heffalump, this is a rubbish theory!'

Is Thomas right?

Dilemma 53
Infantile ethical egotism

Thomas has been caught stealing sweeties from the special tin on the headteacher's desk reserved for rewarding pupils who have done particularly good work. 'Thomas! Naughty boy! What do you think would happen if EVERYONE were to help themselves to sweets whenever they felt like it?' says Mr Bollard. But Thomas, far from being humbled, being a precocious young chap, and also a typical infant, tries to excuse his disgraceful behaviour by offering a spurious explanation: 'Please, sir, if anyone who is hungry and tired and normally responsible and there are lots of sweeties there and no one likely to notice, then, I think, it would be all right for everyone like that to help themselves.' Mr Bollard is inclined to just clip him on the head with the blackboard duster (his favourite trick), but then he hesitates. Has Thomas got a point?

Mrs Cook, the school dinner lady, overhearing this, intervenes to help the boss. 'Thomas, ducky, what you did is just wrong, because the sweet did not belong to you. It was very naughty because you stole it.' Mr Bollard nods vigorously, relieved to have been offered so final an argument. But the dreadful child is arguing again, unabashed.

'Mrs Cook, "stealing" is a value-laden term. Anarchists (for example) may have different "universal" values to aim for – you have to provide some reason why something is wrong, not just say that it is.'

'I beg your pardon, young man!'

'*Petitio principii!*'

'That will do, Thomas!'

Out comes the board duster and it certainly seems to settle the immediate argument in Mr Bollard's favour.

But had Mrs Cook served it up right?

Searching for the good life

Dilemma 54
The rich man's dilemma

Poor Justin Megabucks. He has so much money he does not know what to do with it all. He has no children, so the conventional solution is out, and anyway, he reckons he would rather spend it than save it for them. Yet he already has all the things he could possibly want – posh houses, cars, jets, boats – the lot. Sometimes, he gets bundles of US$1,000 dollar notes delivered to his mansions and burns them on the open fire, just for the fun of it.

The local newspaper once tried to run a story criticising him for his extravagance but Justin pointed out that it was all his own money, he worked hard for it (well, fairly hard – he used to be a pop singer) and anyway, there are plenty of other people around with more than him! So what the heck. It may seem like a bit of a waste to some people, but then they're not zillionaires, he points out, reasonably. It's just envy that makes people criticise him, he adds. He is under no obligation to help others.

Could Justin have the right of it?

Then one day, whilst busy burning wads during an orgy (or as much of one as he can manage after years of overeating and drinking, not to mention . . .) his housekeeper, Mrs Jones, bringing a tray of cocaine in, says: 'It does seem an awful waste, Mr Megabucks, to burn all that lovely money, and me and Mr Jones were wondering, well, couldn't you find something a little bit more, well, you know, *social* to do with it?'

Thus challenged by his faithful old retainer, Megabucks is stirred to action. His long dormant conscience is pricked. He stops burning money to consult around a bit. First of all, he asks his mates (not real ones, of course, paid ones) for advice. Some say he should give it all to charity – but Mr Megabucks doesn't believe in *them*. They only spend it on administration, and any money that doesn't go on that actually only makes things worse. At this point, Samantha (his glamourous PA) suggests he could spend it on having a *flower party*, with thousands of exotic orchids planted in the windswept crevices of Mount Justin (which he bought a couple of years ago). 'Why?' asks Justin. 'As a *concept*,' she replies, sweetly. Megabucks likes the idea, so he does it.

But is that any solution?

Dilemma 55
The beauty trap

Mr and Mrs Plain were very happy after the birth of their first daughter, whom they christened 'Birdy'. She was a very normal girl, of very plain appearance and very normal abilities. Their second daughter, christened 'Wolfie' after her big dark eyes, also appeared normal enough. Unfortunately, it became clear that this wasn't quite true. By the time the two girls had reached school age, it was obvious that Wolfie *was not plain at all*. She was spectacularly intelligent (catapulted a year ahead at school, into Birdy's year), good natured, and worst of all, beautiful. She had such an excess of all the virtues, that it left her ordinary sister struggling to keep up.

Both girls were beautiful to their parents of course, but increasingly it became evident that Wolfie was beautiful to everyone else too. For a start, when Birdy had higgledypiggledy teeth and numerous fillings, Wolfie just had perfect white ones attractively revealed by a generous smile. Wolfie had a particularly flawless complexion, and while Birdy suffered the usual teenage angst over spots, blemishes and even a few nastier things, Wolfie just radiated warm vitality. Wolfie's hair was always cascading elegantly over her slim shoulders – Birdy's slunk limp and dandruffy to her bumpy skull. Wolfie had those big dark eyes, Birdy had ordinary ones which blinked nervously, as if dazzled by her sister.

This last fact was particularly vexatious to her parents, because wherever they went people would stop and stare at Wolfie and often assume that they had somehow pampered and doted on her, whereas they were scrupulously democratic in outlook. But matters came to a head on Birdy's sixteenth birthday, after Birdy invited 'Big John', the ultra-popular captain of the football team, to her party. Birdy spent the whole day getting ready, buying a new pair of jeans with gold highlights, and sewing sequins onto a white jacket to make it look like a football shirt, but when Big John arrived he gave her only a cursory 'hello' and instead spent the whole evening gazing fixedly at Wolfie as she glided around helping with the party by distributing pretzels and fruit punch. (*And is Big John a rotter or what?*)

Poor Birdy. She certainly thought so. At one point she rushed upstairs and flung herself on her bed bemoaning the injustice of it all. Noticing she was gone, Mrs Plain went upstairs to see what was the matter. Then it all came out pitifully. 'Everyone likes Wolfie more than me, just because she's beautiful and I'm not! The boys, the other girls, even the teachers!'

'Nonsense, dear,' said her mother firmly. 'Teachers are paid to be impartial.'

But inconsolable, Birdy explained her theory about what had happened at the party. The boys all want girls to look like Wolfie and have perfect faces and hip ratios x and waist ratios y – like we're all just controlled by our genes or something and not *thinking* people!

Now Mrs Plain was cross. 'Now that's just not true, dear,' she said. 'Everyone knows notions of beauty are completely subjective – socially constructed – mainly as a way of disempowering women. Think of the Chinese foot-binding! Anyone who is considered less attractive than someone else is actually a victim of a form of discrimination!' At this, Birdy sniffed, but was slightly reassured.

Unfortunately, warming to her theme, Mrs Plain continues. 'You see, our notions of so-called female beauty in particular change over the ages and between places. You know, the Maori people admire plumpness in a woman, whilst the Padung admire drooping breasts – you would be considered more beautiful than Wolfie in many cultures!'

But, strangely enough, this last comment had the reverse effect to the one intended, and Birdy burst into tears. Even Mrs Plain's thought 'Is a butterfly any "better" than a cockroach – just because it is considered pretty? We need them both' didn't help. So it was left that the next day the family would hold a 'council of war' and work out ways to combat the social conditioning that caused such unhappiness and discord.

Wolfie was of course very shocked to hear that she had inadvertently been partly responsible for causing her sister such upset, and wanted to take steps at once to remedy the situation. She explained too how horrid it was for her to be followed around by boys and pestered for dates all the time. Birdy had never thought of it like this, and graciously said that Wolfie too was just as much a victim, trapped inside other people's notions and definitions of how to look.

At this, Mrs Plain got a pudding basin, put it over her head (Wolfie's that is) and snip snip! the long flowing tresses fell to the floor to be replaced by a spiky crop. 'No one's going to pick and choose between my two lovely babies!' said Mrs Plain. She then took Wolfie on a special 'unshopping' trip to get unfashionable clothes, and finally at Wolfie's special request they went to the opticians and bought her a pair of very large bright blue spectacles, even though, as the optician protested, she had excellent eyesight, 'as well as the most lovely big eyes' (said gushingly).

Actually, whatever Wolfie wore, no matter how in itself unattractive, invariably ended up looking glamorous and setting new standards in desirable fashion, and these outfits were no different. The spiky crop too immediately looked stylish. Nonetheless, the next morning as Wolfie tucked into a large fried breakfast (part of a new diet) she beamed confidently through the new glasses at Birdy. 'Really, I feel much happier now,' she announces, 'I feel as though I have been set free from being trapped in a prison of other people's notions of beauty! Notions that are supposedly universal but are in fact just socially constructed.' But then her pretty forehead puckers in puzzlement. For this morning, instead of her usual large, healthy breakfast, Birdy is putting out on her plate just two dry looking crackers and some grated carrots.

Now who's in the trap?

Dilemma 56
The good life

Siddhartha Gautama (563–483 BC) was the son of a king, married to a beautiful princess, and looking forward to all the pleasures life could bring. But one day, finding himself separated from his princely minders, he struck off on his own for the first time, and wandered amongst the ordinary townspeople of his native India.

He came across an old wizened man, sitting half-dozing under a tree, staring unseeing at the ground and tapping his hand mindlessly up and down. He came across a house with terrible sounds coming from it, and peering through a window, in a dirty dark room found a huddled figure, lying on a dirty bed, wracked with illness and pain. Shuddering, he hurried quickly on, deciding to return to the cool fountains of the palace. And, even as he approached the safety of his home, he was forced aside into the dirty gutter as a procession of people carrying a corpse went past.

That same night, chastened, Siddhartha reassessed his life and his plans. Perhaps truly, life was not, as he had always optimistically imagined, a series of enjoyable events, parties, elephant hunts, fine meals with good friends? Perhaps, in contrast, life was truly a series of futile banalities, disappointment, and tragedies. A process of inevitable decay and collapse: pain, sorrow and finally death.

Some weeks later, with these melancholy thoughts still going through his mind, a monk with the characteristic orange gown and shaven head passes, and to Siddhartha his calm and composed appearance seems to be a sign, perhaps even an answer. He announces he is leaving the palace for ever, to begin a strict life of monastic asceticism. This is the 'virtuous life'. But it is not the end of the story. After a period of self-denial and starvation, he becomes ill himself and, one day, even collapses in the street. Fortunately, friends nurse him back to health, and so now, convalescing, he sits under a flowering fig tree in the sun. Sitting and pondering there, he realises that what he has just tried is not, in its way, any more 'principled' than his empty life of privileged indulgence was before – the asceticism had simply become another form of self-indulgence.

Which way now to the good life?

Three more trolley dilemmas (that no one really cares about anyway)

Dilemma 57
Flight 999 to Shangri-La

During a vicious snowstorm, Flight 999 is thrown massively off-course and crashes
in the Himalayas. By a miracle, three people on board survive. Or maybe we
should say two and a half, as one of them is a young boy so badly injured he
cannot move. The pilot, who knows about such things, says that because they are
so far off-course there is no prospect of rescuers finding them. As if that was not
bad enough, if they stay put another day or two, he says the cold will finish them all
off too. The only chance is to leave the shelter of the plane and walk over the top of
the mountain range and down to the monastery there. If all goes well, this will take
two days. Now the other survivor is a fit young man and he cheerfully agrees to
attempt the hike. But he points out that to have any chance of surviving they will
have to eat something. Taking the pilot aside, he points out grimly that the only
food available is the injured boy!

Since the boy has no chance of surviving if left, and since they must take food on
the hike immediately if they are themselves to have the energy to get to the
monastery, surely the best thing is to 'humanely' kill the young boy and cook him to
make provisions for the journey? Of course, they would rather eat snow rabbits or
something, but circumstances alter cases . . .

Or do they?

The pilot does not agree. He refuses to allow the boy to be killed. At this the other
man gets very indignant. 'I'm not a murderer, you know!' he exclaims. And he asks
the pilot to consider a 'real' case he had read about in the paper.

A small cruise yacht had hit a rock in the Caribbean, and was sinking. It had two
rubber dinghies for the six people on board, but most unfortunately, one of the
dinghies was broken. At a pinch, each dinghy could take five people, but only that.
Any more and it would sink. Someone will have to sacrifice themselves to save the
others. But no one is prepared to. The captain took a rapid decision. He himself
could not be the one to stay on the sinking boat (of course) as he would be needed
to lead the others. But there was one of the holidaymakers who was already

vulnerable as he was in a wheelchair and would probably not survive long in the dinghy anyway. He says that the wheelchair passenger can be left on the sinking boat. Everyone agrees except the handicapped passenger, who quickly manoeuvres himself in front of the ladder to the one working lifeboat. But (ignoring the shouts of the wheelchair passenger) they quickly push him out of the way, rush into the dinghy and sail off.

Now, says the first survivor to the pilot – would you say that all those passengers did the wrong thing?

Dilemma 58
Dangerous nibbles

Sam is a bright, chirpy, bargirl. One evening she happens to overhear a handsome man (whom she herself fancies a bit!) in a group of customers say that he has found out that he has got the HIV virus (which causes the potentially fatal disease AIDS). This man tells the others, in a way that leaves no doubt at all that he is deadly serious, that he now intends to go on a sexual spree, spreading the virus. The others are laughing and encouraging him.

Now Sam happens to know that the man (who has been into the bar before) has both a critical allergy to peanuts and a strong penchant for the free 'nibbles' that the bar gives out sometimes. If she 'accidentally' puts some of the nibbles in a dish which has previously been used for peanuts, and puts it on their table, then it is very likely that the man will get such a strong allergic reaction that he will be hospitalised for too long to be able to 'go on a sexual spree' afterwards and infect other people with HIV.

It might be rough justice, but, she thinks . . .

. . . surely it would be justice nevertheless?

Dilemma 59
The terrorist

President Settee is dealing with a terrorist crisis. A group of fanatics have acquired a 'dirty' bomb that they intend to detonate in the capital unless their demands are met. The leader of the terrorists is in contact via the internet and has sent a picture of the bomb all set up in place, whilst delivering a long speech about post-industrial hegemony and neo-imperialism.

But in so doing, although hooded, he has given away his identity and the President's aides have identified the terrorist and know that he has two young children attending a school in the country.

Is it acceptable for President Settee to attempt to use the children as a kind of lever in the negotiations with the terrorist group?

The President thinks it is. He tells the terrorist leader that if he carries out any of his threats, his children will be the first to suffer. They will be imprisoned 'as enemy combatants' in one of the government's 'holding facilities, the dreaded secret camps in remote countries'. There, the President warns, they will be subjected to 'interrogation' – and you know what that means, he adds pointedly.

The terrorist leader laughs and tells President Settee to do what he likes. He says that the President is responsible for the deaths of thousands of children throughout the Third World so what will one or two more matter? But voice analysts discern that this bravado conceals a strong concern for the children, and the President's experts advise him that if he applies some severe pain to the children then the leader of the terrorists will probably seek a compromise. One of them says he should send the terrorist a video of one of the children apparently being beheaded. Another one says, why stop there? Why not actually 'execute' one of the terror leader's children? Seeing the President look appalled, the expert adds sanctimoniously that the aim would be to save thousands of innocent lives. After all, the advisor says, the children of terrorists invariably grow up to be ones themselves. If the President could have gone back in time and assassinated Hitler, he would have done that! Why should 'future terrorists' be treated any better than present day ones?

How ethical is that?

Watching brief

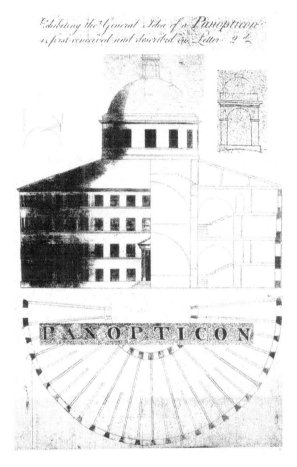

Exhibiting the General Idea of a *Panopticon*
as first conceived and described in Letter 2 &

PANOPTICON

Jeremy Bentham's *Panopticon* – the circular prison where every action of every prisoner is watched all the time.

Dilemma 60
The Panopticon

The good people of Democratia were suffering an upsurge in chronic criminality. A minority of anti-social people were stealing, vandalising, robbing, and every so often murdering other citizens. How bad was the situation? Well, scarcely a day went by without something awful being reported in the papers. So that's bad. Anyway, everyone agreed: something must be done.

An ambitious programme of surveillance was launched to find the culprits.

They watched them on closed circuit cameras as they drove or cycled to work; they watched them when they got there; they watched them at their desks. They even watched them in the staff canteen and the staff toilets. They watched people do their shopping, or cheering the football. Hidden cameras kept a baleful eye over the pubs and clubs. Powerful computers matched faces to names and names to places.

The same computers whirred tirelessly through the night, checking up on people. They sifted emails for suspicious correspondence, cross-referencing the internet histories of every terminal in the land. They checked bank accounts and credit cards for evidence of improper dealings; they even watched shopping bills for evidence of, well, shopping habits.

They listened to telephone calls, collating details of who called whom, and where and when. They used the handsets of phones as microphones to listen in on people in their houses. Devices deciphered reflected light so that they could watch people as they watched television.

And being a great democracy, the government debated its new policy in cabinet (behind closed doors), because the monitors picked up and recorded much mumbling of discontent in the posh newspapers.

Hmmm, the ministers asked, had they preserved the delicate balance between individuals' rights to privacy and the social necessity of data gathering – or overstepped the mark?

Dilemma 61

The Panopticon: second section

The government decides the mark is still some way off yet. There is, after all, a way to have both individual privacy and social controls, and that is to continue with the watching, but have a new Data Protection Act giving individuals the right to check up for themselves on what information on them has been collected. If it's not an official secret, of course – and the police don't mind.

Encouraged by this safeguard, the Minster for Total Security suggest that medical records, tax files, social security files, all kinds of data from the various branches of government should now be carefully collated and brought together in one massive super database, instantly available to all government agents and agencies. New genetic profiles on citizens would be created too, listing useful information on likely future illnesses and predisposition to mental instability.

Again there are complaints from 'the usual suspects'. But as the Minister says (on chat radio), it is all government information, they gathered it, and they only need it to help people.

What possible objections could there be to using it more effectively?

But then there comes a new challenge to the system – a lobby group starts demanding access to information on cameras monitoring nuclear installations, another group wants data on local councillors' financial interests to see if they're profiting from developments – and now some newspapers even want details on ministerial holidays!

Must the 'inspection principle' be applied to the 'Inspector' too?

Dilemma 62
The Panopticon: third section

The government explains that in the interests of efficiency, certain things, such as their own plans, must remain shielded from scrutiny. And despite this hiccup, the collection of information otherwise seems to be going well. Soon it became (official figures showed) much more difficult for anyone to commit any crimes without them being recorded and detected. In fact, the government found it possible to stop crimes even happening, by identifying likely offenders and apprehending them in dawn swoops before they had even thought of doing something wrong.

Later on, the range of behaviours that were tackled was expanded to move beyond the merely criminal to the more generally undesirable. Persons exhibiting all manner of anti-social characteristics, be it sexual deviancy, political extremism or workplace disloyalty. Schoolchildren and students were found to particularly benefit from early intervention. Potentially, the files gave the government great power over the individual, but the government of Democratia was good and scrupulously proper, and no one (except the criminals, of course!) seemed to mind.

It was a straightforward choice between enhancing the collective well-being or allowing individuals the 'luxury' to cause trouble. 'Wars and storms are best to read of, but peace and calms are better to enjoy,' quoth the Minster for Security and Social Harmony to the lobby journalists, although when pressed, he was not sure where the quote came from. ('And this conversation is off the record,' glowered the Minister menacingly.) Anyway, that was how the issue would be presented.

But schools, for goodness sake – can't the children be left to play in peace?!

Dilemma 63
The Panopticon: final section

Unfortunately, the costs of the operation in money terms were huge. The Minister had to ask for permission to allow the data collected to be used by businesses and services seeking to target consumers more effectively. In this way, the Minister explained, the surveillance operation could also become a valuable social tool for more efficient production. Businesses had already started to build up their own sophisticated databases, using information on buying habits, 'postcode profiling', and the like, culled from credit and store cards: now the whole economy would begin to benefit with additional information available from official records, such as health and social security information (for a fee).

Some of the information was very valuable to newspapers, of course. Illnesses of pop and film stars, earnings of politicians, and so on. Video clips of people 'caught in the act' became a popular staple of the TV schedules, sold to the highest bidder, while the newspapers were full of photos and transcripts of lewd and revealing conversations by celebrities.

But at this point, one or two of the other ministers begin to get cold feet. They began to remember some small, 'youthful peccadilloes', just passing youthful ones, they murmur to each other, but nonetheless, in the wrong hands, 'liable to be misunderstood'.

Perhaps there was a need for legislation to protect the individual's right to privacy after all – at least from private enterprise?

101 Ethical Dilemmas

Animals too:

The vegetarian's dilemma

Dilemma 64
Plutarch's uncongenial fare

In Philosophy Heaven (or is it Hell?) a great debate is raging. Should anyone who chooses to eat meat be allowed in?

Plutarch (AD 46–120) opens, for the vegetarians:

'It is not *natural* for men to eat meat. This is shown first of all by the shape of our bodies. The human body has no resemblance to that of a carnivorous creature. It has no hooked beak or sharp talons or pointed teeth, no stout stomach or hot breath able to convert and dispose of such heavy and fleshy fare . . .

'And if you insist it is your nature to eat such food, do you yourself then kill first what you want to eat? Do it yourself without the help of a chopping knife, club, or axe, but as wolves, bears, and lions do, who kill for themselves all they devour. Bite an ox to pieces with your teeth, or a pig with your jaws. Tear a lamb or a hare to shreds and eat it quickly, still alive as they do. If you wait until the dying animal is quite dead and are *ashamed to enjoy the flesh while the spirit is still in it*, why, against Nature, see food at all in a living thing? Actually, no one wants to eat even a dead and lifeless thing as it is, but they boil it and roast it and transform it with heat and sauces, changing and altering and smothering the taste of gore with thousands of sweet spices, so that the palate being thus deceived, may accept this uncongenial fare . . . '

Mmmm. . . . Food for thought anyway . . .

Test your voting buttons please! Meat eaters *in* or *out*?

Dilemma 65
The beast

Appearing for the meat eaters is Nazi philosopher Oswald Spengler, with his mentor, Friedrich Nietzsche, nodding enthusiastically in the background. 'Erst kommt das Fressen, dann kommt die Moral, hein?'* whispers Bertolt Brecht (1898–1956) encouragingly to his fellow countrymen. 'The beast of prey is the highest form of active life,' announces Spengler (looking around cautiously, mindful that 'the Führer' himself was actually a vegetarian).

'It represents a mode of living which requires the extreme degree of the necessity of fighting, conquering, annihilating, self-assertion. The human race ranks highly because it belongs to the class of beasts of prey. Therefore we find in man the tactics of life proper to a bold, cunning beast of prey. He lives engaged in aggression, killing, annihilation. He wants to be master in as much as he exists.'

Shocked and quivering, the sensitive philosophers huddle amongst themselves. What to respond to that?

The cunning beast! But should he be allowed in – or kept out?

* 'First comes the food, then come the morals'.

Dilemma 66
Plutarch's response

Plutarch warms to his theme:

'It all began the same way that tyrants began to slaughter men. At Athens the first man they put to death was the worst of their informers, who everyone said deserved it. The second was the same sort of man, and so was the third. But after that, the Athenians were accustomed to bloodshed and looked on passively when Niceratus, son of Nicias, and the general Thramenes, and Polemarchus the philosopher were executed. In the same way the first animal that was killed and eaten was a wild and mischievous beast, and then a bird and a fish were caught. And murder, being thus tried and practised upon creatures like these, arrived at the labouring ox, and the sheep that clothes us, and the cock that guards our house. And little by little, our desires hardening, we proceeded to the slaughter of men, wars and massacres.

'Can you really ask what reason Pythagoras had for abstaining from flesh? For my part I rather wonder both by what accident and in what state of soul or mind the first man did so, touched his mouth to gore and brought his lips to the flesh of a dead creature, he who set forth tables of dead, stale bodies and ventured to call food and nourishment the parts that had a little before bellowed and cried, moved and lived. How could his eyes endure the slaughter when throats were slit and hides flayed and limbs torn from limb? How could his nose endure the stench? How was it that the pollution did not turn away his taste, which made contact with the sores of others and sucked juices and serums from mortal wounds . . . '

'Hear! Hear!' interjected George Bernard Shaw (1856–1950), 'Animals are my friends . . . and I don't eat my friends.'

Mmmmm . . .

But should people who *do* eat George's friends be allowed in?

Dilemma 67
St Paul's view

A long-haired figure now approaches the lectern, dressed in a shabby white gown. It is Paul, the controversial 'false' apostle. He chuckles, revealing yellow, tobacco-stained teeth.

'You may eat anything sold in the meat market without raising questions of conscience; for the earth is the Lord's and everything in it'

he says, grinning lopsidedly, 'One Corinthians ten fourteen thirty-three.' Then, sitting down he looks self-satisfiedly around awaiting approval.

Voting begins: meat eaters *in* or *out*?

Dilemma 68
Chrysostom's warning

'Wait!' A thin ascetic-looking figure with long black and oily hair trailing over his eyes appears clutching a sheaf of notes with his pale white hands. It is Chrysostom, averting his gaze all the while from a furious Paul. Quivering, he wails: 'We the Christian leaders practise abstinence from the flesh of animals to subdue our bodies . . . the unnatural eating of flesh-meat is of demoniacal origin . . . the eating of flesh is polluting . . . '

Raising his eyes upwards, rocking back and forth, his voice drops to a sinister whisper: 'flesh-meats and wine serve as *materials for sensuality*, and are a source of danger, sorrow, and *disease*. Let him who can be satisfied with pulse, and can keep in good health, seek for nothing more. . . . For, when all his time is spent between feasting and drunkenness, is he not dead, and buried in darkness? Who can describe the storm that comes of luxury, that assails the soul and body?'

Certainly not Chrysostom, by the look of it. Yet he has a go anyway. 'For, as a sky continually clouded admits not the sunbeams to shine through, so the fumes of luxury . . . envelop his brain . . . and casting over it a thick mist, suffers not reason to exert itself . . . ' Then, his voice deepens almost to a groan: 'If it were possible to bring the soul into view and to behold it with our bodily eyes – it would seem *depressed, mournful, miserable, and wasted* with leanness; for the more the body grows sleek and gross, the more lean and weakly is the soul. The more one is pampered, the more the other is hamper . . . '

'Nonsense! Absolute nonsense!' It is Pope Pius XII, making a quite disgraceful interruption, brandishing a poker.* 'Animals have no feelings! Their cries should not arouse unreasonable compassion any more than do red-hot metals undergoing the blows of the hammer!' So saying, he smashes the poker on the lectern splitting it in two, thereby ending the discussion in disarray.

Now what's the verdict?

* Like Wittgenstein. But that's another story . . .

Ethically suspect fairy tales

Dilemma 69
The Frog-King

In olden times when wishing still helped one, there lived a king whose daughters were all beautiful, but the youngest was so lovely that the sun itself, which has seen so much, brightened whenever it shone on her face. Now, close by the King's castle under an old lime tree was a pond, and when the day was very warm, this girl would take a golden ball, and play with it under the tree throwing it high up in the air and catching it, and the golden ball became her favourite thing.

But on one occasion the princess's golden ball did not fall back down. It was stuck in the tree. Seeing this she gave the branch it was on a big tug, and the ball dropped down . . .

. . . straight into the pond! The girl followed it with her eyes, but it vanished, and the water was deep, so that the bottom could not be seen. At this she began to sob, and sobbed louder and louder, until, as she lamented, a little voice croaked, 'What is the trouble, lovely one? Why, even a stone would show pity!'

Surprised, she looked round from side to side to see from where the voice came, and saw a frog stretching forth its squat, ugly head from the water. 'Ah! old water-splasher, is it you?' said she; 'I am weeping for my golden ball, which has fallen into the middle of your pond.'

'Be quiet, and do not weep,' answered the frog, 'because I can help you. But will you do something for me, if I do so?'

'Whatever you want, dear frog,' said the girl. 'My clothes, my pearls and jewels, and even the golden crown which I am wearing are all yours if you like.'

The frog croaked, 'Pah! I do not need your clothes, pearls or jewels, or your golden crown! But if you will love me and let me be your companion and play-fellow, sit by you at your table and eat off your little golden plate, drink out of your little cup and sleep in your bed – if you will promise me this – then I will dive down, and bring back your golden ball for you!'

'Anything, I promise you it all, water-splasher – if only you can bring me my ball back!' But she thought to herself, 'How silly frogs are! They live in the water with other frogs, and cannot live with people!'

However, the frog thought only of the promise, and sprang with his long legs in to the water and dived down before, after a short while, swimming back up with the golden globe in his mouth, and triumphantly throwing it onto the grass by the princess. The girl picked it up, delighted to see her pretty plaything once more, and ran away with it. 'Wait, wait,' cried the frog. 'Take me with you. I can't run as fast as you can!' But what did it avail him to croak, croak, croak after her, as loudly as he could? She did not listen, but ran home and forgot the poor frog, who was forced to go back into his watery world again.

But, wait a minute – she promised! And promises have to be kept – even to frogs – don't they?

The story continues

The next day when the King and all his daughters were eating caviar from their golden plates, a sound could be heard distantly. Splish-splash, splish-splash, splish-splashing up the marble staircase, growing louder until, when it had got to the top, it stopped and a little voice croaked: 'Princess, princess, open the door for me.' The youngest princess ran hurriedly to the door, and there indeed sat the frog, in a puddle of pond water, looking up expectantly at her with big frog eyes. She slammed the door and in great disarray, sat down to dinner again. The King saw all this, and said, 'My child, what are you so afraid of? Is there perchance a giant outside who wants to carry you away?' And he guffawed.

'No, no,' replied the princess. 'Worse than that – not a giant but a disgusting frog!' And she told her father the story of the previous day. In the meantime there came a knock a second time, and the croaky cry: 'Princess! Princess! Open the door for me! Remember your promise to me by the cool waters of the pond?' Now the King cleared his throat and pronounced on the matter: 'That which you promised you must perform. Go and let him in!'

With sinking heart, the daughter went and opened the door, and in hopped the frog jauntily, flip-flop, flip-flop, over to her chair. There he stopped and croaked, 'Lift me up beside you!' She delayed, but the King commanded her to do it. When the frog was on the table he said, 'Now, push your little golden plate nearer to me that we may eat together.' She did this too, but it was easy to see it was not done willingly. The meal continued in silence. The frog enjoyed what he ate, but almost every mouthful the princess took choked her. At length he said, 'I have eaten and am satisfied; now I am tired, carry me into your little room and make your little silken bed ready, and we will both lie down and go to sleep.'

The daughter began to cry, for she did not want the dirty, cold wet frog to sleep in her pretty, clean little bed. But at this the King grew angry and said, 'Those who helped you when you were in trouble ought not afterwards be despised!' So she led the frog slowly upstairs and, after some thought, sat him in the furthest corner. But when she was in bed he crept to her and said, 'I am tired, I want to sleep as well as you, lift me up – or I will tell your father!' At this she became terribly angry, and picking him up gingerly between two fingers, hurled him against the wall above the little bed. 'Now, you will be quiet, odious frog!' she screamed. But even as the frog lay there on the sheets where he had fallen, he was no longer a frog but a king's son with beautiful kind eyes.

Because, by her father's command, he *was* now her dear companion and husband.

The dilemma's gone – but where's the moral?

Dilemma 70

The Juniper Tree: a diabolical fairy tale

Long, long ago, there was a couple who loved each other dearly but had, however, no children, although they wished for them very much. In front of their house was a courtyard in which a juniper tree grew.

One day, in winter, the woman was standing beneath it and peeling an apple, when she cut her finger, and a drop of blood fell on the snow. 'Ah,' said the woman, and sighed, 'ah, but if I had a child as red as blood and as white as snow!' And, as she spoke, she became quite happy in her mind and suddenly felt just as if that were going to happen. Then she went into the house and a month went by and the snow was gone, and two months, and then everything was green, and three months, and then all the flowers came out of the earth, and four months, and then all the trees in the wood grew thicker and the green branches were all closely entwined and the birds sang until the wood resounded and the blossoms fell from the trees. Then the fifth month passed away and she stood under the juniper tree, which smelt so sweetly that her heart leapt and she fell on her knees and was beside herself with joy. And when the sixth month was over the fruit was large and fine, and then she was quite still, and the seventh month she snatched at the juniper berries and ate them greedily. Then she grew sick and sorrowful and when the eighth month passed she called her husband to her, and wept and said, 'If I die then bury me beneath the juniper tree!' Then the next month was over, and she had a son. As white as snow and as red as blood.

But it is said that her joy was too great and so she died. Then her husband buried her beneath the juniper tree. And, after some time, took another wife. They had a daughter called Marilena, and when the woman looked at her daughter she loved her very much, but when she looked at the little boy, it seemed to cut her to the heart, and she slapped him here and cuffed him there, until he had no peace or place. Until one day, the little boy came in at the door, and the Devil made her say to him kindly, 'My son, would you like an apple?' [An old image there!] 'Mother,' said the little boy, 'Yes, please give me an apple!' Then it seemed to her as if she were forced to say to him, 'Come with me,' and going into the pantry she opened the great heavy lid of the oak chest and said, 'Take an apple for thyself,' and as the little boy was stooping inside, crash! she slammed the lid down, and his head flew off and fell among the red apples.

Then she was overwhelmed with terror, and so she took a white handkerchief and set the head on the neck again, and folded the handkerchief so that nothing could be seen, and she sat him on a chair in front of the door, and put the apple in his hand. After this Marilena came into the kitchen to her mother, who was standing by the fire with a pan of hot water before her which she was constantly stirring.

'Mother,' said Marilena, 'brother is sitting at the door, and he looks quite white and has an apple in his hand. I asked him to give me the apple, but he did not answer me.'

'Go back to him,' said her mother, 'and if he will still not answer, give him a box on the ear!'

Marilena did as she was told, and said, 'Brother, give me the apple.' But he was silent, and so she gave him a blow on the ear, at which his head fell off!

Marilena was horrified, and began crying and screaming, and ran to her mother, and said, 'Mother, I have knocked my brother's head off!'

'Marilena,' said the mother, 'Clumsy oaf! What have you done? but be quiet and no one need know it; it cannot be helped now, we will make him into black puddings.' Then the mother took the little boy and chopped him in pieces, put him into the pan and made him into black puddings; but Marilena stood by weeping and weeping, and all her tears fell into the pan and there was no need of any salt.

When father came home and sat down to dinner, the mother served up a great dish of black puddings, but Marilena wept and could not eat. The father saw this and was concerned but only said: 'Ah, wife, how delicious this food is, give me some more.' And the more he ate the more he wanted to have, and he said, 'Give me some more, you shall have none of it. It seems to me as if it were all mine.' And he ate and ate and threw all the bones under the table.

Look, this is all very interesting, but this isn't learning about ethics. Or is it?

After supper, Marilena went away to a cupboard, and took her best silk handkerchief out and got all the bones from beneath the table and tied them up in it, and carried them outside the door, weeping tears as she did so. Then the juniper tree began to stir itself, and the branches parted asunder, and moved together again, just as if it was applauding. And then, a mist seemed to arise from the tree and in the centre of this mist it burnt like a fire, and a beautiful bird flew out singing and flew high up in the air, and when he was gone, the juniper tree was just as it had been before, *but the handkerchief and bones were no longer there.*

The bird flew away and lighted on a goldsmith's house, and began to sing, 'Kywitt, kywitt, what a beautiful bird am I!' The smith was sitting in his workshop making a gold chain, when he heard the bird singing on his roof, and very beautiful the song seemed to him too. 'Here,' said the goldsmith, 'here is a golden chain for you, now sing me that song again.' Then the bird came and took the golden chain in his right claw, and went and sat in front of the goldsmith, and sang, 'Kywitt, kywitt, what a beautiful bird am I!'

Then he flew away to a shoemaker, and lighted on his roof and sang, 'Kywitt, kywitt, what a beautiful bird am I!' The shoemaker heard it and ran out of doors in his shirt sleeves, and looked up at his roof, and saw how beautiful he was, and what fine red and green feathers he had, and how like real gold his neck was, and how the eyes in his head shone like stars. 'Bird,' said the shoemaker, 'sing me that song again.' 'Nay,' said the bird, 'I do not sing twice for nothing; you must give me something.' 'Wife,' said the man, 'upon the top shelf there stands a pair of red shoes, bring them down.' Then the bird came and taking the shoes in his left claw, sang, 'Kywitt, kywitt, what a beautiful bird am I!'

And when he had sung the whole song he flew far away to a mill, and sat on a lime tree and sang whilst the millstone went, 'klipp klapp, klipp klapp, klipp klapp.' 'Bird,' said the miller, 'how beautifully you sing! Do that once more for me.' 'Nay,' said the bird, 'I do not sing twice for nothing. Give me the millstone, and then I will sing again!' And the bird flew down, and the millers all set to work with a beam and raised the stone up. And the bird stuck his neck through the hole, and put the stone on as if it were a collar, and flew on to the tree again, and sang, 'Kywitt, kywitt, what a beautiful bird am I!'

Now the bird spread his wings and flew back to the house, where he sat in the juniper tree, singing. Hearing this, the mother stopped her ears, and shut her eyes, and would not see or hear, for there was a roaring in her ears like the most violent storm, and her eyes burnt and flashed like lightning. 'Ah, mother,' says the man, 'that is a beautiful bird! He sings so splendidly, and the sun shines so warm, and there is a smell just like cinnamon. I am going out – I must see the bird quite close.'

'Don't go, don't go,' said the woman, 'I feel as if the whole house were shaking and on fire.' But the man went out and looked at the bird as it sang: 'My father, he ate me. Kywitt, kywitt, what a beautiful bird am I!' On this, the bird let the golden chain fall, and it fell round the man's neck, and so exactly that it fitted beautifully. Delighted, the father went back and said, 'Just look what a handsome gold chain that bird has given me, and how pretty he is!' But the wife was terrified, and fell down trembling on the floor in the room. 'Ah,' said Marilena, 'I too will go out and see this bird.'

As she approached, the bird sang: 'My sister, little Marilena, gathered together all my bones, tied them in a silken handkerchief, laid them beneath the juniper tree!' And then, throwing down the shoes to her, 'Kywitt, kywitt, what a beautiful bird am I!' Marilena put on the new red shoes and danced and leaped into the house. 'Ah,' said she, 'I was so sad when I went out and now I am so happy; that is a splendid bird, he has given me a pair of red shoes!'

'Well,' said the woman, and rising to her feet her hair also stood up, like flames of fire, 'I, too, will go out and see if the bird can make my heart feel lighter.' And as she went out of the door, CRASH! The bird threw down the millstone on her head, and she was entirely crushed by it.

The father and Marilena heard what had happened and went out, and smoke, flames, and fire were rising from the place, and when that was over, there stood the little brother, and he took his father and Marilena by the hand, and all three were content, and they went into the house together.

(Freely adapted from the 1812 version by Jacob and Wilhelm Grimm, in *Household Tales*)

And the moral is?

Dilemma 71

A cautionary tale

The Dreadful Story of Pauline and the Matches

Mamma and Nursie went out one day,
And left Pauline alone at play;
Around the room she gayly sprung,
Clapp'd her hands, and danced, and sung.
Now, on the table close at hand,
A box of matches chanced to stand,
And kind Mamma and Nursie had told her,
That if she touched them they would scold her;
But Pauline said, 'Oh, what a pity!
For, when they burn, it is so pretty;
They crackle so, and spit, and flame;
And Mamma often burns the same.
I'll just light a match or two
As I have often seen my mother do.'

When Minz and Maunz, the philosopher-cats, heard this
They held up their paws and began to hiss.
'Meow!!' they said, 'me-ow, me-o!
You'll burn to death, if you do so,
Your parents have forbidden you, you know.'
But Pauline would not take advice,
She lit a match, it was so nice!

It crackled so, it burned so clear,
Exactly like the picture here.
She jumped for joy and ran about,
And was too pleased to put it out.

When Minz and Maunz, the catty Kantians, saw this,
They said, 'Oh, naughty, naughty Miss!'
And stretched their claws,
And raised their paws;
'Tis very, very wrong, you know;
Me-ow, me-o, me-ow, me-o!
You will be burnt if you do so,
It is absolutely forbidden, you know.'
Now see! oh! see, what a dreadful thing
The fire has caught her apron-string;
Her apron burns, her arms, her hair;
She burns all over, everywhere.
Then how the philosophers did mew
What else, poor pussies, could they do?
They discussed the position, 'twas all in vain,
So then, they said, 'We'll discuss again.
Argue points, make papers! me-ow! me-o!
She'll burn to death, we told her so.'
So she was burnt with all her clothes,
And arms and hands, and eyes and nose;
Till she had nothing more to lose
Except her little scarlet shoes;

And nothing else but these was found
Among her ashes on the ground.
And when the good cats sat beside
The smoking ashes, how they cried!
'Me-ow, me-o!! Me-ow, me-oo!!
What will Mamma and Nursie do?'
Their tears ran down their cheeks so fast.
They made a little point at last.

But did Pauline really deserve this?!

Dilemma 72

The Illegals: a modern fairy tale

The airforce klaxon sounded 'Boat sighted! Scramble! Scramble!' Immediately Captain Wiggles finished his neat gin in one swift draught, and pausing only to adjust his goggles, strode out to the plane. In a moment he was taxiing down the dusty strip straddled by weary Coolibah trees, on another mission to deter illegal boat people. Minutes later the little plane was airborne and swooping over the leisurely green swell of the South Pacific.

'There they are, old boy,' chattered a voice in his earphones. It was Dickie, the navigator. 'Crikey, the beggars are only twenty miles from land!'

'Roger, I have them,' snapped Wiggles crisply. The plane swooped down towards the tiny dot on the sea which, as they approached, became clear was an old dilapidated fishing boat with several hundred human figures on it, faces upturned, waving their shirts at the plane. 'Give them a shot over the bows, Bulgy, so they know the game's up,' snapped Wiggles grimly. The twin cannon chattered their message to the illegals in cold lead, and the figures on the deck below began to run around in panic. 'That'll show them there's no back door for illegal boats,' smiled Wiggles sardonically.

'Chatter chatter chatter!' The tracer leapt towards the boat and holes appeared in the deck. 'Just warning shots, Bulgy! You know the rules!'

'Yes, dammit!' crackled Bulgy on the radio, heartfeltly. 'But it's a bit of nonsense, doing this job, day after day, with our hands tied behind our back! Why can't we send 'em a clear signal just once – so we shoot a few up, but many more lives would be saved from those leaking rustbuckets – just from the waves!'

Wiggles chuckled. Good old Bulgy! Always joking. Wiggles began radioing for his mate Captain 'Mad' Harry in the fast patrol boat *Hammerblow*, to take over. 'Harry, got a little job here for you – taking another boat load of natives out into the middle of the Pacific.'

But Dickie was frowning in his cockpit. Surely, dammit, Bulgy was right? More lives _would_ be saved if they shot up a few boats and put a stop to the evil 'people trade' as the papers put it! But, even as he wondered aloud, he spotted something queer written on the deck of the little boat far below them. What the deuce . . . were the merchants up to. . . . That looked like an 'S' . . . an 'O'? And what was that last one? Dickie's eyebrows shot up. They were spelling out 'S.O.B', damn them! The international code for 'Son Of a Bitch'! Dickie grabs the radio mouthpiece again. 'Sir! Letters on the boat! Let Bulgy show 'em some lead!'

'Hold on, Dickie,' said Wiggles firmly. 'That's an "S.O.S" and you know what that means . . . '

'Crikey,' said Bulgy, grimly. 'Trouble.' But Wiggles was barking into the mike already. 'Wiggles to _Hammerblow_, that little job here I gave you – watch out – it may be sinking!'

Standing orders were for the navy to avoid refugee ships which were sinking, as the illegals might then clamber on board, where they could claim refugee status. Swooping over a second time to check, so low the little plane's wheels almost seemed to touch the ship's mast, it was clear even as they watched that the boat was already sinking at the stern. 'Harry, it's listing at the bows already!' radioed Wiggles shrugging grimly, pulling hard back on the joystick.

'Roger,' said Harry, 'we're changing course.'

Good as his word, as Wiggles, Bulgy and Dickie flew back home, they passed the little frigate, with its jaunty twin 200mm cannon pointing defiantly skyward, steaming leisurely away from the refugees and back to base.

And the refugees? No one knows. But none of them reached the coast.

Another highly ethical success for Wiggles and Bulgy of the Coast Patrol?

Stories of Relatavia

Dilemma 73
The Baldies of Hairland

In Hairland, there are two ethnic groups, the Long-hairs and the Baldies. In fact, there are slightly more Long-hairs than the latter, and over time, they have gradually taken over all the most important and responsible roles in government. But nonetheless it is a happy (if rather patriarchal) state, everyone knows the system, and their place within it. There is even a very democratic programme of birth screening in place to try and help parents eliminate the possibility of having 'Baldie' offspring. So it is with some annoyance that the Chief Minister finds a typically mixed delegation from neighbouring Relatavia there to discuss trade between the two countries, objecting to certain aspects of Hairland.

'We are concerned that the Baldie people are not getting equal access to health, education and employment opportunities,' says one of the delegation.

'Well now mmm . . . that *is* so,' replies their tall, hirsute host, butting in smoothly, whilst stroking his beard, 'but you must understand, in our culture, only Long-hairs can carry out high- and medium-level jobs of any kind, and so it is impractical and unnecessary to devote limited resources to Baldies. And furthermore,' he goes on, loftily, casting a cold eye over the delegation, most of whom are shuffling their feet and looking ashamed, 'furthermore, it is essential for public order and morals that education and health be provided separately for the two sectors in our society. We consider it extremely dubious ethics to mix up the two groups in public as *your* society seems to think is normal.' Then, in more conciliatory tones, 'Given the relative economic value of a Long-hair to a Baldie, naturally we must target resources and opportunities at Long-hairs. You have similar systems, I think, in your land.'

The Relatavian delegation are grateful for this frank answer. They all pride themselves on being highly tolerant of cultural differences, and many of them consider talk of one system being better than another system to be a sort of imperialism. All but one, that is, the short, balding and excessively studious deputy leader of the delegation.

'But what about the killings of Baldies?' It is him talking now.

There is a nasty hush around the table. Then the leader of the Long-hairs clears his throat with a nasty snarling sound. 'Are you referring to our birth screening programme? Which I may say is particularly in demand from *Baldie* parents?'

'I am, but not only that!' replies the deputy leader.

'Then would the honourable delegate care to explain what they do mean?' asks the Minister.

'Certainly. How can it possibly be right that whenever there is a natural disaster, such as the recent floods, or a so-called national crisis, such as the devaluation of the Hairlandic 'Rigmarole' last week, or even the defeat of the Hairlandic national side in the world croquet series, that members of the Baldie clan are rounded up and publicly flogged? Reportedly in some towns, even stoned to death?'

The Hairlandic hosts look most insulted and offended by this impudent attack on their way of life. It is part of their traditional politics that when the fates seem to be angry with the Hairlandic nation, in whatever form it manifests itself, it is necessary to make a display of power and might to appease them. Besides which, everyone knows it is good politics, every now and then, to make an example of a few Baldies (otherwise they get out of hand).

'Let me ask you a question, gentlemen of Relatavia, before I answer that,' says the Hairlandic minster. 'Are you seeking to impose your values on us?'

What should the Relatavians say to that?

Dilemma 74
The Baldies of Hairland II

The Relatavians confer amongst themselves. Clearly, one argues, the Hairlandic people have a well-established system here, and it seems to have almost universal support (although since disagreement is punishable by death, one cannot be sure). The deputy leader, who has already caused so much consternation and doubtless diplomatic harm, is still agitated. He says that the oppression of Baldies has to be rejected as violating universal human rights, notably the right to life. It cannot be considered a 'cultural' anomaly. But the leader of the group snaps back that it is essential to respect the views of other societies. Yet still the deputy continues to argue: he doesn't even accept there is a way of dividing up the world into these sorts of 'societies', they make no geographical or historical sense. Fifty years ago, he points out, there was no particular distinction in Hairland between Long-hairs and Baldies, there was even a Baldie chief minister, and it is only since the radical Church of the Follicularly Aware grew in influence (and wealth) that Hairlandic society became so determined to eradicate the Baldie influence.

'That was then, this is now,' snaps back another of the delegation. 'You know as well as anyone else that as a Relatavian we accept that values vary equally from time to time as from place to place.'

'Yes,' says another, a prim-looking lady delegate, who has a formidable habit of reciting texts, 'what is right now is right now, even if it was wrong yesterday, will be wrong tomorrow and already is considered wrong everywhere else.'

'Well,' struggles the beleaguered deputy, sensing the mood of the group going against him, 'the geographical definition you are using of the society is based on a misconception. Most of the Baldies we see being killed, are from the southwest of the country, an area which properly belongs to Loveland, but was taken from them by force just ten years ago! (The Lovelanders did not resist, of course.) I have no doubt that if we surveyed the people of that region, Baldies and Long-hairs, they would still believe in the spirit of tolerance and fraternity that I thought we in Relatavia were also keen to put into practice!'

At this point, the Chief Minister, watching the wrangling, grows irritable (Baldies will suffer for this later!) and demands an answer. Are the Relatavians attempting to impose their way of doing things, or can business continue?

The delegation leader replies, in Relatavian fashion, that each member of the delegation will now give their own personal view, at that point in time.

But what to say?

Dilemma 75
Just desserts

The Chief Minister has listened to the shambling equivocations of the Relatavian delegation long enough, and finally cuts it all short with a wave of his hand. 'Silence! I think we are broadly in agreement. *Veni Roma veni Romani*!' (When in Rome, do as the Romans do! Latin was unfortunately still taught in Hairland schools.) 'Now, good friends, some of your views – but by no means all! – having affronted our deeply held values, a small sacrifice must be made before we can continue as partners again. It is our custom, having had a disagreement, for the visiting party who have been cause of the unpleasantness, to join with us in a "Baldie Hunt" to provide us later with something to banquet on! Just for desserts, I do assure you, we have plenty of other dishes (including our special quiche) for the main meal!', he adds, misreading the look of alarm on the Relatavian's faces. And so saying, he turns on his heel and sweeps magisterially out, leaving the unfortunate Relatavians to continue to bicker amongst themselves.

Now the party reach a rapid decision. All but one (the deputy leader), agree that the customs must be respected, and that as Baldies are always being persecuted in Hairland anyway, they will not really be responsible for adding to it. (After all, if a small disagreement necessitates one human sacrifice, it seems likely that a larger difference of opinion might result in a pogrom or even seriously damage trade relations, something that would be very unpopular back home.)

'Have we no principles at all? Are we going to sacrifice lives now, just to oil the wheels of the Relatavian Arms Trade?' asks the Deputy leader, rhetorically, we presume. And in fact, it is a very exciting hunt, followed by an excellent, jolly meal, that night.

The next day the Relatavians sign a number of important trade agreements and return home in triumph. Only years later does a troublesome Loveland newspaper get hold of the background to the deals and insist that it is all rather unethical: 'a betrayal of principle'. 'But whose?' exclaims the Relatavian government in exasperation. And the story fizzles out, because – really – eating people is the least of the ethical problems – particularly when it's all done amicably.

Surely, it's just a different custom?

Dilemma 76

Another problem with the relatives: a matter of honour

Actually, within Relatavia, one of the exciting things is to see so many different cultures living side by side, with no one trying to tell other people what to do. But there can be problems when members of different communities get too close.

Mrs Jones is shocked to hear from a neighbour that her son, Jonathan, *is going out with a girl*. So, when Jonathan gets back the next evening looking pleased with himself, she asks in a quivering voice if he has been 'seeing someone'. 'Why, yes, mother,' says Jonathan naively, 'Sally and I have been out to the cinema together.' Mrs Jones is white-lipped and furious. She has not given her permission for Jonathan to see Sally, and doesn't approve. She considers it her job to arrange who her son can see, and then eventually who to enter into a proper marriage with. She is not even really annoyed with Sally, as she knows she is a 'Lovelander', whom she considers to have very little moral sense. But Jonathan certainly should have known better. Furthermore, although she does not reveal this, *she thinks she can see lipstick on Jonathan's collar*.

That night, Mrs Jones calls all the other lady members of the family together for a special 'conference'. Grandmother Jones is there, Auntie Jo and Auntie Ethel. And so too are Jonathan's sisters, Flo and Kate. Grandma says it is quite clear, Jonathan has been having an unauthorised affair, and the traditional penalty must be applied. As Flo squeaks indignantly – her brother has been behaving like a 'horrible male prostitute'.

The next day, when Jonathan comes back from seeing Sally, Grandma has been busy, and has given the girls a revolver with eight bullets. Flo and Kate are very determined: Bang! Bang! Bang! Jonathan falls to the floor. Bang! Bang! Bang! Click! But it is enough – poor Jonathan is dead, and now not just Mrs Jones but all the family are greatly relieved. *The family honour has been satisfied*.

When a policewoman comes round to see what all the noise has been about (the neighbours have complained) Mrs Jones explains the situation, and says that it is all right, thank you, just now a body to get rid of.

But the policewoman is not so sure. She pulls out a book from her top pocket and starts to writes out a fixed penalty fine. 'You must pay this, Madam,' she says sternly, 'it's the new law.'

'New laws – rubbish!' says the matriarch indignantly, 'Has everyone lost their sense of right and wrong nowadays?'

Is the policewoman right to try to impose the fine?

War ethics

Dresden lies in ruins ... February 1945.
© Hulton Archive.

Dilemma 77
The good fight

In 1939, after Hitler's occupation of Poland, Britain and France declared war on Germany, and the Second World War opened to a new type of air war, despite pleas from President Roosevelt for restraint. In particular, 'under no circumstances [to] undertake the bombardment from the air of civilian populations or of unfortified cities'. This diabolical form of warfare was already known to the world – the Italians had pioneered it against the peasant villages of Abyssinia, the German dive bombers had refined it in Spain.

But by May the following year, with Denmark, Norway, Holland, Belgium and now even France falling to the German advance, Britain reneged on the understanding and began to use the bomb. Churchill broke the conventions step by step. Initially, only 'military targets' were bombed, but this allowed for what is now called 'collateral damage' (civilian deaths) as the targets included things like railway stations and ports, and the bombs were only accurate to within half a mile. From 20 June 1940, the military targets included industrial centres. In September, the Germans launched the Blitz against English cities and civilians, and in October, Churchill allowed the new head of Bomber Command, Arthur Harris, to start 'area bombing'. These were raids designed to destroy whole cities – men, women and children. The story goes that one night, 'Bomber' Harris was caught speeding home from London to High Wycombe. The police officer chastised him: 'Drive like that, sir, and you could kill someone!' Harris replied: 'Officer, I kill thousands of people every night.'

Churchill described the changes as merely one of 'somewhat broader interpretation' of the convention of seeking only military targets. Yet the 'Valentine's Day' memo, Directive 22, from Sir Archibald Sinclair, Air Minister, to Bomber Command in 1942 said that bombing should aim to destroy 'the morale of enemy civil population, in particular industrial workers', and that the bombers' aiming points were to be 'built-up areas, not for instance, the dockyards or aircraft factories'. Nonetheless, throughout the war, MPs and the British public were assured that bombing raids were always scrupulously confined to 'military targets'.

Hitler, of course, issued his orders to his troops with little mincing of words:

> Poland shall be treated as a colony . . . I have issued the order to my SS troops – for the time being only in the East – to kill mercilessly and without pity men, women, and children of Polish origin.

On 30 May 1942, in one of the most successful raids, a 'big wing' consisting of 1,000 Lancaster bombers, destroyed most of Cologne. A year later, the raid on Hamburg killed more people in one night than all the German air attacks on England put together. Using clouds of aluminium foil to fool the city's defences, the bombing was particularly accurate and the old wooden houses blazed in a firestorm, the like of which had never been witnessed before. The civilians huddled in their air raid shelters were often reduced to a fine dust. Rescue workers after the raids could remove the remains of whole families in a single tin bucket.

One civilian clerk in Bomber Command, Freeman Dyson (later a famous nuclear physicist), recalled years later how it felt to collate all the reports on the bombing – reports so carefully kept from the British people. 'I sat in my office until the end, carefully calculating how to murder most economically another hundred thousand people.' Dyson was sickened by the policy. Although he knew that Hitler's extermination squads were then in the process of killing unimaginable numbers (perhaps 12 million) of defenceless civilians, he could not believe that what Bomber Command was doing was so very different.

Dresden itself was the old cultural centre of Germany – full of history and architectural and artistic masterpieces. It was also full of refugees fleeing the Russian advance, and effectively defenceless when the decision was taken to bomb it in February 1945. The firestorm that had been so successful in Hamburg returned. A cauldron of flame consumed an estimated 100,000 people.

Did the ends justify the means?

Dilemma 78
Just some wars

Erasmus, the great Dutch exponent of humanism, was one of the first to condemn war: 'there is nothing more wicked, more disastrous, more widely destructive, more deeply tenacious, more loathsome, in a word, more unworthy of man,' he wrote. And 'whoever heard of a hundred thousand animals rushing together to butcher each other, as men do everywhere?' But the funny thing about wars is that when they are declared, normal rules cease to apply. In particular, good becomes bad, and bad becomes good.

Activity	Peacetime status	Wartime status
Killing people	Bad	Good
Stealing things/smashing things up	Bad	Good
Telling lies and deceiving people	Bad	Good
Killing yourself to harm lots of other people	Very bad	Very good

Small wonder that most philosophers would say the explanation must be that *war itself is bad*. (Nietzsche excepted. And some of the Ancients.) But is it that simple?

Recent 'good' wars* have been to save peoples from genocidal killing by militias and fanatical regimes, wars to save defenceless people from being slaughtered in their millions, the rivers running with blood and the fields covered in human bones (just like Erasmus describes in his time).

Not of course to forget those against Germany to stop the Nazis from their 'ethnic cleansing' of the whole of Europe in the name of racial purity, and against Japan to destroy the cult of Japanese militarism with all its cruelties and massacres. But maybe to leave out the many wars supposedly against 'communism' and in favour of 'democracy'. The dilemma for the peace lovers is – if war is always bad, then all this sort of policing activity must stop too.

Just leaving rulers to massacre their own people, and maybe their neighbours as well?

* With or without UN approval.

Dilemma 79
The unjustified false belief

Not many years ago, when the British Prime Minister was trying to drum up support for a war (in this case against the Iraq of Saddam Hussein), he told an American news station, that

'we *know* that he has stockpiles of major amounts of chemical and biological weapons, [and] we *know* that he is trying to acquire a nuclear capability'.

However, subsequent events showed that the claim was false. Brass, tub-thumpingly plain false. Saddam had no weapons. What's more, it turned out that the 'reason' the Prime Minister offered for believing there to be Iraqi weapons of mass destruction, that is the 'secret assessments' by the British intelligence services, far from supporting his view, rather worked the other way, saying that 'Intelligence on Iraq's weapons' of mass destruction was 'sporadic and patchy'. In fact, far from 'knowing' about Saddam's weapons, the most they claimed was that 'Iraq retains some production equipment and small stocks of CW precursors [things useful to make Chemical Weapons with], and may have hidden small quantities of agents and weapons.'*

Talking later about this complex matter, or 'lie', the British Prime Minster offered the justification that the claim was 'true' in that he 'believed it at the time'. When people say they believe something, we have to take their word for it.

But did he believe that he KNEW it?

* The TV station was NBC, on 3 April 2002, and the 'secret intelligence' was from the Joint Intelligence Committee (JIC) assessment, of 15 March 2002, quoted in *The Rise of Political Lying*, by Peter Oborne, 2005.

Dilemma 80
The deterrents

In Little Dumpling, two neighbours have a long-running and terrible dispute. It is over the shared area between their houses. The Meanies want the hedge between the two properties to be cut down – 'It's an eyesore!' they cry – but the Ingrates want it to be left to grow. However, for their part, the Ingrates want the old outside loo, also on the boundary, knocked down and turned into more hedge. 'Now *that* is an eyesore,' they say, but the Meanies will of course hear none of it – they find it very 'convenient' and want it left 'just as it is'. (Both the hedge and the loo are sort of jointly owned, of course.)

Over the years the dispute has caused a lot of unpleasantness. Trees have been vandalised, the window of the old loo was smashed. And one time the lavatory pan itself mysteriously cracked.

Now, after another spell of ill-tempered and unpleasant wrangling, Mr Ingrate decides enough is enough. He goes out to the Greater Dumpling hardware store and buys a job lot of high explosive. He then attaches forty sticks of it to the rear wall of the privy (on his side of the boundary) and shouts to Mr Meanie that if he hears someone so much as slam the toilet lid, he will detonate the explosive. In fact, this would destroy the much loved convenience, but it would also blow up his neighbour, most of the neighbour's garden and at least half of their house. It is not that he wants to do *that* – he bellows through the beloved hedge – it is just a 'deterrent'.

It certainly is a deterrent. Mr Meanie stops making any physical alterations to the loo, terrified of being accidentally blown up. And there is another effect. Mr Meanie goes out and buys some of his own explosives, and via a complicated set of trip wires and so on, arranges things so that any attempt to prune the hedge will result in a large detonation, destroying the hedge, whoever was cutting it and, he estimates, at least half of the Ingrates' house. It is not that *he* wants to do that, he snarls from behind the privy to his neighbour, 'it is just an insurance policy'.

And peace at last reigns in Little Dumpling. The other residents remark on the quiet, as the Meanies and Ingrates confine themselves to checking regularly on their new explosive charges, and setting up cameras to ensure that no tricks are being played that might undo the 'deterrent effect' of the new arrangement.

In the pub, everyone says that they are mad, of course. But Mr Meanie objects to the term. Now at last, he says, his family who have lived in constant worry, can go to the loo at their own convenience. And he chuckles because he thinks he has really been very clever.

A similar tale is told in the village's other pub by Mr Ingrate. But the irony is not lost on the audience, That now, for the very first time, both families are living in very real danger of the most awful calamity – not merely of losing their outside loo or their hedge – but of suddenly being blown up in the middle of the night!

The barman says to Mr Ingrate: 'What if the Meanies' little boy accidentally slams the loo door – you wouldn't really want to blow up the lad, would you?' Ingrate bristles, 'Look, Phil,' he says, 'no one will get blown up as long as they simply obey the rules, and leave my family in peace. That's not much to ask is it?' The barman looks doubtful, but Ingrate warms to his theme. 'See, Phil, up to now the Meanies' sole interest in life has been how to win battles with us. Mrs Ingrate has got angina, and little Lucy* is not eating, she's so worried. Since I got the explosives, the Meanies's avoid causing trouble. That can't be bad, can it?'

Are the Meanies and Ingrates mad? Or just coldly rational?

* The Ingrates' cat.

Dilemma 81
The school for terror

In a certain country, not only not far away, but actually very close to home, where Interpol least expected to find it, is a terrible institution which we may call the Academy of Terror. Over fifty years, an impressive sounding 60,000 students have passed through its ranks. The names – Alvarado, Juan Velasco (Peru); Galtieri, Leopoldo (Argentina); Noriega, Manuel (Panama); Rodriguez, Guillermo (Ecuador) – are an international roll call of regimes built on the blood and suffering of their own citizens. Other graduates are less well known, so the Academy must honour them separately (see Table of Distinguished School Boys).

In fact, alumni of the Academy set new standards in state-sponsored violence all over South and Central America. Using what they had learnt at the Academy, they arranged the assassination of Archbishop Oscar Romero (1980) as well as that of six Jesuit priests (plus their housekeeper and her daughter), not to overlook some of the most infamous massacres of the time, like those at El Mozote in which over 900 people perished, or that of the banana workers of Uruba.

Assessors of the Academy often ask 'But how do you organise all this terror anyway? How do these "death squads" work?' One witness, Rufina Amaya, describes the El Mozote massacre in El Salvador, involving at least nine of the Academy's graduates.

> There were 100 of us in all. The children were with the women. They kept us locked up all morning. At ten o'clock the soldiers began to kill the men who were in the church. First they machine-gunned them and then they slit their throats. By two o'clock the soldiers had finished killing the men and they came for the women. They left the children locked up. They separated me from my eight-month-old daughter and my oldest son. They took us away to kill us. As we came to the place where they were going to kill us, I was able to slip away and hide under a small bush, covering myself with branches. I watched the soldiers line up twenty women and machine-gun them. Then they brought another group. Another rain of bullets. Then another group and another.

Distinguished School Boys

Name	Country	Distinction
Garzi Meza Tejeda	Bolivia	Led violent 1979 military coup.
Armando Fernandez Larios	Chile	Pioneer expert in setting car bombings.
Hugo Banzer	Bolivia	Wrote Banzer Plan: a guide to silencing church critics – permanently.
Farouk Yanine Diaz	Colombia	Organised death squads including the 1988 Uruba massacre of banana workers, and another of businessmen.
Gambetta Hyppolite	Haiti	Ordered his troops to fire on electoral bureau in Gonaives to disrupt the elections.
Alejandro Fretes Davalos	Paraguay	Coordinated Operation *Condor*, a secret agreement allowing countries to track down and 'neutralise' political opponents across borders.
Byron Disrael Lima Estrada	Guatemala	Arranged the assassination of Bishop Juan Gerardi.
Paucelino Latorre Gamboa	Colombia	As leader of 20th military Brigade specialised in the killing of civilians.
Juan Lopez Oritz	Honduras	Directed Ocosingo massacre in which soldiers tied prisoners' hands and shot them in the back of the head.
Gustavo Alvarez Martinez	Honduras	Asked whether children needed to be killed as well, said 'these seeds will eventually bear fruit' (i.e. 'yes').
Vladimir Lenin Montesinos Torres	Peru	Carried out the La Canuta (1992) raid in which 30 hooded soldiers abducted students, never heard of since.

In 1996, the school was obliged to provide its training manuals to an official inquiry into its courses. These described how to set up death squads, and how to use blackmail, torture, executions (of both 'suspects' and 'relatives of suspects') and generally how to achieve maximum fear in the population. They recommended that killings should be conducted in a way that would produce maximum horror, for example, involving mutilation, rape and torture.

Enough! Now that Interpol know all this:

Is bombing the school justified?

Dilemma 82
The hate preacher

The Vicar of St Bartholomew's was very concerned. Every Sunday, the number of earnest faces in his congregation dropped. One Sunday soon, he imagined, he would stand there in front of an empty church with no one else but himself and young Jones, the curate and organist, to hear his message of love and peace. It was all particularly upsetting as the Vicar, rightly, perceived the times, with all the talk about terrorism and bombings, to be desperately in need of sound ethical guidance (based on everlasting values). Jones nodded sympathetically when the two of them discussed attendances one day, after another poor Sunday. 'Why, there seems to be more interest in Islamic fundamentalism than in our church,' said Jones, sympathetically.

And that chance remark gave the Vicar an idea. What about harnessing the interest in these political issues, and indeed in radical Islam, to promote interest in the Christian message? How would it be if, instead of the people of Lower Little Whitteringham hearing him week after week, they heard a sermon delivered by a real radical Islamist, offering an alternative message of 'holy war'?

It seemed to both of them that in such an unlikely event, there would surely be much interest, indeed a packed church. But neither of them had the faintest idea how to set about finding a real Islamic fundamentalist. Not in Lower Little Whitteringham anyway.

But sure enough, just two weeks later, the parishioners were astonished to find a 'fiery preacher' promised for the next Sunday, in the form of a debate over the question (and this is our philosophical question too):

Will suicide bombers go to Heaven?

Mullah Al-Jazeera would argue that they would, and their very own Vicar would argue against.

Sure enough, the day of the debate saw a small miracle: every seat in the church full, children sitting cross-legged at the front and even a few standing at the back!

'Standing at the back, who would have thought such a thing?' murmured the Vicar appreciatively to himself.

To start with, Jones played 'O Come All Ye Faithful' on the church organ, once in traditional style, and then once again in what he imagined was an 'Arabian' style, full of strange and discordant notes. The congregation applauded this effort politely and a flushed Jones nodded towards them as he retired to the vestry. The Vicar then set out the terms of the debate and introduced the ideas.

This was that in fact there was a long tradition of holy wars in both Christian and Islamic traditions. 'We remember,' says the Vicar, now donning his gold-rimmed half-spectacles to read that 'The Book of Joshua mentions thirty-one kings defeated in bloody battles (Joshua 12:24) . . . and that after every battle, the city and everyone in it he put to the sword, as ordered by the Lord (8:22; 10:28, 29, 32, 36, 38; 11:11, 12, 17, 20) . . . Mrs Briggs, would you give our first reading, Joshua verses 6:21?'

An elderly lady, with her grey hair in a tight bun, steps forward and in a loud bossy voice reads out about how the Bible describes events after the conquest of Jericho. '"They devoted the city to the Lord and destroyed with the sword every living thing in it – men and women, young and old, cattle, sheep and donkeys",' she finishes.

'Thank you, Mrs Briggs,' says the Vicar. 'But the Bible also, we remember, tells us that God loves the world so much and He does not want any one to perish but comes to repentance (II Peter 3:9). And today, we are going to ask our guest speaker to tell us a little about the Islamic religion and to join in our discussion of whether there can ever be such a thing as a "holy war".'

At this point a murmur arises from the congregation as the door to the vestry opens to herald the arrival of the guest speaker, Mullah Al-Jazeera. Ascending the pulpit, the Mullah draws a sharp gasp for his fearsome appearance. With a big black beard, dark glasses, and his head swathed in a turban, his face can hardly be seen, and he resembles nothing so much as a terrible pirate. When he gesticulates with his right arm, the impression is multiplied manyfold – as Mullah Al-Jazeera has only a hook for his right hand!

Looking over his shoulder and smiling nervously, the Vicar continues quickly: 'And secondly we see in the Muslim Holy books the instruction that all prophets are to

141

be respected – including Abraham, Moses, Jesus and Mohammed. For the Moslems believe that even if the Messiah, the son of Mary was "just an apostle" yet also, it says that God "put in the hearts of those who follow him kindness and mercy" (LVII:27). For Moslems, there is "guidance and light" in the ancient Jewish Torah, and in the Bible alongside the Koran, which together they count as making up "the Book of Allah".' So today, Islamic and Christian churches are untied in faith.

At this the Vicar graciously descends the pulpit and allows Mullah Al-Jazeera to take his place, which he does, clutching his robes uncomfortably. Then he surveys the earnest faces in the pews and pauses for a full minute before saying in a harsh voice with some strange accent:

'"Fight in the cause of Allah those who fight you!" (Sura 2:190).'

The guest speaker then explains, in gruff foreign-sounding tones, that he lost his hand fighting the infidel in Afghanistan. He then starts to read out some sections from the Koran in halting English to the effect that there is nothing holier than to fight for God and to kill non-believers. The Vicar for his part, occasionally breaks in offering passages of the Bible.

'For "Lo!",' says Mullah Al-Jazeera, '"Allah loveth those who battle for his cause in ranks, as if they were solid structure" (Sura 61:4). And whosoever fights in the Cause of Allah and is killed or gets victory, we shall bestow on him a great reward" (Sura 4:74).'

To which the Vicar nervously interjects, 'but remember also, do we not, that the Bible tells us "But I say to you, love your enemies, and pray for those who persecute you" (Matthew 5:43, 44)?'

But Mullah Al-Jazeera continues with magnificent indifference:

' . . . and the reward is, "He will forgive you your sins, and admit you into Gardens under which rivers flow and pleasant dwellings in Gardens of Eternity – that is indeed the great success" (Sura 6 1:12). And Mohammed said, "Before long, you (the Arabs) will conquer many countries and cities. Qazvin shall be one of such places. The person who takes part in that battle for forty nights or forty days, will be given a gold pillar in paradise encrusted with jades and rubies. He will enjoy residing in a palace, having seventy thousand gates, and each gate shall be attended by a houri as his wife!" (Ibn-E-Majah, vol. 2).'

'Thank you Mr Al-Jazeera,' says the Vicar tidily. 'But of course, these days, the Christian church considers killing always to be evil and forgiveness to be our duty.'

'Really, Vicar?' says the guest speaker, fixing his host with a steady gaze from behind his black spectacles. 'But what about the stories of the Flood and of the destruction of Sodom and Gomorrah in the Book of Genesis? These argue for killing as a way of making the world more holy, for "vengeance is mine says the Lord!" (Matthew 5:39, 26:52; Romans 12:19).'

'*Thank you*, Mr Al-Jazeera,' says the Vicar more firmly, 'But the Bible also tells us that: "Our struggle is not against flesh and blood, but against the spiritual forces in the heavenly places" (Ephesians 6:12). And the disciple, Peter, says that our "holy war" is not against flesh and blood, but against the Satanic forces which are blinding their eyes. For "God loves the world so much and He does not want any one to perish but comes to repentance" (II Peter 3:9).'

But Mullah Al-Jazeera it seems is quite unconvinced. After reading a final passage about the rewards of martyrdom in increasingly excited manner, he opens his tunic to reveal a strange vest with tubes apparently tied round it, and calls upon members of the congregation to step forward, to take their part in God's holy war!

'"Paradise lies under the shades of swords!"' he quotes excitedly (Albokhari, vol. 4).

As several of the children began to move forward, a voice booms from the back of the church: 'Now see here, this has gone on quite far enough! I order you to stop!' It is the village policeman!

Mullah Al-Jazeera looks very alarmed, as well he might, and immediately disappears into the vestry, followed by the police constable. The Vicar appeals for calm to the astonished congregation and asks people to file out quietly (making a small donation to the collection if they wouldn't mind – for the church steeple, of course, not for any bombs).

And then he goes to see what has happened in the vestry. If only he had thought to brief PC Boot before the debate! He finds the long arm of the law looking very perplexed. Although he had moved with lightening speed after the Mullah, by the time he got to the back of the vestry, the preacher had disappeared. There is no one there, in fact, except Jones, who it seems has been praying quietly all the while in the back. 'I advise you Vicar,' says PC Boot firmly, 'to avoid getting into bad company – people like that are dangerous tricksters!'

'Oh come, come, officer,' says the Vicar gently, 'all men of God share certain fundamental values.'

'Oh, you think so, Vicar?' says Boot, and then, with a triumphant gesture, reveals what he has found in the vestry wastebasket – a large black beard, lots of bandage – and a prosthetic hook! 'Mullah Al-Jazeera is no more a veteran of holy war than young Jones here!' says the policeman with satisfaction at his powers of deduction. And both Jones and the Vicar look suitably chastened.

Environmental ethics

Dilemma 83
The dodo's call

In an account of the Dutch voyage to the Mascarene Islands in 1598, under a rough sketch entitled 'The Destruction of the Dodos', is a verse on how to catch the dodo:

> For food the seamen hunt the flash of feathered fowl,
> They tap the palms, the round-sterned dodo they destroy,
> The parrot's life they spare that he may scream and howl,
> *And thus his fellows to imprisonment decoy.*

The seamen were very hungry, the dodos were very easy to catch and there were an awful lot of them. At first.

And if it were all right to catch the first one, then it must have been all right to catch the next one, and the next one, and the next.

Well, who was to know when it became not all right?

If indeed it ever was wrong. There are a lot of seagulls left.

Dilemma 84
Killing the wolf

'We were eating lunch on a high rimrock, at the foot of which a turbulent river elbowed its way. We saw what we thought was a doe fording the torrent, her breast awash in white water. When she climbed the bank toward us and shook out her tail, we realised our error: it was a wolf. A half-dozen others, evidently grown pups, sprang from the willows and all joined in a welcoming mêlée of wagging tails and playful maulings. What was literally a pile of wolves writhed and tumbled in the centre of an open flat at the foot of our rimrock.

'In those days we had never heard of passing up a chance to kill a wolf. In a second we were pumping lead into the pack, but with more excitement than accuracy; how to aim a steep downhill shot is always confusing. When our rifles were empty, the old wolf was down, and a pup was dragging a leg into impassable side-rocks.

'We reached the old wolf in time to watch a fierce green fire dying in her eyes. I realised then, and have known ever since, that there was something new to me in those eyes – something known only to her and to the mountain. I was young then, and full of trigger-itch; I thought that because fewer wolves meant more deer, that no wolves would mean hunters' paradise. But after seeing the green fire die, I sensed that neither the wolf nor the mountain agreed with such a view . . .

'Since then I have lived to see state after state extirpate its wolves. I have watched the face of many a newly wolfless mountain, and seen the south-facing slopes wrinkle with a maze of new deer trails. I have seen every edible bush and seedling browsed, first to anaemic desuetude, and then to death. I have seen every edible tree defoliated to the height of a saddlehorn. Such a mountain looks as if someone had given God a new pruning shears, and forbidden Him all other exercise. In the end the starved bones of the hoped-for deer herd, dead of its own too-much, bleach with the bones of the dead sage, or molder under the high-lined junipers.'

Aldo Leopold has been called 'the Father of American Conservation'. But if the message of the green fire is about the need to kill deer, to kill elephants or kangaroos, *what kind of 'conservation' is that*?

Dilemma 85
The Green Revolution

Some environmentalists, tired of waiting for 'green economics' to catch up with them, have adopted their own strategies for tipping the financial calculation in favour of the land. In the forests surrounding Vancouver, where trees are being clear-felled for paper to print philosophy books (well, maybe one or two, but it's worth it), groups have used metal spikes hidden in trees to prevent the chainsaws from operating safely, putting up the price of harvesting the trees. The saboteurs announce areas 'spiked' to avoid casualties.

In Phoenix, Arizona, where mountain nature reserves have been encroached on by new houses, hooded vigilantes have burnt down the new residences. That's not only expensive for the would-be holiday home owners affected, but it prices out a wider group who find their insurance premiums have gone up.

The arsonists, according to the local paper, pray before they burn down a house that no one will get hurt, thinking primarily of the fire-fighters – the new houses are torched while still empty. 'We don't pray for ourselves not to get caught – that's God's will,' one is quoted as saying.

But the greenest form of 'direct action' to protect the land, is of course, trashing crops. Wherever 'Frankencrops' – that is genetically modified crops such as maize, wheat, soya or tomatoes – are grown, green vigilantes are there too, smashing and destroying the new varieties.

Mind you, there are a lot of crops to be trashed. In 2001, a remarkable two-thirds of the United States soya bean crop was genetically modified – that's 20 million hectares.

But you've got to start somewhere.

Yet with habitats being destroyed all over the planet, how can trampling more plants be the answer?

Dilemma 86
Pain is good

The idea of the *Benthamistas* – that pain is always bad and pleasure is always good – breaks down from an ecological perspective. Pain is nature's way of telling us to see the dentist. After all, 'A living mammal which experienced no pain would be one that had a lethal dysfunction of the nervous system', as one environmental philosopher, J. Baird Callicott, put it, before going on to add that 'the idea that pain is evil and ought to be minimised or eliminated is as primitive a notion as that of a tyrant who puts to death messengers bearing bad news on the supposition that thus his well-being and security is improved'.

Well, that's easy for him to say. *But I would want a second opinion.*

Money matters

Dilemma 87
Greed is good

That canny Scot, Adam Smith, friend as well as contemporary of that other great and equally canny Scottish philosopher, David Hume, discovered that it is not, as many seemed to imagine, love that makes the world go round – but money.

Money is the hidden hand, which governs all our actions, whether apparently altruistic – or selfish.

Economists, who are philosophers of money, rather than anything grander, love Smith. His account, however, of the role of money in moral decision making, has been overlooked by many philosophers. Instead, they have focused on the somewhat less original or innovative observations of Smith's in the 'Theory of the Moral Sentiments', wherein it is argued that 'sympathy' – we would say 'empathy' – is the root of social life. Somehow, his important statement of morality within a capitalist system has been overlooked. And it is really quite a simple message:

Greed is good

This is because self-interest is actually the basis of social cooperation. For example, trade. And this is Smith's special interest. As Smith says:

> Nobody ever saw a dog make a fair and deliberate exchange of one bone for another with another dog.

So, if greed really is good, and self-interest the human thing, the practical dilemma for the bakers, the butchers and the candlestick makers (who want to do the moral thing) is:

Should they sell their goods for just enough to make an honest living – or charge as much as they can get away with?

More money

Smith thinks it is better to charge the highest price as then there will be more money to *save*, which he sees a bit like missionaries see their duty towards souls. So, grasping the pulpit earnestly, he goes on to say in the *Wealth of Nations*:

> With regard to profusion [spending our money], the principle, which prompts to expense, is the passion for present enjoyment; which, though sometimes violent and very difficult to be restrained, is in general only momentary and occasional. But the principle which prompts to *save*, is the desire of bettering our condition, a desire which, though generally calm and dispassionate, comes with us from the womb, and never leaves us till we go into the grave.

Compare *that* with the 'moral impulse', which even on the most generous estimate would leave a large proportion of people unaffected for the greater part of their lives.

Perhaps, rather than study morality, to work out what to do with money, shouldn't we *study money,* and work out *what to do with morality*?

Dilemma 88
Death and taxes

Since time immemorial, there have been taxes. Taxes on water, on grain, on ale, beards, or windows. Naturally, clothes, tools and 'goods in general' have all been taxed. Nowadays everything is routinely taxed, with the possible exception of beards.

But perhaps the most hated tax of them all was the salt tax. The ancient Chinese invented the tax 4,000 years ago, and the French version of the tax – the hated *gabelle* – notoriously included a stipulation that people had to buy a minimum quantity each week – or be whipped or imprisoned.

And it was the salt tax that provoked Gandhi into staging one of the most famous acts of non-violent* resistance in history: the march to the sea and a ceremonial distilling of salt from the seawater.

Less well known is the related fact that during the days of the British Raj a huge hedge was constructed running for thousands of miles across central India, an edifice comparable in scale to China's Great Wall. Only, this hedge was not to keep out invaders, but to keep out cheap supplies of salt. Within the area enclosed by the hedge, the colonial masters taxed the Indian people for the use of this unassuming but essential mineral. But why choose salt? Well, the choice was a pretty logical one. The British relied on the help of the rich and wealthy Indian princes and landlords to maintain their grip on this huge and populous colony. So they dare not tax *them*. On the other hand, they also needed revenues to pay for the cost of their rule, and most people in India had little or no money and little or no goods to be taxed.

So the British came up with a new version of that very ancient tax. Levied at a rate equivalent to almost a week's work in every month, it was significant enough to occasion salt smuggling, and that's where the hedge came in. Planted between the salt-producing areas and the rest of India and guarded by troops at regular intervals, it gave the locals a stark choice.

Pay your salt tax or die.

* It was non-violent on his part, see the discussion of Dilemma 23.

Legal dilemmas

William Spiggot: charged with robbing on the highway.

Do the ends justify the means?

Dilemma 89
Rough justice

At the Old Bailey in January 1720, William Spiggot and Thomas Phillips were tried for committing several robberies on the highway; but they refused to plead either 'guilty' or 'not guilty', much to the court's annoyance. No arguments could convince them of 'the absurdity of such an obstinate procedure', as the official record puts it; so the court ordered that the following should be read, which was the law in such cases:

> That the prisoner should be sent to the prison from whence he came, and put into a mean room, stopped from the light, and shall there be laid on the bare ground, without any litter, straw, or other covering, or without any garment about him, except something to hide his privy members. He shall lie upon his back, his head shall be covered, and his feet shall be bare. One of his arms shall be drawn with a cord to one side of the room, and the other arm to the other side; and his legs shall be served in the like manner. Then there shall be laid upon his body as much iron or stone as he can bear, and more. And the first day after he shall have three morsels of barley bread, without any drink; and the second day he shall be allowed to drink as much as he can, at three times, of the water that is next the prison-door, except running water, without any bread; and this shall be his diet till he dies; and he against whom this judgement shall be given forfeits his goods to the King.

(Hmmm . . . That should do it . . .)

Or do even highway robbers have 'rights'?

Dilemma 90
Son of Sam

When, on 1 June 1953, newborn baby David was given up by his natural mother to Nat and Pearl Berkowitz, the adoptive parents showered him with gifts and attention, and no one imagined that a serial killer was making his debut. But David Berkowitz was not only a school bully and hyperactive 'loner' who would not obey his parents, and became not only an arsonist who claimed to have started 1,488 fires (recording each in his diary, celebrating the sense of power they gave him), but was also to be one of New York's most notorious mass murderers.

At age fourteen, David lost his second mother to cancer, and had sunk further into mental isolation, brooding on 'the conspiracy' that meant no one had warned him that this might happen. At age eighteen he left home and joined the army where he stayed for three years. He was particularly keen on the rifles. He briefly converted from Judaism to the Baptist faith, but then lost interest.

At one point, David found his biological mother – Betty Falco. She and her daughter Roslyn did everything they could to make David feel welcome in their family, but he drifted away from them too, making excuses for not coming to visit.

On the morning of 29 July 1976, 'Son of Sam' first struck. For over a year, he would strike at random, shooting or stabbing lone women. Growing in confidence, David would goad the police with letters like the one reproduced here.

The attacks on the women pacified David's demons for a while. After them he was relaxed and would go out for a burger and fries. He was caught eventually, of course. But then the questions had only just begun.

Who to blame? Betty? Nat and Pearl? Society?

Dilemma 91
The Twinkies: not a normal act

Act I, scene I

Nathan Leopold and Richard Loeb were two eighteen-year-old American youths with an ambition; they wanted to do the perfect murder. Richard's fourteen-year-old cousin, Bobby, had the misfortune to be passing by on the day the dream came to fruition. They bludgeoned him to death and left him in a storm drain. Unrepentant, when they got back to their comfortable home they carefully typed out a ransom note and sent it off – to confuse the authorities.

Unfortunately (for them), far from confusing the authorities, the note led the police straight to them, and so it came to be that they found themselves in court on trial for first degree murder. Not that their lawyer saw it that way. The boys' families had hired one of the most famous attorneys to defend them, one Clarence Darrow. Here is some of what he had to say:

'They pull the dead boy into the back seat, and wrap him in a blanket, and this funeral car starts on its route. If ever any death car went over the same route or the same kind of a route driven by sane people, I have never heard of it, and I fancy no one else has ever heard of it.

'This car is driven for 20 miles. First down through thickly populated streets, where everyone knew the boys and their families . . . straight down The Midway through the regular route of Jackson Park, Nathan Leopold driving this car, and Dick Loeb on the back seat, and the dead boy with him. The slightest accident, the slightest misfortune, a bit of curiosity, an arrest for speeding, anything would bring destruction. They go down The Midway, through the park, meeting hundreds of machines, in sight of thousands of eyes, with this dead boy.

'For what? For nothing! The mad acts of the fool in *King Lear* is the only thing I know of that compares with it. And yet doctors will swear that it is a sane act. *They know better*.

'They go down a thickly populated street through South Chicago, and then for three miles take the longest street to go through this city; built solid with business buildings, filled with automobiles backed upon the street, with street cars on the track, with thousands of peering eyes; one boy driving and the other on the back seat, with the corpse of little Bobby Franks, the blood streaming from him, wetting everything in the car.'

It's actually a pretty sickening tale. One you might think makes the crime worse. Not at all! Darrow thinks the very unpleasantness reduces the boys' (as he calls them) responsibility:

Because they must be mad. Or are they?

Act I, scene II

'They tell me that this is sanity; they tell me that the brains of these boys are not diseased. You need no experts, you need no X-rays; you need no study of the endocrines. Their conduct shows exactly what it was, and shows that this Court has before it two young men who should be examined in a psychopathic hospital and treated kindly and with care. They get through South Chicago, and they take the regular automobile road down toward Hammond. There is the same situation; hundreds of machines; any accident might encompass their ruin. They stop at the forks of the road, and leave little Bobby Franks, soaked with blood, in the machine, and get their dinner, and eat it without an emotion or a qualm.

'Your Honour, we do not need to believe in miracles; we need not resort to that in order to get blood. If it were any other case, there could not be a moment's hesitancy as to what to do.

'I repeat, you may search the annals of crime, and you can find no parallel. It is utterly at variance with every motive and every act and every part of conduct that influences *normal people* in the commission of crime. There is not a sane thing in all of this from the beginning to the end. There was not a normal act in any of it, from its inception in a diseased brain, until today, when they sit here awaiting their doom.'

Although rather a circular argument, there's no answering that. And now Darrow allows a hint of a tremor to enter his voice.

'Before *I would tie a noose around the neck of a boy* I would try to call back into my mind the emotions of youth. I would try to remember what the world looked like to me when I was a child. I would try to remember how strong were these instinctive, persistent emotions that moved my life. I would try to remember how weak and inefficient was youth in the presence of the surging, controlling feelings of the child. One that honestly remembers and asks himself the question and tries to unlock the door that he thinks is closed, and calls back the boy, can understand the boy.'

Is it in the genes?

Act I, scene 3

'But, your Honour, that is not all there is to boyhood. Nature is strong and she is pitiless. She works in her own mysterious way, and we are her victims. We have not much to do with it ourselves. Nature takes this job in hand, and we play our parts. In the words of old Omar Khayyam, we are only

Impotent pieces in the game He plays
Upon this checkerboard of nights and days,
Hither and thither moves, and checks, and slays,
And one by one back in the closet lays.

'What had this boy to do with it? He was not his *own father*; he was not his *own mother*; he was not his *own grandparents*. All of this was handed to him. He did not surround himself with governesses and wealth. He did not make himself. And yet he is to be compelled to pay.

'There was a time in England, running down as late as the beginning of the last century, when judges used to convene court and call juries to try a horse, a dog, a pig, for crime. I have in my library a story of a judge and jury and lawyers trying and convicting an old sow for lying down on her ten pigs and killing them.'

Stop a moment, Darrow! Surely that's enough. Ladies and gentlemen of the jury: *will you show mercy*?

Dilemma 92
The Twinkies: the villain enters

Act II

But Darrow thinks it is not yet a strong enough case. (It was them Nietzsche books wot dun it . . .)

'Babe [Nathan] is somewhat older than Dick, and is a boy of remarkable mind – away beyond his years. He is a sort of freak in this direction, as in others; a boy without emotions, *a boy obsessed of philosophy*, a boy obsessed of learning, busy every minute of his life. . . . He was just a half boy, an intellect, *an intellectual machine going without balance* and without a governor, seeking to find out everything there was in life intellectually; seeking to solve every philosophy, but using his intellect only. . . . He became enamoured of the philosophy of Nietzsche. Your Honour, I have read almost everything that Nietzsche ever wrote. He was a man of a wonderful intellect; the most original philosopher of the last century . . .

'Nietzsche believed that some time the superman would be born, that evolution was working toward the superman. He wrote one book, *Beyond Good and Evil*, which was a criticism of all moral codes as the world understands them; a treatise holding that the intelligent man is beyond good and evil; that the laws for good and the laws for evil do not apply to those who approach the superman.

'At seventeen, at sixteen, at eighteen, while *healthy* boys were *playing baseball* or working on the farm, or doing odd jobs, he was *reading Nietzsche*, a boy who *never should have seen it*, at that early age. Babe was obsessed of it, and here are some of the things which Nietzsche taught:

- Become hard.
- To be obsessed by moral consideration presupposes a very low grade of intellect.
- Substitute for morality the will to our own end, and consequently the means to accomplish that.

'Nietzsche held a contemptuous, scornful attitude to all those things which the young are taught as important in life; a fixing of new values which are not the values by which any normal child has ever yet been reared – *a philosophical dream* – containing more or less truth, that was not meant by anyone to be applied to life . . .

'Many of us read this philosophy but know that it has no actual application to life; but not he. It became a part of his being. It was his philosophy. He lived it and practiced it; he thought it applied to him, and he could not have believed it excepting that it either caused a diseased mind or was the result of diseased mind.'

Now who is to blame?

Final curtain: the deprived childhood defence (the too much money gambit)

Darrow continues indefatigably.

'What do we know about childhood? The brain of the child is the home of dreams, of castles, of visions, of illusions and of delusions. In fact, there could be no childhood without delusions, for delusions are always more alluring than facts . . .

'*The whole life of childhood is a dream and an illusion*, and whether they take one shape or another shape depends not upon the dreamy boy but on what surrounds him. As well might I have dreamed of burglars and wished to be one as to dream of policemen and wished to be one. Perhaps I was lucky, too, that I had no money. [no penny dreadfuls . . .] We have grown to think that the misfortune is in *not* having it. The great misfortune in this terrible case *is* the money. That has destroyed their lives. That has fostered these illusions. That has promoted this mad act. And, if your honour shall doom them to die, it will be because they are the *sons of the rich*.

'Is Dickey Loeb to blame because out of the infinite forces that conspired to form him, the infinite forces that were at work producing him ages before he was born, that because out of these infinite combinations he was born without it [a moral conscience]? If he is, then there should be a new definition for justice. Is he to blame for what he did not have and never had? *Is he to blame that his machine is imperfect?*

'Who is to blame? I do not know. I have never in my life been interested so much in *fixing blame* as I have in *relieving* people from blame. I am not wise enough to fix it. I know that somewhere in the past that entered into him something missed. It may be defective nerves. It may be a defective heart or liver. It may be defective endocrine glands. I know it is something. I know that nothing happens in this world without a cause.

'Society, too, should assume its share of the burdens of this case, and not make two more tragedies, but use this calamity as best it can to make life safer, to make childhood easier, and more secure, to do something to cure the cruelty, the hatred, the chance, and the wilfulness of life.

'I am pleading that we overcome cruelty with kindness and hatred with love. . . . I am pleading for the future; I am pleading for a time when hatred and cruelty will not control the hearts of men. . . . If I can succeed, my greatest reward and my greatest hope will be that I have done something for the tens of thousands of *other* boys, for the countless unfortunates who must tread the *same road in blind childhood that these poor boys have trod* – that I have done something to help human understanding, to temper justice with mercy, to overcome *hate* with *love*.'

Yes, yes, but what has all this got to do with Twinkies?

Dilemma 93
Diktatiaville City Square

At the centre of Diktatiaville is a rather nice neo-classical city square, laid out in a grid and surrounded by the City Museum, the President's Palace and other important buildings. In the middle is a fountain, with several large metal dolphins spouting water.

Altogether, the square presents an imposing and elegant face for the city. Alas, whenever it is hot, the younger residents of the city strip off and bathe in the fountains with the dolphins. At these times, the sober square presents a quite different aspect, of lawlessness and loose morality.

So at least said the Mayor of Diktatiaville, to his colleagues in proposing some new regulations to tighten up on the use of the square.

Rule number one, to be posted up prominently in the square, is to be NO bathing in the fountains. If anyone defies the order and jumps in, then they will face fines and up to 100 hours of compulsory 'community' service – for example, scrubbing graffiti off the railway bridges or dissolving chewing gum off the pavements.

The councillors nod approvingly at this, although some think privately that as bathing in the fountains doesn't really do anyone any harm, 100 hours is a bit harsh.

The Mayor nods but reassures them. The penalty is put very high so that no one will dare to risk offending. It is a 'deterrent', rather than a measure of the nuisance. And then he goes on:

'Rule number two is that anyone who has already been convicted of bathing in the fountains and hence evidently not learned from the 100 hours of community service to behave better, will on the second offence face a *12 month prison sentence.*'

At this the councillors are a little alarmed. Just for bathing in the fountains? What about if there is a heatwave – if people are a little tipsy and forget the rules? If . . . ? But the Mayor brushes the objections aside. This penalty, he says, will surely never be needed. Only a mad person would risk bathing in the fountains in such circumstances. It is better to have penalties that deter effectively, than weak penalties that encourage people to take the risk of breaking the law.

Naturally, this being Diktatiaville, the proposals become law. The next summer, some students are fined, and one or two are given the long community service orders. No one reoffends. The fountains are left to spurt in peace.

It's rough, maybe – but is it justice?

Island ethics

The Black-pawed Rock Wallaby, endangered due to new predators on its land. So-called as it likes to spend the day sitting on rocks. And it has black paws.

Dilemma 94
Sanctuary Island

Sanctuary Island has just been sold, some way off the Scottish west coast. It is only small, but very very ancient. A volcanic and generally rather desolate place, it was believed to support only seabirds. So it is a great wonder (actually, inconvenience and annoyance) to its new owner, Mr Crofter, to find all sorts of unexpected wildlife exist there. In fact, in amongst some of the old extinct volcanic vents, primeval forest can be found, sheltering:

- the Spotted-tailed Quoll, a kind of bizarre mixture of rat and monkey;
- the Toolache Wallaby, a beautiful, agile creature with silver and russet fur;
- Boyd's Forest Dragon, a large mythical-looking lizard with its crown of white triangular scales;
- a kind of big fox, the Thylacine, with stripy fur and dog-like face.

Meanwhile, scurrying busily about the undergrowth is the Bush-tailed Bettong and something that looks very like a Desert Rat Kangaroo, a creature, like the Toolache, otherwise presumed extinct. And what's that strange croaking noise? Up in the trees, by the Double-Eyed Fig Parrot – most unexpected of all (for a frog) – is the Torrent Tree Frog. That's not to mention the sight of the Golden Bandicoot, or the Woylie, that uses its tail, curled around in a prehensile manner, to carry bundles of nesting material, or the tall, stately figure of the Great Auks, a type of penguin and . . .

. . . some large ugly pigeon-like birds which can't even fly.

They're first to go. Mr Crofter has plans for the island. He wants to make it into a golf course, and they keep swallowing the golf balls. In addition to that, they make rather a good stew. The wallabies don't do that, but the staff whose job it is to clear the forest on the island and lay the turf for an international-standard golf course, find that having had roast giant pigeon every week for months, the gap left after the last one has been caught has to be filled somehow.

Lara, his beautiful PA, timidly suggests that couldn't just a few of the funny birds be kept? For posterity? People might like to come and see them? But Mr Crofter just spits derisively. 'Pah! Let them go to Trafalgar Square if they want to see pigeons!'

As acre by acre the forest is cleared, the other animals begin to look a bit thin and mangy, and out of common humanity the staff take to running over any animals they find rashly crossing the new tarmac highway. Hearing of this, Mr Crofter is very angry. He puts an email round pointing out that Toolache and Quoll fur is very valuable and henceforth the animals must NOT be run over, but captured instead. He has plans to use the fur for the clubhouse furnishings – very distinctive.

But before half the island has been cleared, who should come over to the island in an old motor boat but a tall willowy figure in black, the local chaplain, Father McMoor. Being anxious not to offend the locals, Mr Crofter invites him into his office and shows him the plans for the island. Explosives experts will blow off the top of the mountain, and use the crushed rock to fill in some of the lakes. There will be a heliport, and a multiscreen cinema as well as a one-thousand bed hotel and . . . but McMoor is not listening. 'Blow up Black Mountain! One of the oldest . . . ' and he pauses melodramatically, ' . . . *darkest* of the island peaks!' McMoor rolls his eyes for effect.

And he tells the ancient story of how the Black Mountain came to be named. It seems there were two warriors who fought over a beautiful maiden, the battle creating the strange shape of the mountain peak, as well as turning the maiden into one of the tarns (recently drained and filled in with spoil for the heliport). Although the tale is very violent and seems to have involved much duplicity, Crofter loses interest long before the end, instead turning to his estate manager, who whispers that they *could* use some of the rock blown up to build a small replica mountain somewhere else. At this, Crofter turns back to the old Scot, clears his throat and announces grandly 'Ahem! Although yes, it will cost the company a *great deal* of money, Mr McMoor, I can personally assure you the children will still have a "Black Mountain" to play on! My expert here says we can rebuild –'

'Nooo, nooo, Mr Crofter, Black Mountain cannot be "rebuilt",' McMoor waves his white hands dismally, '– he just is!'

It's a clash of cultures certainly. But how about that offer – it must be better to save *something*, anyway?

Dilemma 95
Sanctuary Island II: the blackbirds

And Mr Crofter, what about the animals? 'Well, they'll be a bit in the way, if you're trying to run a golf course!' chuckles Crofter, but McMoor has no sense of humour. They part on chilly terms. As McMoor steps back into the boat he half-turns and says 'Crofter, I call on you – remember yer duty!'

But Mr Crofter thinks his duty is to his bank balance and, likewise, his employees – how could it possibly be otherwise?

'Do yer mean to the bluidy blackbirds, man!' he shouts after McMoor (but only after the boat has gone well out of range). A solitary looking figure lifts his hand in a slow salute and waves back.

Crofter orders work to be carried on at a faster pace.

What duty can there be to animals anyway?

Dilemma 96

Sanctuary Island III: the sourpuss

By the time the island is ready for the first jet-setter guests, the danger of attack by the animals has been reduced to the odd snake bite, and a programme of spraying is fast reducing that too. There is just one blot on the landscape to Crofter's eye. Indeed, as he arrives in his launch at the new jetty, to congratulate his manager on a job well done, a terrifying seal appears, as big as a bus, with ugly mottled skin.

'Blast and Bugger! I can't have people arriving and seeing that!' exclaims Crofter, prudently (thinking of the 'primacy effect'). 'Get a harpoon and clean up the coast line too.' But Lara, having watched reluctantly the animals being cleared out as 'in the way', has a better idea – to advertise the seals as 'big game', and charge for hunting them instead. She thinks by giving the beasts an economic value, it may be possible to spare them the fate of the other animals. Crofter claps her on the back, guffawing – 'I like that! I like that very much!'

And in fact, the resort is a great success. The seals are one of the main pulls for the new resort, helping to create extra jobs in what had previously been a pretty desolate, useless island. As a mark of appreciation, the Scottish Humanist Society erects a statue of Mr Crofter in Glasgow City Square.

Although, typical of the Scots, there are those sourpusses who disagree, saying he has not really earnt the honour.

Can businessmen be friends of the environment too?

Some really rather implausible ethical dilemmas that could only happen in the movies, and what do they tell us about ethical decision making anyway?

Dilemma 97
B-movie openers

Part 1: the bombmaker's dilemma

An Irish housewife, with a secret bombmaking past, is kidnapped, along with her little girl, and forced to build a huge bomb at the top of a skyscraper in the centre of London. If she builds the bomb, maybe hundreds of people will die, if she doesn't, her daughter certainly will. They mean business, these terrorists, because they keep the little girl in a dungeon and only produce home videotapes of her every weekend, or whenever her mum seems to worry about the ethics of making the bomb.

What *should* she do?

[Tea-break]

Part 2: the witness's dilemma

Over a period of several weeks, the bombmaker's little girl (who we should recall is kidnapped), befriends one of her guards, who is a very nice cheery Irishman of the old sort, who plays a fiddle and sings Celtic songs to keep the girl's spirits up. They have a high old time! Unfortunately, in the middle of all this, the order comes through to kill the girl. The kidnappers have a fight and the nice one kills the nasty one. The nice terrorist wants to run away then, but what is he going to do about the little girl? She could give him away. . . . Then the little girl says that if he lets her go, she will never tell the police on him. So, he does let her go and makes a run for it, but is soon caught. In a dramatic *finale*, the little girl is brought into the police station to pick him out in an identity parade.

What should *she* do?

Dilemma 98

The main feature: *Clockwork Orange* dilemmas

Stanley Kubrick's *A Clockwork Orange* is a mainstay of film ethics courses. It encapsulates many of the main moral issues: namely, sex, violence and politics. There's even a bit of plot too. Basically, this is that a handsome but morally dysfunctional young man, called Alex, and his unpleasant gang, 'the droogs', are fed up with society which is seen (because of its totalitarian institutional violence) as in its own way completely immoral too. Abandoned, deprived, unloved, Alex responds to the violence of bankrupt liberal society. The four faces of which are:

- the emotional violence of the nuclear family;
- the economic violence of capitalism;
- the anarchic violence of hooliganism;
- the organised violence of modern science.

So Alex is obliged to use his own psychopathic tools to achieve pleasure. The result is many vicious cruel assaults, murder, rapes. Violence simply becomes Alex's day job. In return, Alex and the droogs obtain the trappings of conventional success: cars, hi-fis, and drugs – and find freedom.

Is that the way life really is, you know, out 'on the street'?

Nearly at the ends if not the means

Dilemma 99
100 Person Village

100 Person Village is in a far away land. It is a charming place full of exotic marvels and surrounded by all the good things that nature has to offer.

The villagers are a mixed lot. Of the 100 inhabitants, most of them are dark-skinned, just about thirty of them are what we would sometimes call 'white', and in fact just one person in eight is of African 'stock', although it is said that once, long ago, everyone was.

There are about half and half men and women, slightly more women in fact, but not all the villagers are in mixed couples – half a dozen of them are in same-sex couples and have declared themselves to be homosexual. The villagers are all encouraged to worship in a little straw Christian church, as the current head of the village is keen that they do so, although only about thirty of them actually are Christian.

It all looks perfectly balanced and harmonious. But a group of visiting anthropologists finds a few of the other things in the village less acceptable. Why, they wonder, does one hut in the village, containing just six people, claim to own well over half of all of everything there – not just the built things, but the natural resources as well? Such as the branches and straw to make and repair huts. Many of the other villagers live either in dilapidated and leaking huts, or have to sleep rough on the borders of the village itself. Walking around one night, whilst the Head Man is hosting yet another feast at the 'top table' of the village, the anthropologists record the astonishing fact that just over half of the villagers are showing symptoms of malnutrition, one third seriously. Many of them also seem to be suffering from diseases, most of which ought to be preventable. Disturbingly, one of these villagers dies during the night. A lot of it seems to be connected with the rules regarding the village well, as one in six of the villagers are not allowed to draw water from it, but have to rely on the ditch which surrounds the houses instead. Unfortunately, for nearly half of the village, the ditch is also the main 'sewer'.

Challenging the head of the village (a white European-descended man living in a hut equipped with all the latest electronic and mechanical devices) about this, the anthropologists are told that anyone who wants resources for whatever purpose has only to apply to the village council, who will then normally authorise it. He even shows them the form on the village computer, kept in the hut. It is all just there waiting to be printed out for anyone who asks. Of course, the applications for resources must be in writing. 'But how many can read?' ask the anthropologists, bemused at this mix of high technology and extreme poverty side by side. Patiently, the Head Man says that he understands seventy of the 100 villagers are unable to read. But the deputy head of the village, he adds proudly, has actually had a university education. He is the only one.

As one of the anthropologists leaves the village, to return to their own university, they bump into two of the 'rich six', who are just setting out, clutching the village's two machine guns. 'Come and see!' they shout excitedly. 'There's been trouble in Hut Seven! We're going to restore order!' But the anthropologist just hurries away.

Now who would create a silly village like that?

Dilemma 100
Voltaire's dilemma

The scene:

Voltaire is sitting in a cane chair, in his garden in the late September sunshine, watching the bees busy with his nasturtiums, and two finches playing in the shrubbery.

VOLTAIRE: How absurd, how platitudinous, to say that beasts are machines devoid of knowledge and feeling which perform all their operations in the same manner, which learn nothing, which perfect nothing!

What? This bird which makes a semi-circular nest when it builds against a wall, which builds in a quarter-circle in a corner, and in full circle on a tree – this bird does everything in the same fashion? Doesn't the hound you have disciplined for three months know more at the end of that time than it did before your lessons? Does the canary you teach an air repeat it immediately? Don't you employ considerable time to teach it? Haven't you seen it making mistakes and correcting itself?

Is it because I speak to you that you decide I have feeling, memory, ideas? Well suppose I don't speak to you; let's say you see me enter my house with a distressed air, look uneasily for a paper, open the bureau in which I remember putting it, find it, and read it with joy. You decide that I have experienced feelings of distress and pleasure, that I have memory and knowledge.

(Just then, his faithful hound, Blackie, pads up, and puts his nose on his master's lap, looking blindly up at Voltaire with quiet devotion.)

Then extend the view to the dog who has lost his master, who has looked for him all over with piteous cries, who enters the house agitated and restless, who goes upstairs and down, from room to room, and at last finds the master he loves in his study, and shows his joy by the gentleness of his cries, by his leaps, and his caresses.

Barbarians seize this dog, who surpasses man so greatly in his capacity for friendship; they nail him to a table and dissect him alive . . .

(Voltaire strokes Blackie's ears)

 . . . and what you discover in him are the same organs of sensation you have in yourself.

Now, is that any kind of philosophical argument?

Dilemma 101
The pragmatic response

Nicholas Fontaine reports in Philosophy Heaven to George Bernard Shaw of what he found when visiting the laboratories of a large pharmaceutical company (*Memoirs pour servir à l'histoire de Port-Royal, 1738*):

'They administered beatings to dogs with perfect indifference, and made fun of those who pitied the creatures as if they felt pain. They said the animals were [like] clocks; that the cries they made when struck, were only the noise of a string pulled, and the whole body was without feeling. They nailed poor animals up to boards by their four paws to vivisect them.'

George is appalled: 'You do not settle whether an experiment is justified or not by merely showing that it is of some use.' And he wags his finger. 'The distinction is not between useful and useless experiments, but between barbarous and civilised behaviour. Vivisection is a *social evil* because if it advances human knowledge, it does so at the *expense of human character*.'

Yes, but it is useful, isn't it? After all, you wouldn't rather a thousand people – including your whole family – die from the washing up liquid, just to save the life of one measly rat, would you!

Now (at last!) a *real* argument?

(It certainly looks like one . . .)

Discussions

Dilemmas 1 and 2
The lifeboat and Sinking further

To what extent should an individual risk their own well-being for the well-being of others (and in this case a responsible captain risks the lives of others under his command)? This is a slightly glorified version of the biologist Garrett Hardin's so-called 'lifeboat' scenario. In a bit of applied utilitarianism, it is designed to show that rich countries do not have any obligations to poor countries, as they would endanger the well-being of their own populations were they to attempt to admit the world's poor in the rich world's 'lifeboat'. If the world's wealth was shared out equally, it might only mean that everyone had too little. Hardin argues that 'altruism' can only apply on a small scale.

Professor Hardin is not interested too much in rescuing individuals, as he sees the problem as one of too many people anyway. The 'population problem' is the 'root cause of both hunger and poverty', he insists. Or rather, he says, it is the '180 separate national population problems'. (That's enough for another book, albeit not a very interesting one.) The only important ethical principle here is that no one must try to solve their population problem by exporting their excess people to other countries. Expanding his famous metaphor, Hardin continues, saying that each rich nation is a lifeboat full of comparatively rich people, some of whom feel sorry for the people in 'more crowded' lifeboats. These 'heart-on-sleeve' people, he says, should 'get out and yield their place to others'. Yes, Bert can help Tom – by jumping overboard! The net result of conscience-stricken people relinquishing their unjustly held positions, Hardin concludes with Nietzschean zeal, is the elimination of their kind of conscience from the lifeboat. 'The lifeboat, as it were, purifies itself of guilt.'

But there is one other possibility open to Bert. He can rescue Tom, and save the lifeboat too – by pushing the captain overboard. And wouldn't that be ethical? No wonder Professor Hardhearted's position is that social systems are rendered unstable by such altruistic tendencies . . .

On the larger scale, survival of some necessitates and requires the non-survival of the rest. (Biologically speaking – think 'fruit flies'.) The 'starvation hunger process' is essential to the balancing of the human population. However, like the lifeboat, the global example risks foundering on the practical question of whether the boat/rich world will *really* sink – or is it just a question of squashing up a bit, maybe taking a risk on behalf of others, which is a slightly different question.

And the bit of captain's schoolboy Latin? Doubtless Flintheart is saying *impossibilium nulla est obligatio* – nobody is obliged to do what is impossible, one of the fundamental principles of the old Roman civil law. Naturally, not all philosophers agree on *that*.

Dilemma 3
The psychologists' tale

One of the great challenges of philosophy is the riddle posed by the ancient oracle at Delphi, the simple injunction: 'know thyself'. Aren't most people basically good, with just a few secret sadists and repressed killers lurking amongst us?

Unfortunately, it seems the difference is often only skin deep, not at all as many philosophers imagined. Just in the last few generations we have seen the good people carrying out the slaughter of the First World War, the concentration and extermination camps for the enemies of the Third Reich, the prison camps and mass starvations of the Stalinists, not to mention the 'saturation bombings' of civilians all over Asia, the carefully planned genocidal killings in Rwanda, Cambodia and the Balkans – the list goes on and on. Perhaps more chilling than the bald facts are the details caught forever in the photographs – of the passers-by pausing to spit or throw stones at Jews on their way to the concentration camps, or the proud small-town American folk posing in their Sunday best by poplar trees, from which hang, in the words of the song, that 'strange fruit / swinging in the Southern breeze'. The fruit here being the mutilated corpses of blacks, some of the estimated 5,000 lynched in the seventy or so years leading up to the Civil Rights victories in the 1960s.

Stanley Milgram of Yale University devised a simple test to see whether people need to be 'bad' before they can be persuaded to do bad things. Alas, it seems not. They can be persuaded to 'adjust' their moral beliefs very easily. In one experiment, Milgram asked students to give another student an electric shock every time they got answers wrong, in a sort of memory test. The 'experimenter' encouraged them to keep 'punishing' the students in the interests of science – even when they started to scream and writhe in pain. (It is of only small consolation that the student being electrocuted was in fact an actor and part of the experiment. The indifference of the 'ordinary person' inflicting the pain was real enough.)

Philosophers have traditionally been suspicious of unguided human nature, with the noteworthy exception of Jean-Jacques Rousseau – who was a rogue himself. Most of the Ancients thought that only a few people could be trusted to be ethical: and that societies needed a 'virtuous man' to rule over them. Confucius, like Aristotle, meant by this, a 'noble' man, others reinterpreted it to be a 'superior man' with certain qualities instead: wise, courageous, humane. Plato is almost alone in including women in his definition of suitable 'guardians'. The superior man both thinks and acts well – virtuously – modelling his behaviour on the great men of the past. He understands that life is a quest for perfection and learning, a quest that is unending and necessarily never completed. Confucius identified the pitfalls on the way, the *Tao*, as greed and aggression, resentment and pride, and self-interest. The best protection is education – knowledge. A key component of which is offered in the *Analects* (*c*.550 BC). In reply to an entreaty to sum up the moral life in a single word, Confucius offers: 'Reciprocity'. By which he meant, do not inflict on others what you yourself would not wish done to you.

Some centuries later, Mohammed recommended the *velayat-e faqih* – the clerical rule of Guardians in Islamic lands. In the twelfth century, Moses Maimonides, the Spanish North African rabbi-philosopher (1155–1204) advised in his *Guide to the Perplexed* (*c*.1190) that virtue is simply a means of becoming good at following the religious code. That other great Chinese philosopher, Mencius (371–289 BC) however, differed from Confucius significantly, as he thought people were born good, but were corrupted by their miserable lives (and circumstances). From his perspective the crucial thing is to look inward for virtue, to find our original nature.

> Benevolence is the heart of man, and straightens his road. Sad it is indeed when a man gives up the right road instead of following it and allows his heart to stray without enough sense to go after it. When his chickens and dogs stray, he has sense enough to go after them, but not when his heart strays.

So the answer is? With only three *ethical dilemmas* so far, we have only just scratched the surface of the complexity and downright contradictoriness that is the human psyche.

Mrs Goebbels does 'the right thing'

Actually, the Nazis often appear in ethics books as examples of people who were clearly evil. They can be offered as an illustration of the reality of evil to even the most blasé of would-be relativists. Funny thing is, lots of ordinary Germans, people who we can no more explain away as 'evil' than we can Zimbardo's students, did not seem to realise this, even as evidence of the horrors of the National Socialists and indeed their hypocrisy and failure could be measured in the piles of bodies lying in the streets during the regime's 'last few days' in 1945.

Mrs Goebbels, 'Magda', sums up the apparently inexhaustible ability of people both to whitewash their own motives, and the ostensibly magnificent aspirations of the Nazis, in the last days in the Berlin bunker. As her husband, the terrifying propogandist, was preparing their suicide, along with their six little children, she wrote a letter to her son by an earlier marriage living in another part of the country. In it, she explains that she had decided to put an end, 'the only possible, honourable end', to her National Socialist life. 'I want you to know that I stayed with Papa [Goebbels] against his will, that as recently as last Sunday the Führer still offered to help me get away. But I did not have to think twice. Our glorious idea is in ruins, and with everything I have known in my life that was beautiful, noble and good.'

Gobbles himself, the insatiable propogandist, could not resist penning, in neat letters, his own postscript:

'One day the lies will crumble and the truth will triumph. That will be the hour when we will tower over everything, pure and spotless . . . '

The next day, Magda, wearing her golden Nazi Party badge (given to her by Hitler just three days before) poisoned her six small children with hydrogen cyanide, and was in turn shot by her husband, who then turned the gun on himself.

Dilemma 4

Custom is king

Actually, no one could agree over the UN Declaration of Human Rights either. The Saudis expressed the doubts of many other countries by objecting to the inclusion of women's rights and 'freedom of religion' particularly. They thought these were not 'universal', or 'natural' at all. Certainly their customs tell a different story. But the opposition between nature and culture is an ancient one, presented by the Sophists (fifth century BC) as between *pysis*, nature, and *nomos*, law or custom, and it is hard sometimes to know which one is worse. But here are the facts backing up our alternative declaration:

1 We assert the fundamental right to torture and kill people in all sorts of ingenious and cruel ways.

People generally have favoured the use of torture, over the ages merely devising new and more horrible forms of it. Dungeons were part of the process too, ingeniously constructed to destroy the will of the prisoner. One in the Bastille in Paris was constructed to be a downwards pointing cone so that it would be impossible to lie down, sit, let alone stand.

After confessions of misdeeds have been obtained through torture, a painful death is also the historical norm, with burning probably the most cruel and yet the most easily arranged. In 1252, the church gave torture its seal of approval when Pope Innocent IV issued a papal bull authorising the setting up of the 'machinery for systematic persecution', the so-called Inquisition, as a way of obtaining confessions to heresy. Four years later, with licensed secular torturers struggling to keep up with demand, Pope Alexander IV authorised church officials to use torture too. For twelve generations the Inquisition did an imaginative job in providing an advance view of Hell for the people of Europe on Earth too.

Even so, throughout the Middle Ages, there was one 'out-of-step' European country, England, which declined to adopt the use of torture as a judicial method – other than the 'pressing of prisoners', as described in Dilemma 89. Barbaro, a Venetian ambassador of the sixteenth century, observed that the English were concerned that torture of the innocent 'spoils the body and an innocent life' and strangely thought it better to 'release a criminal than punish an innocent man'!

Today, torture is alive and well in many countries.

2   We assert the inalienable right to own slaves and declare that some people are fit only to be slaves.

Another historical constant is the use of slaves, be they slaves from birth, from conquest or whatever. Aristotle and Plato both produced justifications for slavery centred on the lower abilities of slaves, seen as more akin to animals. Both Christianity and Islam have been apologists for the practice, despite Mohammed setting free his own slaves and instructing that all men should be brothers and treated as equals. (Well, that's half the human race freed, anyway.)

For 300 years, the infamous African slave trade was based on and facilitated by African customs of selling their neighbours. The peculiar contribution of the Europeans was to develop a theory of racial superiority to justify their own involvement. The prevalence of this custom can be shown by the fact that when the British undertook a census of India in 1841 they found a mind-boggling 10 million slaves. (They passed laws forbidding the custom in 1862.) Today, there are still thought to be at least 200,000 child slaves sold by African nations alone. Countries like Benin maintain this is a 'custom', in which children are given 'work experience' abroad. In 2001, the world's interest was briefly kindled when one such modern day slave ship, the *Etireno*, en route to Gabon, was accused of having thrown 250 children overboard (as surplus to orders).

3   We claim the natural right to kill babies for any reason we care to think of.

Killing newborn babies (infanticide) is another worldwide customary norm with, until very recently, only the odd country like Egypt and Cambodia having divergent customs suggesting that ALL children must be reared. Usually it was girl babies that were killed, but it could be, as in Madagascar, any child born on an 'unlucky day'.

A long line of ethical thinkers from Seneca to Peter Singer write of killing 'defective' children. They even see it as a wise and prudent action suitable for use as a policy benchmark. Singer *et al.* seem to see childbirth as a bit like getting coffee from a vending machine. The babies are all infinitely replicable, some are just 'better' than others. Preventing the birth of 'defective' children is only like blocking off a button marked 'weak coffee' on the human slot machine. (And no wonder feminists object to the way women are portrayed in the fertility debate.)

185

Customary rights

When the Icelanders accepted the moral guidance of the Christian church, they insisted on just two cultural exceptions: they wanted to be able to continue to eat horses, and to kill children. Curiously, it was the Christian emphasis on the dreadfulness of children dying 'unbaptised' that had more effect in changing practice than anything else.

4 And demand the right to kill the old and infirm and eat their bodies afterwards.

Killing old people was widespread until recently, but never universal. Herodotus' story of the Massagetae, who boiled their old folk with beef, and ate the mixture as a treat, is perhaps the best known, but there are many other equally queasy-making stories. One tribe in Niger were said to kill their old people, smoke and pulverise the bodies, and then compress the powder into little balls with corn and water. These unedifying burgers were kept for long periods as a basic food. Some people rationalise this today by saying that it reflected the cruel necessity of life in harsh conditions, citing stories of Inuits (like the Hudson Bay Inuit who strangle the old), or the Tupis (of Brazil, who killed any elderly person who became ill, and then ate the corpse) or the Tobas (of Paraguay, who were reputed to bury their old folk alive) to illustrate both the necessity and the good intentions of the tribes. However, these customs were never universal – some tribes had found other solutions. American Indian tribes like the Poncas and Omahas, as well as some Incas, created a role for the old and infirm by leaving them at home, with supplies, while the rest of the tribe hunted or gathered. The old watched the cornfields and scared away birds, so they were of use and the 'cruel necessity' is exposed somewhat.

Eating people is not wrong, as such. A Miranhas cannibal explained to the anthropologists Spix and Martius, that 'it is all a matter of habit. When I have killed an enemy, it is better to eat him than to let him go to waste. Big game is rare because it does not lay eggs like turtles. The bad thing is not being eaten, but death . . . you whites are really too dainty!'

See also Dilemma 75 for some peculiar tales of Herodotus.

Dilemmas 5–7

This type of 'personal dilemma' is very common – hardly any of us will avoid finding ourselves in such a dubious situation, be it just an opportunity to travel without paying on the train, or leave the shop with some unintended purchases. We are caught between the two horns of 'personal interest' and 'impersonal principles', which is precisely where Thomas Nagel thought most ethical dilemmas were to be found. Not that Kant would have any of it – he denied that there were any dilemmas at all, that a 'perfect duty' always could and always should be obeyed. Otherwise it would not be perfect. The danger of allowing that there might be 'irresolvable dilemmas' is that the only 'logical' response might be that unspeakable ethical hobgoblin: relativism. In this fear, Kant is temporarily in unlikely alliance with the utilitarians, whose system was also supposed to make impossible such ambiguities. Even so, John Stuart Mill himself acknowledged that:

> There exists no moral system under which there do not arise unequivocal cases of moral obligation. These are the real difficulties, the knotty points in the theory of ethics, as in the conscientious guidance of personal conduct. They are overcome practically, with greater or lesser success, according to the intellect and virtue of the individual.

So now let us apply our ethical principles to a few knotty points.

Dilemma 5
The internet bargain

For most people, the first reaction (as with most ethical matters) is to calculate the likely consequences – can you *really* get away with it? Second, if you suspect you may be unable to – will there be some unpleasant consequences? If you think the computer company will eventually note the discrepancy or if you think the railway inspector may pounce at the ticket barrier the next day, having videotaped the whole thing, then you will probably not find it much of an ethical dilemma at all, just a matter of cowardly self-interest to get the due money to someone as soon as possible.

But if you calculate that even if it is noticed you could always pay up and pretend you had not noticed, then you may tell yourself that you are only doing 'what most

187

people would do'. Mind you, that is not to say very much. Plato had a well-established contempt for the opinion of the 'majority' as merely another form of anarchy.

Perhaps you could cite in support the example of the great 'Brains Trust' moral expert, Professor Joad, from the 1940s, observing even he was tempted by Beelzebub to dodge his train fare . . . but then he *was* found out and disgraced. Or perhaps you could cite Bertrand Russell, and argue that you are resisting the tyranny of public opinion:

> One should as a rule respect public opinion in so far as it is necessary to avoid starvation and to keep out of prison, but anything that goes beyond this is voluntary submission to an unnecessary tyranny, and is likely to interfere with happiness in all kinds of ways.

Bertrand Russell wrote that pithily in one of his 'Sceptical Essays'. Then again, Russell rightly notes that we have in fact, 'two kinds of morality side by side: one which we preach but do not practise, and another which we practise but seldom preach', and that everyone is surrounded in this way by a 'cloud of comforting convictions, which move with him like flies on a summer day'.

Generally, the number of people following objective rules like 'always pay the correct amount' is less than it might seem. At least with our internet 'bargain', there is no breach of 'personal trust'. This is not a cornerstore, with some sort of nodding acquaintance to the store-keeper. In practice, this seems to be another factor – the relationship matters – a nice helpful cashier will get more money returned than the nasty grumpy one. But the ethical status of such distinctions is not really there under most theories. Which maybe is a deficiency in the theories.

But next time you get an extra note in the change, or find some other temptation – bear in mind the possibility that you may be being filmed as part of a programme on social values. Recall, as Adam Smith wrote in his *Moral Sentiments*, if we could see ourselves as others see us, 'a reformation would be unavoidable – we could not otherwise endure the sight!'

Dilemma 6
The toaster

This involves personal freedom, privacy and choice. Not much, but a bit. Clearly if it is addressed, even by some automatic database, to your partner, you have no right to interfere with the mail. Second, right or wrong, clearly Sam's partner is the sort of person who likes such catalogues and indeed making such purchases. On the face of it, there is not much of an ethical issue here – you shouldn't throw it in the bin at all.

If Sam is the sort of person who might be tempted to – after all, 'they would never know', and it might save everyone a lot of bother and expense – then Sam might be claiming some sort of 'utilitarian' justification: to be increasing the sum of happiness, even if not recognising certain 'rights'.

Certainly (as mentioned above), in one of the most famous ethical thought experiments of them all, Socrates asks his friend Glaucon whether it is always correct to follow a 'rule', such as returning property to its owner, or to adopt a strategy – calculating the consequences of returning it – for good or evil. The example Socrates uses is of friend who wants his knife back so he can stab someone. It seems all right to withhold a knife – but a nick-nack catalogue?

In another Platonic dialogue, the *Protagoras*, it is suggested that what is needed is the ability to weigh up the pleasures against the pains likely to result from an activity (or catalogue) – an early kind of 'hedonic calculus', of the type, in fact, normally associated with the Utilitarians of the eighteenth century. (*Hedone* being Greek for pleasure – we have the word 'hedonist' still in common usage for anyone who seems particularly motivated by it.) But in fact the Greeks could not agree on the correct approach. While the astronomer Eudoxus went so far as to claim that 'pleasure' was the sole good, Speusippus, on the contrary, held that pleasure (and pain) were two sides of the same thing – and that thing was evil.

Dilemma 7
The liar

Lying is as old as speech, it could hardly be otherwise. Everyone does it. God, doctors, teachers, philosophers – even some clever birds lie to each other. (They hide their store of food in one place, knowing other birds are watching, and then secretly return later, dig it up, and hide it in another place.)* Winston Churchill once said that truth was so important and so valuable, that it must always be accompanied by a bodyguard – of lies.

But the philosophical status of the lie is another matter. With the tale of the 'mad knifeman', Socrates argues with Glaucon over the conflict between the ethical imperative to always be truthful and the negative practical consequences that may follow, and the founders of Plato's *Republic* are allowed to lie to the people about their origins – the 'gold, silver or iron' in their souls.

In the Middle Ages the issue still rated highly in learned debate, with Thomas Aquinas writing at length 'On Lying' – even making a case for it occasionally. Although Aquinas agreed with the earlier warnings of St Augustine that 'the mouth that belieth killeth the soul', that 'every lie is a sin', and that generally 'lying is in itself evil and to be shunned', he then like so many of us, went on to muddy the waters a bit. In fact, Augustine's ability to take a firm stand on lying depended mainly on his decision to put the emphasis entirely on the individual (soul)'s self-interest in all these matters. (Consequences be damned!) If Bernard is *really* weighing up everyone else's happiness when he lies, then he is talking a very different moral language to St Augustine.

Perhaps, like Abraham, who we see (in Dilemma 47) lying about where the sacrifice is to come from (and Abraham is also known in Biblical circles for being evasive about his relationship with Sara, whom he calls 'his sister'), Bernard only 'wished to hide the truth', not to actually tell a lie. That is the line, at least, that Aquinas waffles on Abraham's behalf, but the policy was also recorded more recently by Britain's most powerful civil servant, Sir Robert Armstrong, in court in New South Wales to explain the 'Spycatcher' case. Prevaricating vigorously for England, he admitted of his and the British government's evidence: 'It contains a misleading impression, not a lie. It was being economical with the truth.'

Another device, for liars, as the Ancient equivocator Seneca observed, is to appeal to the flux and change of the universe:

* If no other birds are watching, the ravens leave the food in the first hiding place.

for a man to be bound by a promise it is necessary for everything to remain unchanged: otherwise neither did he lie in promising – since he promised what he had in his mind, due circumstances being taken for granted – nor was he faithless in not keeping his promise, because circumstances are no longer the same.

(*De beneficiis*, IV)

Meanwhile, a lone figure on the other side, brandishing the trusty sword, Kant warns that the liar causes contracts to be voided and to lose their force, and 'this is a wrong done to mankind generally'. A lie does not need to cause harm directly to be wrong, and even when it appears to do good, it instead must be judged by this general collapse of the truth. 'To be truthful in all declarations, therefore, is a sacred and absolutely commanding decree of reason, limited by no expediency', he concludes. (If Bernard can lie about this, then he could lie about other things too – and probably will.) But let's see how Kant's system works in practice, for fortunately, there is an apt historical case.

Impressed to see a philosopher assume the precarious pulpit of moral conviction, one Maria von Herbert wrote to Kant, in 1791, to say that she had long been a fan of his, and had recently applied the 'truth telling principle' in her most intimate affections.

'As a believer calls to his God', Maria begins fervently, 'I call to you for help, for comfort and for counsel to prepare me for death.' It seems that by telling her lover of a previous affair, she caused him to be offended because of the 'long drawn out lie'. Although 'there was no vice in it', she relates, 'the lie was enough, and his love has vanished'. As an 'honourable man', her lover offers to continue as a 'friend'. 'But that inner feeling that once, unbidden, led us to each other is no more – and my heart splinters into a thousand burning pieces!'

So far so tragic. Maria says it is only Kant's strictures against committing suicide that have thus far stopped her from taking that way out. Kant wrote back the following spring (this is before email slowed up the rate of correspondence of course.) After a few kindly words on her evident good intentions he speaks sternly of duty: 'A love like that wants to communicate itself completely, and it expects of its respondent a similar sharing of heart, unweakened by distrustful reticence.' If such full frankness leads a couple to split asunder, this is because their 'affection was more physical than moral' and would soon have disappeared anyway. Sighs Kant, the confirmed bachelor, this is a misfortune often to be encountered in life.

Fortunately, the value of life itself, when it depends on the enjoyment we get from people, 'is vastly overrated'.

Maria replies a year later, saying that she has now achieved the high level of moral exactitude outlined by Kant, albeit she finds life now rather empty. She says she is indifferent to everything, and suffers from ill health. Like the best moral philosophers, 'each day interests me only to the extent that it brings me closer to death'. She thinks she would like to visit Kant, however, as in his portrait she has discerned 'a profound calm there, and moral depth – but not the acuity of which the *Critique of Pure Reason* is proof'. She entreats 'her God' to 'give me something that will get this intolerable emptiness out of my soul'.

But for that, apparently, Kant had nothing to offer.

Dilemma 8
The dodgy donor clinic

Discussions

Is it ethical? Much more than that, Dr Dedicated thinks it is his duty. But other colleagues in the clinic's tea-room warn that the plan is contrary to the hypocritical oaf, 'to do no harm' – and that is the end of that.

Dilemmas 9 and 10
The famous footbridge dilemma and The human cannonball

'Trolley dilemmas' appear in many forms, sometimes down deep mines or in exotic jungles, sometimes in very spartan logical form, sometimes as here in elaborate 'Penelope Pitstop' dramatic style. But the most interesting thing about them is not what the 'answer' is, but what people think the answer is.

For it seems a large majority of people will say that Fred can switch the trolley onto the other track – but not push the stranger into the path of the runaway trolley. Psychologists as much as philosophers think this is very significant, arguing (in the words of the psychologist Jonathan Haidt) that moral reasoning is really intuitive and emotional, and that any 'reasons' for decisions are in reality generated after these intuitions have already decided the case. So people may agree to switch the trolley onto the other track saying 'it is better to save five lives even at the price of one', the usual 'utilitarian' line – but then refuse to push the stranger into the path of the trolley this time saying it would be wrong to take an innocent life – for whatever reason. They thus switch over their mental 'points' onto lines of 'Kantian' reasoning about 'Categorical Imperatives' and inviolable principles. The psychologists have impressive brainscans too: ones that show the logical parts of peoples' brains quietly processing the first part of the problem, and the 'emotional' parts of their brains working overtime on the second part.

Another way of looking at it is to say that the difference lies in the 'intention', even if the consequences are 'arithmetically' equivalent. This is also what philosophers call the doctrine of 'double effect' – a bad action intended to achieve a good end is unethical, but a good action with equally harmful 'side effects' is 'justified'. It is this doctrine that allows, for instance, the dropping of bombs on restaurants by the US to kill 'terrorists' but forbids the bombing of restaurants by terrorists, to 'attack the US'. Of course, the devil is always in the detail.

'Trolley dilemmas', at least a little like these (of course, less interesting) have been shown to 'volunteers' in university research labs, and their responses carefully calibrated. In the United States, researchers found that when the situation arouses an emotional response, for example, pushing someone off a bridge, the decision to 'not act', so to speak, is taken quickly and 'irrationally', but if the situation is processed by the 'logical centres' of the brain, the decision is taken slowly. The reason is not so much because logic is very difficult and rather confusing, but rather, as one Princeton University professor put it, that 'you've got an emotional response saying, "no, no, no," so anyone who's going to say "yes" will have to fight that response . . . you can see it in how it slows people down when they go against emotion.'

Myself, for what it is worth, which is not very much (but then this is a trolley dilemma), agree that the trolley can be switched onto the other track, for the very excellent fuzzy reasoning that maybe the butterfly lady will hear it and jump aside anyway, 'or something'. In this sense, I am not absolutely certain that I am killing her. Of course, it is fuzzy reasoning, as we could claim the same kind of exceptional change might save the five workers too if we let the trolley run towards them. Similarly, someone might claim that in pushing the youth off the bridge they 'weren't sure' what would happen to him either. In such dilemmas, as in real life, it is often easiest to simply appeal to not 'being sure' what would happen – as we allow the trolleys to hurtle towards their grim rendezvous . . .

193

The first stage of cruelty

William Hogarth's *The Four Stages of the Descent into Cruelty* is a series of eighteenth-century engravings, popular then, if today less well known than his *Rake's Progress*. These attractive room decorations depict, as the artist puts it, 'some vices peculiar to the lower class'. In this scene, Tom Nero and the street urchins are enjoying the torture of animals. Tom is doing something unspeakable to a dog, cats are being hanged – even thrown from windows top left – and in the foreground, with childish ingenuity, a bone is being tied to a dog's tail.

The second stage? This also involves cruelty to animals, featuring wanton destruction of sheep and horses. By the third stage, Tom has graduated to humans, cutting the throat of a woman that it seems he may have raped. The fourth gruesome scene depicts the knife of justice dissecting Tom himself, whose body is now being used as part of an anatomy lesson. A dog nibbles happily on his discarded stomach.

The Four Stages of Cruelty is perhaps the only 'great work' of art to have the depraved underworld of the criminal classes as its intended audience. William Hogarth (1697–1764) lived at a time when it seemed that decent folk faced a rising tide of unprecedented wickedness that was threatening to engulf society, and the only hope was to stamp on the first signs of incipient moral error.

Plus ça change.

The four stages of Descartes' descent into cruelty: stage 1

Are we machines? Certainly, and indeed many philosophers have pointed out the similarities. As, for example, David Hume (1711–76) put it: 'I assert [all kinds of behaviour of animals] . . . proceed from a reasoning, that is not in itself different, nor founded on different principles, from that which appears in human nature'. And this 'mechanical view' of the world has had profound implications.

When the father of 'modern' philosophy, French biologist and mathematician René Descartes (1596–1650), split the world into two parts – the *mental* world of minds and the *physical* world of bodies ('dualism') – all the things philosophers valued belonged to the world of ideas and thoughts, a world peopled by souls. Animals, unfortunately for them, belonged only to the physical world. Descartes pioneered a particularly clinical kind of reductionist thinking that taught that animals are simply machines, without souls, reason or feeling. The cry of a dog in pain, according to Descartes, is merely a mechanical noise, *like the creak of a wheel*.*

Science was progressing quite rapidly in the seventeenth century, and Descartes' beliefs found enthusiastic acceptance in both ecclesiastical and scientific circles. They also offered the removal of all moral objections to animal experimentation. Only a few voices of objection remained. One such was that of Henry More (1614–87). In an exchange of letters with Descartes, More wrote that no one can *prove* animals lack souls or share an afterlife. To deny animals souls and an afterlife was done only out of 'narrowness of spirit, out of overmuch self-love, and contempt of other creatures'. More recalled that the world was not made for people alone, but for other living creatures as well. Quoting the Bible in support, More says that humans were meant to rule over the animals with compassionate stewardship and warns that unrestrained human violence and abuse towards animals must result in humans behaving likewise to one another. 'He that slights the life or welfare of a brute Creature', wrote More, 'is naturally so unjust, that if outward laws did not restrain him, he would be as cruel to Man.'

Dilemma 12
Stage 2: free to do otherwise

Free will is a fiction, and a very useful one at that. It says that when we *think* we make a choice – we really have done. Of course, no one can ever know whether that freedom is real or just an illusion. Some people – determinists – say that every decision is, well, determined: by circumstances, genes, chemicals, even Nietzsche books – or whatever (see Dilemma 92). As far as that sort of determinism goes, a straw offered by William James (1842–1910) is that there is a sort of 'randomness' in the physical world that makes everything just a little uncertain. Of course, even if we are not really free at all, it might still be best that we be treated as though we were.

Why is free will definitely a fiction then? Because to be responsible for your behaviour, you have to be not only taking a decision freely, but you also have to be

* See also the discussion of Dilemma 24.

held responsible for being the sort of person who, given all the circumstances, will freely take that sort of decision. You have to be held accountable for being what you are. In a sort of logical sense, the responsibility is infinite. Kant says that although we cannot understand how human freedom is possible, we must accept that it exists, and that the freedom belongs to the 'noumenal' self (not the everyday physical one), the noumenal world being outside the usual rules of cause and effect.

Why did Descartes make this the key to being human, then? Well, Descartes was a very innovative mathematician, and a very competent scientist. His work on the laws of refraction was a milestone in optics. But his philosophy drew excessively on Aristotle, who in turn had tried to mix both science, mathematics and philosophical speculation, with erratic results. Descartes' contemporary, Thomas Hobbes, said of the 'Ancients', at the end of the *Leviathan*:

> Their Logic which should be their method of reasoning, is nothing else but captions of words, and inventions how to [i.e. designed to] puzzle such as should go about to pose them . . . there is nothing so absurd that the Old Philosophers have not some of them maintained. And I believe that scarce anything can be more absurdly said than that which is now called Aristotle's *Metaphysics*; nor more repugnant to Government, than much of what he hath said in his *Politics*; nor more ignorantly, than a great part of his *Ethics*.

Of course, not everyone would agree. But it certainly pays to be sceptical even of the greatest philosophers. Many people believe it was Descartes' greatest triumph – the division between mind and matter – that was also his greatest mistake. In fact, William James was one of the 'pragmatist school' (which included John Dewey and C. S. Pierce) of the turn of the twentieth century, which specifically condemned Descartes for having misdirected philosophy away from understanding people as part of nature and towards a false 'ideal' of the human essence, outside language, culture and social life.

And it was from Aristotle that Descartes had got fixed in his head the notion that 'man is a rational animal', a view which is really little more than a (category) mistake. All animals are rational: they have aims and strategies, memories and feelings. The Chinese philosophers said instead that 'man is a moral animal'. And this is much more plausible as a way of distinguishing humans from non-humans. But with this notion of humanity fixed in his mind, Descartes goes on to build an entire theory of the world on Aristotle's distinction.

It is also a very remarkable fact that although there are many animals which exhibit more dexterity than we do in some of their actions, we at the same time observe that they do not manifest any dexterity at all in many others. Hence the fact that they do better than we do, does not prove that they are endowed with mind, for in this case they would have more reason than any of us, and would surpass us in all other things. It rather shows that they have *no reason at all*, and that it is nature which acts in them according to the disposition of their organs, *just as a clock, which is only composed of wheels and weights is able to tell the hours* and measure the time more correctly than we can do with all our wisdom.

And we ought not to confound speech with natural movements which betray passions and may be imitated by machines as well as be manifested by animals; nor must we think, as did some of the ancients, that *brutes talk, although we do not understand their language.* For if this were true, since they have many organs which are allied to our own, they could communicate their thoughts to us just as easily as to those of their own race.

Dilemma 13
Penultimate stage: the two tests

During the third century AD, Porphyry made allusions to the golden age in his writing. According to Porphyry, animals have rights. Animals are our brothers and sisters. Animals have been endowed with life, feelings, ideas, memory, and industry. The only thing animals may be said to lack which sets humans apart from them is the gift of speech. 'If they had it', asked Porphyry, 'should we dare to kill and eat them? Should we dare to commit these fratricides?' Porphyry further observed that, in reality, animals do possess language, which the Ancients were said to have understood. The birds and beasts communicate, but men no longer understand their language.

In any case, perhaps it is more like Brigid Brophy (b. 1929) says:

'Sentimentalist' is the abuse with which people counter the accusation that they are cruel, thereby implying that to be sentimental is worse than to be cruel, which it isn't . . . I don't hold animals superior or even equal to humans. The whole case for behaving decently to animals rests on the fact that we are the superior species. We are the species uniquely capable of imagination, rationality, and moral choice – and that is precisely why we are under an obligation to recognise and respect the rights of animals.

Descartes raises important questions not only for the treatment of animals – but for the treatment of humans too. We shall have to return to it after he has finished his dissection.

Dilemma 14
Final stage: the immortal member

According to many Biblical passages, animals have the same 'breath of life' as do humans (Genesis 7:15, 22) But, influenced by Aristotle, followed by the saintly sages Augustine and Aquinas (echoed by Descartes), the Church changed its position, henceforth maintaining that animals lack souls or divinity. (During the Synod of Macon (AD 585), again following Aristotle's lead, the Church debated whether or not women had souls!)

The Ancient Greeks were generally more inclusive though. Hippocrates (c.460–377 BC) states flatly that 'the soul is the same in all living creatures, although the body of each is different', whilst Pythagoras famously told a man abusing a puppy: 'Do not kick him: in his body is the soul of a friend of mine. I recognised the voice when he cried out.'

Dilemma 15
Gyges' ring

On the surface, the story of Gyges' ring is one about human nature. But in Book Two of Plato's *Republic*, where the tale is to be found in its original form, it is part of a wider discussion of society. There, Glaucon tells it to Socrates as a way of illustrating his view that the origins of 'right' and 'wrong' have more to do with plain self-interest than anything greater. It is simply a compromise between doing what is most desirable – doing wrong and getting no punishment and doing what is most undesirable – suffering wrong and being unable to do anything about it. In this sense, the story of Gyges' ring is also the story of the social contract, the imaginary agreement citizens sign where they exchange liberty for security.

Is Glaucon right? Certainly, Socrates doesn't think so, and uses the 'larger' case of the community to illustrate his belief that any individual who allows themselves to misbehave will suffer a heavy penalty in terms of loss of their own internal harmony and balance. Someone like Gyges, Socrates might predict, would become debauched by his excesses, and lose the spiritual benefits of the moral way he (presumably) used to follow, when he was but a simple shepherd.

In fact, we have all come across plenty of debauched people who don't seem to mind losing those benefits, so the response is rather unconvincing. But that is looking at it as advice to an individual. Since the Greeks considered the community to be more important than the individual, in any case, Plato's argument about maintaining a 'balance' and internal harmony is more persuasive. The city of Melbourne is a case in point. When Melbourne's 800 police went on strike in 1923, it didn't take long for the previously most placid and law-abiding citizens to turn into a dishevelled mob intent only on riot and looting. Everyone was very pleased, apparently, when the 6,000 troops from the national guard came in to restore 'visibility' and force them to be moral again.

Dilemma 16
The woeful tale of St Augustine

Augustine is actually rehearsing the same old issue as Plato did with the story of Gyges. Only Augustine takes the opposite view – it is possible for self-interest to tempt us to knowingly choose the wrong thing. Fortunately, it does not end there. The tale has a happy twist of positive logic to it.

> And it was made clear to me that all things are good even if they are corrupted. They could not be corrupted if they were supremely good; but unless they were good they could not be corrupted. If they were supremely good, they would be incorruptible; *if they were not good at all, there would be nothing in them to be corrupted.*

> Either, then, corruption does not harm – which cannot be – or, as is certain, all that is corrupted is thereby deprived of good. But if they are deprived of all good, they will cease to be. For if they are at all and cannot be at all corrupted, they will become better, because they will remain incorruptible. Now what can be more monstrous than to maintain that by losing all good

199

they have become better? If, then, they are deprived of all good, *they will cease to exist*. So long as they are, therefore, they are good. Therefore, whatsoever is, is good.

Evil, then, the origin of which I had been seeking, has no substance at all; for if it were a substance, it would be good.

Which is very reassuring, at least for the owners of pear trees.

Dilemma 17
A balanced tale for the Yellow Emperor

The Ancients understood that everything is interconnected and the health of a person is much more subtle than the mechanical model both doctors and philosophers since Descartes have largely followed. Qi Bo recommended practices such as *Dao-in*, an exercise involving stretches, massage and special breathing techniques to improve the flow of *Qi* in the body, and also to return it to harmony with the rest of the universe. He advised that people should eat moderately, at regular intervals, awake and retire at sensible times, avoid overindulgence in general and excessive stress on either their bodies or their minds in particular.

And the Yellow Emperor's approach has many echoes in the writings of Plato and Aristotle, who emphasised the need for moderation and balance and were of the view that if people were behaving badly, it was because they had become ill. Or more precisely 'unbalanced'. Of course, this point of view is very much the thing nowadays. We use this sort of language to speak of even those who are particularly evil as having 'sick minds'.

Yet just as modern medical science attempts to treat bodily disorders as (solely) physical problems with physical solutions, many 'psychological' problems, from exotic ones such as 'frotteurism' (the compulsion to rub oneself against others in a sexual manner while on public transport) or 'pogonophobia' (a disabling fear of beards) or more mundanely, 'ADHD' are blamed on, and perhaps to be treated with, chemicals.

Attention Deficit Hyperactivity Disorder is a rapidly spreading disease – apparently affecting one fifth of US children, and identified by their being inclined to be bad tempered, uncooperative and to attack other people. As one of the traits of ADHD is a refusal to accept responsibility for your behaviour, this approach (with its panhandling of blame onto 'everyone else') is not necessarily entirely helpful. Qi Bo offers not only the Yellow Emperor but also the likes of Gyges and Augustine another reason to choose the ethical life, the balanced life, and forego the 'unethical' one, but not yet a conclusive one.

Marshmallow bit

In the 1970s, which was a good time for such experiments, a psychologist called Walter Mischel conducted a classic experiment on children. He left a succession of four-year-olds in a room with a bell and a large, tempting looking, marshmallow (leaving aside the irrelevant but philosophical question of whether a marshmallow can ever really be considered tempting . . .).

He told them if they rang the bell, he would come back and they would then be allowed to eat the marshmallow.

The clever bit in the experiment was that he added, that if they waited, he would be back in a moment anyway and would then give them *two* of these delicious marshmallows.

You see, it was an experiment to see how the children coped in controlling their desires. Some indeed 'cracked' almost immediately, rang the bell and then ate the marshmallow. (Not too many ethical questions for the experimenter there.) Others, however, had considerable internal 'conflict' over the best policy, wriggling and covering their eyes against the dreadful temptation – even kicking and squirming! As Mr Mischel was clearly a dedicated sort, he let them struggle like this for up to fifteen minutes.

What is most interesting about this, is that the children who were best at controlling their wants, were also those who went on to do better at school, and in later life. The children who (on the face of it) lacked self-control, tended instead to have mediocre results and become bullies.

Dilemma 18
The ascetic tale of Chrysippus the Stoic

Actually, there are people who run Chrysippus down as having written a great deal that is very shameful and indecent. In his treatise on the *Ancient Natural Historians*, for instance, he relates the story of Jupiter and Juno *very* indecently, devoting 600 lines to 'what no one could repeat without polluting his mouth'.

And if we're talking disgraceful pleasure (and I suppose we must be), then we are also talking about SEX. Philosophers don't like sex. It is after all, highly irrational. Most of them are against it, at least, as it were, in principle. Plato even has Socrates ask his friend Glaucon, in his usual rhetorical manner, whether 'true love can have any contact with frenzy or excess of any kind'? The answer Glaucon gives obligingly, is, most certainly not, but Socrates, unusually, goes on to spell it out:

SOCRATES: True love can have no contact with this sexual pleasure, and lovers whose love is true must neither of them indulge in it.

GLAUCON: They certainly must not, Socrates.

SOCRATES: And so, I suppose you will lay down laws in the state we are founding [discussing] that will allow a lover to associate with his boy-friend and kiss him and touch him, if he permits it, as a father does his son, if his motives are good; but require that his association with anyone he's fond of must never give rise to the least suspicion of anything beyond this, otherwise he will be thought a man of no taste or education.

GLAUCON: That is how I should legislate.

(The Republic, Book III, 403)

However, the iconoclastic German philosopher, Arthur Schopenhauer (who really was called Arthur – it being a useful even cosmopolitan name for a career in European business, alas he went into philosophy) is surely right, the reproductive urge, be it simply the sexual one or be it the more respectable procreative one, is so strong, it is somehow fundamental and really philosophers are being a bit evasive if they continue to discuss the nature of human life without any reference at all to it. At least Plato did value a sort of filial love, the kind ever since called 'Platonic'. Unfortunately, the Christian church instead taught a rather extreme version of the 'no sex' doctrine for most of the millennia between Socrates and Schopenhauer, which culminated in the most bizarre and hypocritical attitudes towards sex. So, let's consult a doctor instead. As Dr Wilfred Barlow puts it in *The Alexander Principle* (1973):

Innumerable treatises have been written on moral philosophy, on free-will and choice. Innumerable theologies have presented views on the good life; about the heavens and abominations and the wrath to come. You would think that out of all this lot, somewhere someone would be able to give a young (or old) person really useful advice about whether or not, and when to indulge in sexual activity.

Particularly, Barlow notes clinically: *when on your own*. 'Dry textbooks of moral philosophy . . . would surely become best-sellers if they genuinely considered, say, this one sexual dilemma'. Yet 'most of the treatises on moral philosophy' do not offer any guidance to someone who 'feels guilt' about this 'fascinating stimulus and response situation'. One, moreover, Barlow adds wisely, in which 'freewill and determinism are on opposite sides of the pitch'.

Of course, Chrysippus and the Stoics are more generally remembered for preaching the virtues of doing without – whether of second helpings of pudding or by walking to work because the horse is worn out. These are all part of it, certainly, but the Stoic philosophy is actually more subtle. Indeed, comparisons are sometimes made between Stoic notions of the 'cosmic breath', the ripples of which are the material universe, and the latest thinking in sub-atomic physics.

The Stoics start with the concept the Greeks called *oikeiōsis* which is the 'natural' process by which mind takes control of matter. It follows from this, they say, that we have a special obligation not only to ourselves, not only to all other living creatures, but to all things. Chrysippus offers as a metaphor a man entering a running race. It is the duty of the runner to put in all his strength and strive with all his might to win; but still he must never try to trip up or, with his hand, foul a competitor. 'In the stadium of life', people may seek 'what is needful for their own advantage', but not go further and attempt to wrest it from their neighbours.

As for virtues like those Aristotle would later attach so much importance to, such as being 'balanced', honourable, magnificent and so on, these are only valuable in as much as they may assist someone to achieve harmony with the world as it is. Even the difference between 'virtue' and 'vice' is not very important. This is because both are intellectual states. Virtue is the result of the appliance of the science of the good, the activity of the wise. Vice is the result of allowing an excessive role of the passions, leading to errors of judgement.

What the later Stoics, such as Epictetus (c.AD 50–c.120) and Seneca, in Italy, stressed instead was the need to achieve 'freedom' from the passions, to reject pleasure and seek 'equanimity' in the face of (what superficially looks like) misfortune. Seneca even 'retells the uplifting story of Stilbo. After Stilbo's home town was captured and ransacked by invaders and he had emerged to find his children perished, his wife gone and all his possessions destroyed, Stilbo was asked by another philosopher, Demetrius, whether he had lost anything. "Why no," he replied. "I have all my valuables with me."'

Dilemma 19
The sensible tale of Epicurus

A little of what you fancy is good for you. But remember:

> It is common to find a man poor in determining the natural end of life but rich with empty fancies. For no fool is satisfied with what he has, but is distressed for what he has not. Just as men with a fever, through the malignancy of their disease, are always thirsty and desire the most injurious things, so too those whose mind is in an evil state are always poor in everything and in their greed are plunged into capricious desires.

. . . and you can avoid getting stuck in an unhappy state of seeking stimulation for pleasure. Epicurus (341–271) wrote 300 long scrolls on this suggesting a viable strategy namely: a simple life style, and scientific outlook. This last was important as it should ensure that not only are there no troubling fears of either God or death, but only the reassurance of the hugeness and imperturbability of the universe. In fact, the realisation that being dead is only the same as not having been born yet – which is obviously not a problem for anyone.

Dilemma 20
Magnanimous Man

The *Nicomachean Ethics*, that is.

Others may feel this kind of paean to pride to be reprehensible, indeed Christians say it is a sin, as our accomplishments are supposed to be the gift of God, *Soli Dei*

Gloria – the glory is God's alone. The Christian virtues, in fact, are very like the Socratic ones: justice, prudence, temperance, fortitude, faith, hope and charity – but Aristotle's Magnanimous Man has no need of the last three of these. Being so fine a fellow, he is unlikely to suffer from several of the sins either: envy, covetousness, gluttony and sloth, and so can share in the common approbation there. However, pride, anger, even lust, may be for him not only quite respectable but his main reasons for living (just like Nietzsche's later 'Superman').

Certainly Magnanimous Man has a rather different take on morality to today's liberal, sandal-wearing 'Christian' one. To start with, it has to be a man, because, unlike Socrates, Aristotle thought only the male of the species was truly 'rational', indeed, only a small proportion of them. Men reason, women bear children. And as rationality equals virtue, women lack 'virtue'. So what is now called 'virtue theory' in ethics courses, applied originally only to men, and even then, only rich political leaders. Nietzsche is famous for saying that most were born to be slaves, a few to be masters. But it was Aristotle who gave him the idea.

Dilemma 21
The Magnanimous Man in heaven

Aristotle is the hero of course. Indeed, as this is a story made up for the glorification of the 'Magnanimous Man', Kant gives in very easily to Aristotle, perhaps concerned that he did allow the 'spirited' part of his soul to temporarily overrule the reasoning part (with the usual disastrous results). But there is another view possible of the matter, that says on the contrary, good intentions are all that matters.

> Even if, by some especially unfortunate fate or by the niggardly provision of stepmotherly nature, this will should be wholly lacking in the power to accomplish its purpose, if with the greatest effort it should yet achieve nothing, and only the good will should remain (not to be sure, as a mere wish, but as the summoning of all the means in our power), yet would it, like a jewel, still shine by its own light, as something which has full value in itself. Its usefulness or fruitfulness augment nor diminish this value.

So Immanuel Kant wrote in the *Groundwork of the Metaphysics of Morals* in the eighteenth century. For him then, at least, the road paved with these 'good intentions' leads directly to philosophy heaven, and not to any other destination as others would have us think. Virtue, for Kant, Socrates and all the Christians too, is truly its own reward. But Aristotle came to a different conclusion. Magnanimous Man, sometimes called the 'great-souled' man, or the 'magnificent' man, is virtuous in the sense of being excellent in all he does:

> greatness in every virtue would seem to be characteristic of a proud man. And it would be most unbecoming for a proud man to fly from danger, swinging his arms by his sides, or to wrong another; for to what end should he do disgraceful acts, he to whom nothing is great?

It is to be expected that any virtuous man would have the strength to break the bough off a tree, and the skill to throw it into the river too. The Greek word 'virtue' (*arete*) is a quality related to being good at doing things, not just about the 'virtuous' intentions as we nowadays understand it (although there is still a shared emphasis on 'how to be' over 'what to do'). We still respect this cultural value in our celebration of the Olympic champions.

> Further, a slow step is thought proper to the proud man, a deep voice, and a level utterance; for the man who takes few things seriously is not likely to be hurried, nor the man who thinks nothing great to be excited, while a shrill voice and a rapid gait are the results of hurry and excitement.

Aristotle certainly thought that there was a 'golden mean' to be sought for in (nearly) all things. Actually, the oriental philosophers put it more radically, saying that *nothing* is all bad, and *nothing* is all good, but Aristotle allows that some things, justice, for example, are always good. (Conversely, 'the rule of choosing the mean' cannot be applied to some actions and feelings, which are 'essentially evil'.) Magnanimous Man is angry 'in the right way, at the right time', considers those who aim 'at being pleasant with no ulterior object' obsequious; the others irreconcilably 'churlish and contentious'. The next best thing to being magnanimous is to be 'mock-modest' and 'speak not for gain but to avoid parade, as Socrates used to do'.

Speaking of whom, Socrates also thought that not only are some things always good, but some things are always all good. At least one thing is quintessentially 'all good' and not at all bad (not bad at all!). And that is the 'Form of the Good', not only for Socrates, but for God and the many monotheist religions. However, most things are a bit of both. In this case, to be too fearful, as Rousseau is depicted here, is bad, as it prevents you doing anything, whilst to be completely fearless, like Kant here, is also bad, as it results in unnecessary error. The 'golden mean' is fear enough to prompt wise consideration of the options available, but not so much as to prevent you from then acting.

A true story

There is actually an historical illustration of the difference of being 'principled' but maybe foolhardy, and being 'just courageous enough'. It is between Socrates and Aristotle, who never knew each other, but were nonetheless connected by their shared contact with Plato, the pupil of the first, and the teacher of the second. The question was, what to do when the Athenian council accuse you of impiety and threaten to put you to death?

Socrates, as we know so well from Plato's dialogue, the *Phaedo*, which records the 'last days' in prison, chose to stay in the City and make a principled defence of his actions and beliefs. Aristotle, facing the same charges half a century later, chose to flee instead, or, as he put it magnanimously, chose to save Athens 'from sinning against philosophy twice'.

So Socrates chose the short, fearless path which led to his cup of hemlock, and Aristotle chose the prudent path which led to retirement abroad, as well as, incidentally, to his death scarcely any later, from a stomach illness. Almost certainly, however, by choosing to retreat to Asia Minor, Aristotle protected his library and his legacy. Although Socrates' influence was magnified by the manner of his death, and Aristotle's name and influence soon disappeared from Europe, the fact is that it was Aristotle's substantial body of work that was kept in high esteem, particularly by the Islamic cultures of the Middle East, who respectfully called him simply 'the Philosopher', and his work survived the long period of the 'Dark Ages' in Europe. Socrates' influence, by contrast, is mere shadows and reflections on the 'cave wall' of the writing of his friends, students and compatriots.

But in this story, Socrates is the hero.

The Goldilocks table (of Aristotelian virtues and vices)

Sphere of applicability	too much	too little	'just right'
fear	rash	cowardly	courageous
pleasure	licentious	'cold fish'	temperate
spending	prodigal	stingy	generous
honour	vain	pusillanimous	magnanimous
anger	irritable	lacking spirit	patient
expressiveness	boastful	humble	truthful
conversation	buffoonery	boorish	witty
social skills	flatterer	cantankerous	friendly
social conduct	shy	shameless	modest
view of others	envious	malicious	lofty and superior

Dilemma 22

Against e-Ville

The principle of utility judges any action to be right by the tendency it appears to have to augment or diminish the happiness of the party whose interests are in question . . . if that party be the community, the happiness of the community, if a particular individual, the happiness of that individual.

(Opening sentence of Introduction to *The Principles of Morals and Legislation*, by Jeremy Bentham)

It is in 'The Commonplace Book' that Jeremy Bentham (1748–1832) says firmly that: 'The greatest happiness of the greatest number' is the foundation of morality, a famous phrase which actually originated slightly earlier with Frances Hutcheson (1694–1746) who had said: 'That action is best, which procures the greatest happiness for the greatest numbers.'

This is the logic that drives most people and institutions – a utilitarian calculation of kinds in which you weigh up the alternatives and choose the least bad one. And on that basis, having lumped a good part of global poverty onto the balance at e-Ville's expense, the verdict is clear. But, even if we accept the methodology, in fact, there are more than two possible actions. There are any number of responses possible to e-Ville Corps' activities, and to start using 'violence' (or at least produce a good utilitarian case for it) it would have to be shown that this was in some sense 'necessary', that the other methods would not work. Indeed, it would have to be shown that the new methods *would* work. As to that, violence often does seem to be the fast route to social change, albeit not necessarily with the results expected or for the better.

Anarchism

Proudhon said: 'I destroy and I build up'; Bakunin asked us 'put our trust in the eternal spirit which destroys and annihilates' and advised that: 'Bloody revolutions are often necessary, thanks to human stupidity.' Yet even Bakunin thought them to be always an evil, 'a monstrous evil and a great disaster, not only with regard to the victims, but also for the sake of purity and perfection of the purpose in whose name they take place'.

Anarchism – like Buddhism – preaches the virtue of surviving on only just enough. The anarchist not only despises the wealthy – the anarchist despises wealth itself. It only became a mass movement amongst the very poorest peasants of Andalusia and the Ukraine; amongst even middling peasants it had little appeal.

Anarchists despise democracy as enslavement by the majority – voting is the act of betrayal, both symbolically and practically. 'Universal suffrage is the counter-revolution' declared Proudhon, in one of his less catchy rallying cries. ('Property is theft' was perhaps the most famous, adopted by Marxism, but 'God is evil' had its followers too.) William Godwin summed the philosophy up: 'There is but one power to which I can yield a heartfelt obedience, the decision of my own understanding, the dictate of my own conscience.'

Dilemma 23
Stumped

Of course, Lawrence is on the side of 'right', and against 'wrong'. But then so is Lina. They just don't agree on what that is, or the limits of protest. In one of the most famous acts of non-violent resistance in history – Gandhi's march to the sea and his ceremonial distilling of salt from the water – both the power and the limitations of civil disobedience are seen. The campaign was non-violent only on the protesters' part. In May 1930, a column of volunteers tried to march towards the salt heaps and the British toleration of protest came to an end. Three hundred and twenty Indians were injured after being beaten to the ground with steel-tipped bamboo sticks, and two died. Over subsequent protests the violence escalated.

See also Dilemma 88 for the roots of the salt tax.

Dilemma 24
Cracked?

Certainly, on one level, it is. On another level, maybe more is lost than gained. For STUMP are returning people to a 'state of war'. It is not so much 'might is right' as 'might takes the place of right'.

Thomas Hobbes, the seventeenth-century English philosopher who spoke of the central role of violence in society, coining the famous aphorism about the life of man being solitary, poor, nasty, brutish and short, is really the first philosopher to challenge the authority of those who speak of 'good and evil', saying that the terms are really inventions 'fluttered over' by philosophers, who neglect their social origins. Hobbes is if anything rather more radical than STUMP: he writes that human societies are made up solely of selfishness, violence and fear, topped off with a dollop of deceit. (The last there to make things work more smoothly.) Writing in the God-fearing times of the sixteenth century, he even had the temerity to describe this as the 'State of Nature' – a shocking phrase calculated to arouse the wrath of the Church, directly conflicting with the rosy Biblical image of Adam and Eve in the Garden of Eden before the Fall.

Hobbes was consciously attacking the idealism of the Ancient philosophers, with their talk of 'forms of the Good' and men as 'rational animals'.

> Their logic which should be their method or reasoning, is nothing else but the captions of words, and inventions how to puzzle such as should go about to pose them . . . there is nothing so absurd that the Old Philosophers . . . have not some of them maintained . . .

he scoffs. In its place, Hobbes offers a gritty materialism directly challenging Dr Descartes (Dilemmas 11–14). A man or woman is but 'an Artificial Animal', the 'heart but a spring, and the nerves but so many strings; and the joints but so many wheels'. And this automaton is primarily motivated by appetites and aversions.

> These small beginnings of motion with the body of Man, before they appear in walking, speaking, striking and other visible actions are commonly called endeavour. This endeavour, when it is towards something, is called appetite or desire; the latter being the general name, and the other often times restrained to signify the desire for food, namely hunger and thirst. And when the endeavour is fromward something, it is generally called aversion.

Of all these 'appetites' the primary inclination, 'the primary motion', is towards *power*: 'I put for a general inclination of all mankind, a perpetual and restless desire of Power after power, that ceaseth only in death.' Since all the motivations are selfish, they inevitably result in conflict, or causes of quarrel, as Hobbes puts it. There are three main ones: *competition*, for gain; *diffidence*, for safety; and finally the *compulsion for glory*, respect and reputation. But they all lead to the same thing: *violence*:

> the first use violence to make themselves masters of other men's person, wives, children, and cattle; the second, to defend them; the third, for trifles, as a word, a smile, a different opinion, and any other sign of undervalue either direct in their Persons, or by reflection in the kindred, their friends, their nation, their profession, or their name.

It is true, Hobbes agrees, that

> certain living creatures, [such] as Bees and Ants, live sociably one with another . . . and some may perhaps desire to know why people cannot do the same. The reason is that people like to compare themselves each with the other, unlike the creatures beneath them.

Given that people are all so nasty, not to mention so competitive, the only rule, Hobbes says, is that of self-preservation. And it is this that is the foundation for moral systems. In the war of everyone against every other person, which is the natural state, 'this also is consequent: that nothing can be unjust. The notions of right and wrong, justice and injustice have there no place. Where there is no common power, there is no law: where no law, no injustice.'

211

So, perhaps by stepping outside the rule of law, and attempting to dismantle the power of the Leviathan, STUMP destroy the framework that enables them to even talk of justice and injustice.

Dilemma 25
Getting hotter

Even having convinced themselves of the need for some sort of new level of protest, STUMP would probably still want to retain a distinction, as do most radical groups in contemporary political society, between 'combatants' and 'non-combatants', that is between those with a direct 'guilt' and those with only incidental 'guilt by association' or through passivity. So, when Animal Rights letter bombs are sent out, they will be addressed to people perceived to have particular guilt, such as those who work in laboratories that use animal testing – rather than, say, the nurses who prescribe the drugs in the medical practice up the road. There will be some illogicalities to the calculations: the cars of biology teachers who use rats for vivisection would make a rather unconvincing 'target', as would tractors of farm workers – although butchers and hauliers using refrigerated lorries for the meat have been found suitable focal points for protest.

For Western ethicists at any rate, the distinction between deliberate casualties of military campaigns and 'incidental' ones matters; they've even given it a special name: the Doctrine of Double Effect. This states that it is permissible to do anything you like as long as no one can stop you. No, wait! That's the Doctrine of Everyday Life (as one wag put it on the internet recently). The Doctrine of Double Effect is more scientific and more sinister. It states simply that you cannot be held responsible for the foreseeable but 'unintended' consequences of your actions. Now a bomber who blows up restaurant diners has specifically and deliberately targeted the kind of 'non-combatants' that we usually consider to be innocent. On the other hand, the (far greater) toll of equally indisputably 'innocent' land mine and cluster bomb victims as a result of Western military intervention is said to be 'unintended' and therefore not only less bad, but not bad at all. The bomblets are still made, and scattered. Even the money to clear them up afterwards is not considered a moral imperative. Such thoughts will give our STUMP activists succour in their dingy basements: 'Kill a man, and you are an assassin. Kill millions of men, and you are a conqueror', as Jean Rostand (1894–1977) once said.

Some more utilitarian killings

- Throughout the 1980s, the USA funded and trained death squads to kill civilians in South American states whom that they said were becoming 'communist' – a propensity that put them into the category of legitimate target straight away. The USA became the first and only country to be condemned by the World Court for sponsoring terrorism in this way, a ruling which has simply reinforced their perception that only *they* know what terrorism is anyway.

- In recent years the Israeli defence forces have killed men, women and children whose legitimacy as targets rests solely on proximity to earlier 'security incidents'. So, for example, if shooting at one of the fortified 'settlements' near a village takes place, the helicopter gunships or bulldozers will be along in an hour or two to destroy homes in that village. Palestinian police stations have been 'taken out' using a similar elastic version of 'an eye for an eye'. In August 2002 a one-tonne bomb was dropped on a Gaza Strip block of flats to 'assassinate' a terrorist. Of the sixteen other casualties, nine were children in neighbouring houses.

- Following the Gulf War, in the 1990s, sanctions against the defeated Iraq were believed to have been the cause of many thousands of civilian deaths, mainly through illness and malnutrition. In the follow up war, in 2002, intended to remove Saddam Hussein, at least 50,000 more civilians died. The British and US governments insisted the ends justified the means.

Dilemma 26
Feeling drained

How much calculation must go into deciding your actions anyway? What is the 'duty to think'?

Is the assistant responsible – she 'did it' – or no one? (No one *meant* to do it.) If you can't get your head around such a big mistake, then the great and the good J. D. Mabbott offers a few rather more homely examples of this sort of thing. What if Mabbott accepts an invitation to give a paper in Edinburgh this week, but then cannot teach in Oxford because he has forgotten term would have started? Or if a doctor has too much sherry at a party, and when another guest rushes in to announce that he has just passed the scene of a car accident a few miles away and an injured driver needs help – the doctor is unfit to drive to the scene?

Then again, what if the good doctor goes anyway, despite being inebriated and drunkenly overtakes on a bend – not even seeing Mrs Mabbott on her bicycle! Even if there is no crash: was their action really 'right', just because everything turned out that way? (Which is that important thing, 'moral luck'.) Or because the 'mercy mission' was virtuous? (The 'motive' was just?)

Mabbott and the party-going doctor may be being irresponsible (like any drunk driver) but they are not consciously aware of doing anything wrong. A contrast with Lina who is knowingly doing something (taken in isolation) that is wrong, albeit with a calculation of net benefits enabling her to justify it as being 'the right thing' in the long run, if all goes according to plan. An 'ends justify the means' type of argument.

If Lina's plan had worked, some support for her might come in fact from Mabbott's sometime colleague, G. E. Moore, as Moore it is who says that intentions are irrelevant anyway, since only actual results matter. As unfortunately, the plan goes wrong, Lina might need to adopt the position advocated earlier in the twentieth century by H. A. Pritchard, that intentions *are* the decisive factor. Mind you, she doesn't have too long to worry anyway.

Dilemma 27
Breeding experiments

Plato's ideal society is sometimes accused of being rather totalitarian in nature. This is rather unfair. It is *completely* totalitarian. Plato in fact, makes a virtue of the rigidity of the controls (as long as they are being implemented by the enlightened and unselfish philosophers). And breeding is no exception. After all, as Socrates advises his friend Glaucon, 'it would be a sin for mating or anything else in a truly happy society to take place without regulation'.

Other 'medical' controls are:

- weak or sickly babies should be killed;
- people who allow themselves to be captured should be 'the lawful prey' of their captors, who can do what they like to them (typically, they were made slaves);

- the chronically ill, or just old, should not be given medical treatment;
- children should be brought up collectively, ignorant of their natural parents, and family structures abolished;
- private property should be discouraged (presumably other than slaves);

whilst more generally, to protect the psychological health not only the young and impressionable but of people generally, only 'wholesome' music and plays will be allowed. Then there is Plato's suggestion that children should be brought up to believe that people are, by nature, made up of three different types of material (metaphorical of course): 'gold', 'silver' and 'iron'. Of course, once identified, and trained accordingly, only those with 'gold' in their souls would be allowed to rule.

Yet, in fact, Plato is quite progressive in other ways. He advocates total equality for men and women, he insists on equality of opportunity (as, occasionally, 'gold' children may be born even to 'iron' parents) and the detailed plans for schooling start from the progressive assumption that education must be fun, as 'forced learning never sticks in the mind'.

But of all the dodgy aspects of Plato's *Republic* (which was intended as a serious blueprint for a real society), the programme of eugenics, outlined in the 'breeding experiment', must be one of the worst. In fact, the only thing to be said for including the argument is that the notions expressed are becoming increasingly popular, and so need to be considered philosophically again. Today, the idea that genetic testing of embryos can allow the termination of certain potential people is widely accepted as just the set of 'common sense' that Plato is alluding to here – and the development of 'test tube babies' suggests a future where parents choose the characteristics of their children.

Eugenics is the science pioneered by the Nazis, and parodied by Aldous Huxley in his 'Brave New World' of 'Alphas, Betas and Gammas'. There are many objectionable aspects to it. One is that we conventionally value all human life equally, not on some supposed sliding scale of physical and mental perfection. Another is, why should anyone accept simplistic measures of human worth anyway? People are surely not to be measured by the same yardsticks as captive animals bred for eating or specific human purposes. (And that is another story too.)

One target of the Nazis were 'mental defectives', but sterilisation programmes for them were already in place elsewhere. In 1931, just prior to the rise of Hitler in

Europe, there were formal programmes in no fewer than twenty-seven US states. Again, the Nazis devoted a large part of their efforts into the systematisation of race, with the aim of increasing the 'purity' of the Aryan blood, and reducing 'dilution' by Jews and Slavs. That strategy was not unique to them, either. The purity of white races has long been considered to be threatened by such mixing of the genes. The arguments advanced are no different from Plato's. Benjamin Franklin, otherwise hailed as one of the Fathers of the American Revolution, wrote in 1751:

> The number of purely white people in the world is proportionately very small. All Africa is black or tawny. Asia chiefly tawny. America (exclusive of the newcomers) wholly so. And in Europe, the Spaniards, Italians, French, Russians and Swedes are generally of what we would call a swarthy complexion, as are the Germans also, the Saxons only excepted, who with the English make the principal Body of White People on the face of the Earth. *I could wish their numbers were increased.*

In fact, Franklin's opposition to slavery was motivated primarily by concern about the dilution of the white race. Similarly, Thomas Jefferson, writing in 1804 of the continued importation of slaves, warned that 'this blot in our country increases as fast, or faster, than the whites'. To today, there continues to be great concern in government circles over relative birth rates and national demographics, with regular 'horror scenarios' of minorities becoming the majority!

Actually, it was not until the early years of the twentieth century that Native Americans began to be recognised officially to be full citizens. 'Silent Cal' (Calvin Coolidge), famous for telling a lady at a presidential dinner (who had wagered him that he would say at least three words to her that evening) only 'you lose'; did at least write more lucidly of his efforts to combat race prejudice. In his inaugural speech he declared that, 'the fundamental precept of liberty is toleration' (which is seven words) as well as later:

> Divine Providence has not bestowed upon any race a monopoly of patriotism and character. Whether one traces one's Americanism back three centuries to the *Mayflower* or three years to the steerage, we are all now in the same boat. Let us cast off our hatreds.

Even so, as recently as 1977, a Native American physician, Dr Constancy Redbird Uri, claimed to have found that the US government was operating a *de facto* sterilisation programme on the minority races. Out of interviews with a sizeable sample of 1,000 Native American women, who had been sterilised by the 'Indian Health Service', she found just one had freely decided to forego further children.

Finally, attempts in both East and West to rationalise the spate of 'ethnic cleansing' in the Balkans through the 1990s by suggesting the 'solution' was to identify and then split up the different ethnic groups, shows that issues of racial 'purity' continue to be dangerous ones.

Crick and Watson, the scientists associated with the discovery of the double helix structure of DNA, only knew the half of it when they wrote: 'We used to think that our fate was in our stars. Now we know that in large measure, our fate is in our genes.' (But since Crick and Watson really 'stole' their discovery from Rosalind Franklin (academically speaking), they are hardly reliable on these matters.)

Dilemma 28
Designer babies

Designer babies have been around for some time. All attempts to 'select' partners are a kind of natural influence on the genetic make-up of future babies, after all. Nowadays, parents may select characteristics at *KwikBaby*-like clinics when choosing an IVF donor. Advertisements for 'eggs' of brainy young women offer good money and so these are the first designer babies. 'Ordinary' couples (those able to have a baby without medical assistance) may request information, for example on the gender of their baby. Another issue has been whether to allow parents to design their next child to be a tissue donor for another one. It sounds worthy, but it immediately subverts the principle of treating each child *as an end in itself*.

Today, prenatal testing is carried out for an ever wider range of 'defects', and abortion may be compulsory. More recent attempts to 'scan' babies (and embryos and foetuses) for birth defects are, however, the beginning of a kind of eugenics anticipated quite confidently by Plato and so many other philosophers. With regard to that, Pope John Paul II pontificated that screening for a 'malformation or a hereditary illness must not be the equivalent of a death sentence'.

In this one respect, the philosophers tend to assume certain points are 'obviously' bad, and others 'obviously good'. So, for example, being short-sighted, lethargic and none too bright either, is taken as 'obviously' worse than being eagle-eyed, fleet of foot and quick-witted. (And they should know!) But does this justify preventing the less fortunate kind of people from existing, in order to produce more of the 'approved' ones?

A typical debate in medical ethics today is whether to eliminate babies with Down's Syndrome or *spina bifida*. Down's Syndrome children used to be believed to have little chance of survival into their thirties, but recent research has found that those babies allowed to come into the world with it actually survive much longer – until into their fifties. Screening for the latter disease reduced the incidence in the UK by nearly 95 per cent – mainly through abortion. More recently there have been proposals that *cystic fibrosis* should be 'screened out' of the population. This is a lung disease which slowly develops over about half the normal human lifespan, eventually causing the sufferer problems digesting food, and involving a great deal of unpleasant medical activity in the intervening years too. One in twenty-four people carry the gene for *cystic fibrosis*, and if both parents are carriers, the risk of the child being a sufferer is calculated at one in four. The UK charity representing people with the disease supports systematically destroying embryos which may carry the disease. It is thus in the strange position of supporting the elimination of the people it otherwise represents.

Dilemma 29
KwikBaby

Ectogenesis, literally 'birth outside the body', was the process mooted as early as 1923, by J. B. S. Haldane, the evolutionary biologist, who hailed it as the next great leap forward. Unfortunately, as a technique it has always suffered a bad press. For one thing, it has always seemed to be a little too useful to any would-be founder of a totalitarian state. In 1923 Aldous Huxley opened *Brave New World* with the words:

> A squat grey building of only thirty-four storeys. Over the main entrance the words:

> *Central London Hatchery and Conditioning Centre*

'In the Bottling Room', Huxley continues, 'all was harmonious bustle and ordered activity . . . one by one the eggs were transferred from their test tubes to the larger containers . . . heredity, date of fertilisation . . . details were transferred from test tube to bottle'.

Bertrand Russell said of Huxley's nightmare vision that it was all too likely to come true. And indeed now it seems that it has. Contemporary biologist David Bainbridge has even claimed that the gap between the length of time already possible to sustain human life in a test tube, and that of viability for the very premature babies will, within just a very few years, shrink to nothing, making entirely artificial 'baby hatching' a reality.

But, at this moment, despite the scientists keeping busy conducting distasteful experiments on animals (for example into how to create artificial placentas), the technique remains some way off. So the boundary between what is acceptable in terms of 'unnatural' childbirth and natural childbirth is still there, even as it becomes increasingly fuzzy. After all, most of the (now fairly numerous) people receiving 'fertility treatment' are very ordinary people merely trying to have children and would much prefer the 'normal' way. There seems no reason to prevent them from receiving assistance, however 'unnatural' that medical intervention may sometimes seem.

On the other hand, already 'nightmare' scenarios can be summoned to alarm sensitive souls, even in these early days of the new 'reproductive technologies', as it is loftily put. If you can have babies for couples – why not babies for singles? Babies for homosexuals, for sociophobes, for the deceased? (All of which are old dilemmas now . . .) What about clones of great artists or scientists or millionaires . . . or just anyone really?

But perhaps the peculiarly alarming prospect is the old Huxley one. As human beings play a smaller role in bringing new humans into the world, perhaps we are hastening a day when having children will be something done by the state, to its own specification, not by individuals, in the present inefficient, erratic and disorganised way. And although Plato might trust the rulers of such a land to ensure that this is done with an eye to the 'Good', history points to another grimmer, conclusion.

Dilemma 30
The downmarket rival

Funnily enough, although very large amounts of public money have gone into developing laboratory methods of combining male and female gametes, very little public funding is available for more conventional methods, so to speak (like that outlined). But why should the IVF clinics get state approval? The presumption has been that there is, as it is put in the UN Declaration, *a right to have a family*, and that right applies equally to people who either cannot or do not want to start the family the conventional way. Reasons why someone may not be able to can range across lifelong genetic and biological inability, to temporary inability, perhaps from advancing age, perhaps from poor health. People who may be able to start a family (or indeed continue one) but prefer artificial methods include those in homosexual relationships (men or women), people concerned to ensure certain features of the offspring, notably their gender, but sometimes also their physical appearance and intellectual attributes (none of which are necessarily obtainable this way, of course), and those who prefer to delay childbirth. For these people, as one wag put it, the 1960s interest in how to have sex without having babies is reversed into the problem of how to have babies without having sex.

Surprisingly large numbers of babies are now being born, in 'developed' countries, through artificial methods rather than through natural ones. And the services on offer keep expanding. *DIYBabies*' service is probably both cheaper and safer than the present IVF clinics can offer, say for individual women wanting to have babies 'on their own', or as lesbian couples. And, of course, the service would also satisfy a male / female couple seeking assistance at a clinic where the problem is identified with the male 'supplier' of gametes. If Sharon, like many clients of IVF clinics seeking to have a baby with a genetic inheritance drawn from both herself and her life partner, the test tube may still have the advantage.

Dilemma 31
TGN1412

The volunteers were reassured to know that the drug company had been licensed by the European and UK regulators and of course that it had already been tested in much more potent doses, on the usual animal victims, including man's nearest cousins (monkeys) all without causing the catastrophic immune reaction that it would cause them.

But then the human guinea pigs might have been less reassured if they had been told that testing a drug on one species tells you very little about its effects on another species. Indeed, animal testing, whatever its 'psychological value', seems to have a practical role in pharmaceuticals mainly as a kind of 'cash hurdle' enabling large companies to control the lucrative market in drugs.

In this case, 'TGN1412' was designed to affect the immune system, and indeed it did, causing their livers, kidneys and lungs to fail. The six volunteers suffered excruciating internal pains, and vomiting, passed out and had to be rushed to intensive care, to have their blood 'scrubbed'. Some of them were put on ventilators (one of them was still being treated at the time of writing, three months after the events) and if all survived, it was only with unknown long-term after-effects.

Afterwards, there were complaints from the volunteers (or their relatives) that they had not been made aware of the possible risks (especially not to their immune systems), and that they had been injected in a predetermined sequence which meant that the last of them was being given the drug even though the first had already collapsed unconscious!

Curiously, Dr Emanuel, however, went on to tell reporters that although it was clearly a 'terrible tragic event', he himself 'did not see any clear ethical problems'.

Dilemma 32
The Nobodie Rules

One of the 'unplanned consequences' of the new test tube babies, or In Vitro Fertilisation (IVF) techniques, is that it is now possible to scan babies long before they are born, and certainly before they are 'implanted' in their future mother's womb, for diseases, for gender – or for tissue compatibility as a future organ donor. And so issues like this are being very much debated in countries across the world, usually at the level of government committees, made up of not only doctors and philosophers, but representatives of various churches. Such committees then decide what is 'right' as opposed to being 'popular'.

And much of what used to be controversial in IVF is nowadays so everyday that it has become uncontroversial, beyond debate. Instead one of the 'boundary' issues of medical ethics at the moment is the question of 'tissue-typing', where parents with a child needing tissue donation for survival, request testing and selection of embryos in order to ensure that their next child will be one that can be used as a tissue donor. Instead of just having a child, and hoping it will have the right genetic

221

detail for saving its sibling, the scientists scan half-a-dozen 'potential' children, at embryo stage, and select the one that really will be right. It sounds innocuous – compelling even. If the plight of childless couples is not enough to justify the risks and side effects of IVF, surely the plight of a couple with a sick child is?

This is still a controversial issue, and it is recognised that for such a second child to be produced effectively as a source of 'spare parts' for another existing child is a little disquieting . . . that the procedures required of them in later life may include bone marrow transplants, that they may be deeply invasive, even dangerous...

But up against any waves of protest stands the rock of utilitarian logic: that the sum of the total well-being is increased when the procedures are allowed. After all, if the choice for a child is between not existing and existing with some 'marginal' negatives (such as not knowing their natural parents, or being under a lifelong obligation to provide donations to siblings) – surely only the most *irrational* person would claim to prefer the first option?

Discussions

On committees such as the UK's HFEA, the grandly named Human Fertilisation and Embryo Authority, utilitarian arguments take priority. After a philosopher has set out the 'principles', after a chance to hear the church representative's concerns, the hard-headed calculation is made and invariably found to sanction the latest advance in medical technology. But then the members of committees can be chosen precisely to ensure that a certain view prevails. For biotechnology is a large and increasingly profitable global business, and politicians, accustomed to maximising their vote, are inclined to allow the 'happiness of the greatest number' to be the ultimate arbiter between 'right' and 'wrong'.

Yet is it? Although medical ethics has been largely left to those who think the end justifies the means, there are of course still remnants clinging to 'ethical absolutes'. That is why experiments on embryos are justified, but only after a certain date, and in certain conditions. That indeed is why abortion is allowed in the UK but ostensibly not 'on demand' but rather for health reasons. The public policy is neither consistent nor intuitive – merely a pragmatic compromise between two irreconcilable views of when life starts, and whether it is anything untouchably special anyway.

In our story, the Nobodies' case doesn't sound so very strong, let alone ethical. Yet the argument all runs the same way. The second child gets some years of 'happy' existence which 'must' be better on the utilitarian calculus than zero years of no existence.

As one of the most influential figures in forming UK policy, Professor John Harris, puts it: 'unless the child's condition and circumstances can be predicted to be so bad that it would not have a worthwhile life, a life worth living, then it will always be in that child's interests to be brought into being'.

In our story, if the parents manage to save their first child, that child will go on to a full and happy life, whereas otherwise they won't. Naturally, both this child and the parents will feel great sorrow that the second child had to be 'sacrificed' in this way, but if they are convinced utilitarians, they should end up (overall) considerably happier.

Perhaps the fate of humans is only to choose between unattractive choices, but in that case each decision will need to be taken again and again on its own merits, by the people directly affected, and never as it were 'automated' by official edict – especially not the rules of the Nobodies!

Dilemma 33
Witheringspoon-X disease

Surprisingly perhaps, Dr Purplepatch is asking Mrs Blank to undertake an operation she might really not need. In fact, the odds are better than they seem. When a disease is very rare, like this, a test that is only 95 per cent accurate will still throw up a lot of erroneous results: 4,999 for every correct one.

So Mrs Blank may well do better to take her chances . . .

Dilemma 34
The hospital's dilemma

Medical ethics starts with the obligations of doctors and physicians towards their patients, and doubtless its founding father is Hippocrates, who emphasised above all the interests of the patient. Nowadays, this encompasses not only apparently new (but actually very ancient) issues raised by medical technologies such as

'When is the beginning of life?', and 'When is the end?' but also 'doctor–patient' issues such as truth telling, confidentiality and decisions on whether or not to treat. These days, medical ethics also contains a great deal of economics, and social science – with tricky decisions about resource allocation and the structure and nature of society needing to be taken (which is where Plato was, of course, all those years ago, with his authoritarian slant).

Mind you, the Browns do not even know whether heads is 'keep the life support on' – or 'turn it off'. But then people are often invited to take part in medical decisions without actually knowing the details. Perhaps Plato was right to keep these decisions to the philosopher 'experts' (they must be right about *something*)! Hospitals talk of 'informed consent', but being professionals, they have their own criteria and may, in fact, have arrived at a view already, often based on factors which they hesitate to discuss with the relatives, perhaps for the best humanitarian motives. Or, there may be a number of experts, all of whom have a clear view, and whose clear views conflict too. In which case at least relatives and patients get a chance to 'pick' the expert they prefer.

Certainly hospitals – and their staff – do routinely face difficult decisions, such as when to accept the end of life, that for the rest of us are very personal and difficult, but rare. As a result, they have adopted systems for helping to evaluate the merits of cases, such as the utilitarian measure of QALYs or 'Quality Adjusted Life Years'. The adjustment is, for example, that if you will make only a partial recovery, then your remaining years are 'not so valuable'. As babies have a lot of 'life years' ahead of them, usually considered to be 'quality' ones too, the budgets tend to favour younger patients over older ones, not so much in terms of emergency treatment but in terms of things like transplants and replacements.

Yet where health care is provided by the state, decisions are needed to ration it. Where medicine is privately funded, as it is, not only in countries like the USA, but also in 'socialist' countries like China, rationing is more transparent – you can have as much treatment as your money will allow. (If the Browns were paying the hospital, they might be encouraged to keep the life-support machines going.)

The one thing that all hospital staff can agree on is that patients and their families should be treated as 'ends' in themselves too – their views and feelings are also important. One aspect of this commitment is to provide full and considered accounts of any decision that needs to be taken. Too often this ideal is not achieved, but I doubt if many hospital practitioners would instead offer this particular decision making strategy.

Dilemma 35
Foul things

'This is a very bad lad, sir,' remarked the governor sternly; 'he only came in yesterday, and to-day, while out for exercise with the others, he must misconduct himself, and when the warder reproved him, he must swear some horrible oath against him. It is for that he his here. How many times have you been here, lad?'

Lad (gulping desperately). 'Three times, sir!'

Governor (sternly). 'What! speak the truth, lad.'

Lad (with a determined effort to gouge tears out of his eyes with his knuckles). 'Four times, sir.'

Governor. 'Four times! and so you'll go on 'til you are sent away, I'm afraid. Can you read, lad?'

Lad (with a penitential wriggle). 'Yes, sir; I wish as I couldn't, sir.'

Governor. 'Ah! why so?'

Lad (with a doleful wag of his bullet-head). ' 'Cos then I shouldn't have read none of them highwaymen's books, sir; it was them as was the beginning of it.'

(James Greenwood describing 'The Thief Non-Professional' in *Seven Curses of London* (1869) Boston: Fields, Osgood)

The new 'low-brow' pulp publications of the 1830s to 1850s were generally referred to as the 'bloods', for reasons that will become obvious, as opposed to the 'dreadfuls' which followed soon after, 'with a touch less gore and more adventure'. The passage in our dilemma, dreadful as it may be, is actually borrowing from a particularly successful series of illustrated 'story-papers' relating the disgraceful exploits of 'The Wild Boys', printed in the 1860s and again in the 1870s, until, that is, His Majesty's Constabulary put a stop to it (tantalisingly for some, no doubt halfway through the story).

Should they have acted earlier? These 'Penny Dreadfuls', with their stories of sex and violence, panicked the Victorians. They seemed to think (like Plato) that violent plays encouraged violent thoughts, and that it was their duty to prevent the pollution of the young from stories of sewer-dwelling boys battling the bluebottles, salvaging corpses – 'and stuff'. (Aristotle, on the other hand, clinical as ever, thought differently: such tales cleansed the watcher.)

> When it is remembered that this foul and filthy trash circulates by the thousands and tens of thousands week by week amongst lads who are at the most impressionable period of their lives, it is not surprising that the authorities have to lament the prevalence of juvenile crime

warned one commentator in 1890. After all, even the almost respectable story of Werther's unrequited love for the lovely Lotte in the story of the *Sorrows of Werther*, written by the great Goethe (1780–1833), ending in the tragic suicide of the hero, had led to a whole spate of 'copycat' suicides.

So it was that such as Greenwood had dedicated themselves to the task of eradicating 'the plague of poison literature':

> There is a plague that is striking its roots deeper and deeper into English soil chiefly metropolitan week by week, and flourishing broader and higher, and yielding great crops of fruit that quickly fall, rotten-ripe, strewing highway and by-way, tempting the ignorant and unwary, and breeding death and misery unspeakable.

Popular titles (perhaps reflecting the paucity of ideas) included *Sweeny Todd, the Demon Barber of Fleet Street*; *Spring-Heeled Jack, the Terror of London* and *Three-Fingered Jack, the Terror of the Antilles*. Not to mention the *Hounslow Heath Moonlight Riders*, or the *King of the Boy Buccaneers, Admiral Tom*. 'Nasty-feeling, nasty-looking packets are every one of them, and, considering the virulent nature of their contents, their most admirable feature is their extremely limited size', wrote Greenwood in 1874.

Nonetheless, both H. G. Wells and Noel Coward were avid consumers of such savoury titbits, praising the genre highly. They willingly wandered amongst the lonely tarns and stagnant weed-covered pools, slept in whispering hollows in secluded woods, saw the moon shine on the swiftly flowing waters even gasping as they glimpsed heading serenely downstream the white hand of a corpse . . . Never to forget the waiting condemned cell and the creaking gibbet on the lonely common.

But in fact, however horrible some passages, like our one, aspired to be, they were, like the horror genre itself, often only the high points of an otherwise rather pedestrian tale, one dictated by the need to keep the reader wanting (and paying for) more. A successful theme (unlike a philosophical dilemma) could stretch on for several hundred issues. 'At times, in search of novelty', one wit observed, 'the scene would shift to a mutinous convict ship, or to the Australian bush, but sooner or later . . . would return, nostalgically, to the sewers of London'.

We might think it all very tame stuff today, what with contemporary technologies immeasurably increasing the scope for the voyeuristic to sample 'horror', or to witness 'nightmares of depravity' as one presidential candidate put it as recently as 1995. Today's censors would not look twice at the highwaymen stories.

Indeed, today, many of the concerns relate not to what is depicted but what may be involved in the production of the sex, violence or horror images. In so-called 'snuff movies', unpleasant things (such as being killed) happen to people or animals, and the fact that the making of the images involves criminality adds to the appeal. That there is a market out there which appears to prefer unpleasant events to be 'real' than just the result of technical sophistication is a fact which television networks know only too well, falling on amateur video footage of street crimes, suicides and murders like drunkards offered free Scotch.

Dilemma 36
The criminal connection

In an editorial for a new 'safe' boys' magazine, the *Halfpenny Marvel*, founded the year after the dreadful crime described, Alfred Harmsworth, later Lord Northcliffe, opined:

> It is almost a daily occurrence with magistrates to have before them boys who, having read a number of 'dreadfuls', followed the examples set forth in such publications, robbed their employers, bought revolvers with the proceeds, and finished by running away from home, and installing themselves in the back streets as 'highwaymen'. This and many other evils the 'Penny Dreadful' is responsible for. It makes thieves of the coming generation, and so helps fill our gaols.

Steel yourself, so to speak, dear reader, for another sample, this time from the *Hounslow Heath Moonlight Riders*. (And we were warned not to mention them!)

The picture: A poor wretch undergoing some frightful torture. He is extended on the ground, a wagon wheel is lying atop of him, and by his side are various instruments of torment, consisting in a knife, two flaming torches, a glue-pot, and a spokeshave. Gloating over his agony stand two ruffians with (yes) highwaymen's masks on.

> Toby Marks dangled now a dead weight by his legs; the two robbers saw the thick and deep-coloured blood roll sluggishly from his nostrils. Then it burst in a torrent from his ears and mouth, and soon his face presented a horrible spectacle to look upon. The blood had completely saturated his hair, until he looked as though he had been newly scalped. The torture was over. The traitorous wretch could bear no more in safety, and so they cut him down. And thus did they avenge the sad end of the gallant Tom King!

Hence the other name for the genre: 'The Bloods'.

In the 1930s an American-inspired series of films apparently glorifying gangsters caused a very similar moral panic to that of the 'Moonlight Riders'. One typical US story, 'The James Boys as Guerillas' described the (at least partially) true story of how the Boys took on the Feds. And it was published in the context of an ongoing hunt for the Boys. Then too, there were the tales of 'Bonny and Clyde', and even 'Robin Hood' continuing to set a bad example.

A new ethics code drafted by Will Hays, which resulted in additional scenes being added to the films depicting concerned citizen groups or the chief gangster dying in grisly fashion at the end, helped to raise the moral tone. But for many Americans, just portraying gangsters as the main characters was too much. Numerous surveys were conducted to find the link between unsavoury images and delinquency, and came up with testimonies like that of a ten-year-old who confessed: '*The Big House* made me feel like I was a big tough guy. I felt just like Machine Gun Butch', or the eleven-year-old who said 'When I saw Jack Oakie in *The Gang Busters* I felt like a big gangster'. Happily, by the middle of the decade, Hollywood, propelled by the likes of the 'Legion of Decency', thought to reinvent the genre with a law officer carrying out all the exciting car chases and shootings that previously had been the responsibility of the gangsters, thereby making the violence completely ethical.

Dilemma 37
A matter of standards

This sort of interview was similar to that carried out in the famous *Lady Chatterley's Lover* trial of 1959 – in no small part because the lawyer for that was one who had come over from the USA with a series of successful 'gangster' (book) trials under his belt. Attorney Mervyn Griffith-Jones, prosecuting at the Central Criminal Court of the Old Bailey, in 1960, offered the jury this unfortunate advice:

> You may think that one of the ways in which you can test this book and test it from the most liberal outlook, is to ask yourselves the question when you have it through: 'Would you approve of your young sons and daughters – because girls can read as well as boys – reading this book?' Is it a book you would have lying around in your own house? Is it a book you would even wish your wife or your servants to read?'

That was a low point in the campaign against filth, as the case was lost and D. H. Lawrence went on to become the standard-bearer of artistic freedom. In fact, public opinion simply refused to accept that it *was* filth, and half a century on, it is a respected part of the literary landscape. At least, in 1993, an independent bill in the House of Commons did manage to 'fight back' against a new tide of so-called 'video nasties', such as *Driller Killer*, *I Spit on your Grave*, and so on. The minister responsible (David Mellor) supported the bill in the strongest terms, saying: 'No one has the right to be upset at a brutal sex crime or a sadistic attack on a child or mindless thuggery on a pensioner if he is not prepared to drive sadistic videos out of our high streets'.

This marked at last nothing less than 'a return to responsible censorship' by popular demand, cheered that trusty guardian of UK morals, the *Daily Mail*.

Six of the worst: the 1970s and the rise and rise of the video nasties

Ilse: She-Wolf of the SS (1974)
So ashamed was David 'Blood Feast' Friedman, the producer of this nasty, that he took his name off the final film, and left it to sell on the strength only of the stream of castrations, torture, executions and intermittent soft-porn sex (not necessarily in order of popularity). *Morality rating*: Very Nazi.

The Texas Chainsaw Massacre (1974)

Banned twice in the UK, general standards dropped to the point where this French blood feast, featuring a laconic rechargeable appliance, was eventually released to the general British public in 1999. *Morality rating*: Zzzzzz.

Snuff (1976)

Made in Argentina, during a decade of disappearances and massacres, for the princely sum of US$30,000, adverts proclaimed that it could only have been made in South America, 'where life is cheap!' Ostensibly about a hippie cult of mad killers, it included apparently genuine footage of one of the crew themselves being killed, and gave us a new concept to grapple with. (Whether anyone really did die to make it is unlikely – but the concept sold well!) *Morality rating*: Nil.

Driller Killer (1979)

Abel Ferrara both made the film and played the lead as a misunderstood artist who runs amok. (Well, who else would do it?) *Driller* promised 'the blood runs in rivers' and 'the drill keeps tearing through flesh and bone', but somehow retained some 'art house' pretensions. *Morality rating*: Wrong setting.

I Spit on Your Grave (1978)

Goodness knows what Buster Keaton would have made of this sort of 'black humour' (especially as his niece Camille plays the lead), but *Spit* features a lengthy rape scene followed by a role-reversal 'chopping, breaking and burning' of the villainous men by the victim herself (who naturally carries out this task in a state of undress). *Morality rating*: Slightly humorous.

Faces of Death (1978)

For those who don't get enough from the evening news, this Italian collection of autopsies, executions and accidents (Italy, as well as a centre for Renaissance art, is second only to the USA for video nasties) is narrated apparently by a pathologist (or should that be psychopath?) and spawned five sequels. *Morality rating*: That's enough – ed.

Dilemma 38
The exploitative pictures

The acceptable degree of nudity in church (thinking more of the decorations than the parishioners) has fluctuated. Michelangelo battled on artistic grounds for his view that the human form was divine and needed no covering, particularly not in heaven. But, in fact, his statues and frescoes had their 'fig leaves' added, and today feminists and others continue to argue that so-called classical art depicting women in sexually suggestive roles – or simply as naked forms, should be suppressed – removed from display in public institutions such as universities and libraries. There is very little consensus on what constitutes 'exploitative' or 'degrading' representations; censorship of the female form ranges from almost total prohibition in some Islamic countries to almost complete legality in some secular jurisdictions. Meanwhile, sexual activity, which in a way sits strangely alongside 'crime and violence' in the censor's library, has always attracted a disreputable premium for being 'real' as opposed to 'faked'. *Romance* in 1999, and the radical French film *Baise Moi* (2002) with its story of how a rape triggers two women to go on a rape and maiming spree, challenged this tendency and confused censors as they were not sure whether to ban them for the 'glamourless' 'real' sex scenes – or the run-of-the-mill, intermittent 'fake' violence.

The rallying cry that such images are 'violence against women' appears to offer a straightforward justification for intervention, but Maurice's practical problem is that it is hard to define what makes an image pornographic – legislators tend to be dragged along behind the apparently ever liberalising demands of the market.

The supposed roles in such representations – of women as 'sex objects' and men as invisible voyeurs – as *Meluisine* illustrates – is disappearing too, particularly as an expanding homosexual sex industry makes its presence felt. Equally, given the reduced role of women in societies that 'protect' them from such 'violence', other feminists decry censorship of the female form as reactionary and oppressive. After all, it seems that the objection to the naked body applies to men as well as women, to naturalistic figures as well as to 'suggestive' poses.

The female philosopher, Diotima, is found in Plato's *Symposium* making a rare lecture to Socrates – who is cast in the role of 'straight man' for once (see also Dilemma 55, 'The beauty trap'). Diotima says that the attraction to beauty, specifically in the naked body, is fundamental, but yet only a preliminary stage to something else. She even argues that there is an entirely natural link between seeing a beautiful body and wanting to have sex with it – it is the subconscious desire to make the beauty last forever. In this way, sexual attraction and beauty are irrevocably linked.

She advises Socrates, in words clearly later taken to heart, that although the wise philosopher may indeed 'fall in love with the beauty of one particular body', they will then discover that the quality of beauty that attracted them in the first place to one lover, is in fact the same thing that attracts them to another – that the beauty of their lovers is only part of some greater, eternal beauty. In fact (and Diotima here offers the famously ugly Socrates a glimmer of hope), the philosopher will realise that the beauty of mortal bodies is as nought compared to the beauties of the soul, 'so that wherever he meets with spiritual loveliness, even in the husk of an unlovely body, he will find it beautiful enough to fall in love with'. Nor does it stop there: the philosopher finds beauty in laws, institutions and human artefacts too, and thus 'by scanning beauty's wide horizon', the philosopher is saved from 'a slavish and illiberal devotion to the individual loveliness' of a single lover, or a single human construction. Turning their eyes towards 'the open sea of beauty' the philosophers find instead 'a golden harvest of philosophy' centred around knowledge of the good. (If this is the natural process, surely the philosopher-cum-Guardian will be forgiving towards those at an earlier stage in their appreciations?)

Dilemma 39
The nasty pop group

Police said the album was selling well, as tens of thousands of young people did buy it. But they charged the members of the group, in their late twenties and early thirties, with incitement to murder and actual involvement in racial attacks, notably arson.

Some people would say that this was a lost chance to show 'toleration' of different views, or that whilst they might personally abhor the sentiments expressed by Landser, would nonetheless still want to defend to the end 'their right to say it'.

But perhaps 'free speech' is not really the issue here. (Perhaps that is why the case was presumably not referred to Maurice the censor but directly to the German Constabulary?) Perhaps, like the evergreen case of the woman who shouts as a joke 'Fire! Fire!' in the cinema, and watches people stampede and some of them die underfoot, the words are also deeds, and the deeds are what the public is defending itself from. *But then again, that is exactly what the Victorian moralists were arguing too.*

The US Supreme Court, charged with upholding the rights of the citizen or, more specifically, attempts to interfere with the

> establishment of religion, or prohibiting the free exercise thereof; or abridging the freedom of speech, or of the press, or the right of the people peaceably to assemble, and to petition the government for a redress of grievances

was asked to mark out the boundaries for this sort of issue in 2002, specifically to rule whether 'freedom of expression' included the burning of crosses by the Klu Klux Klan, part of the KKK's campaigns to intimidate black Americans.

Nothing in the amendment lends itself to protecting 'expressive actions', as we might classify burning crosses to be, or indeed burning effigies perhaps on political demonstrations. However, banning the latter might seem to many to be a restriction on 'freedom of speech'. Fortunately, extra guidance is given by a decision in 1919 when the court ruled that where there was a 'clear and present danger' of criminality, even words would not be tolerated. Satisfactory? Well, *that* ruling was in relation to pacifists campaigning against conscription in the First World War.

These days, many so-called rap singers, particularly in the USA, also sing about killing pigs (by which they do not mean the pink farm animals) and raping bitches (by which they do not mean dogs). In these cases, it is often not clear whether the lyrics *are* a serious recommendation to their listeners for action, or some sort of (rather nasty) macho ritual. These cases blur into ones not so unlike the Penny Dreadfuls, where it is not directly demonstrable that it was the songs 'that made me do it', but certainly leave a doubt.

When a fundamentalist religious state was set up in Afghanistan in the 1990s, one of its first acts was to create a Ministry for the Propagation of Virtue and the Prevention of Vice. Its edicts included the banning of all television, music, photographs of living people, shaving and the showing of flesh in public. As well as forcing women to wear top-to-toe garments to hide themselves (and even then confining them to the home except when accompanied by a male), the men were also required, for example, to wear long trousers when playing football.

In due course, these restrictions, which echoed similar programmes in Iran under the Ayatollahs, came to undermine the very moral authority that the governments imagined they were protecting.

Censorship is part of social life – inevitable and desirable. For example, the rules on where people can and cannot be naked are a form of censorship. We don't want to find the milkman standing outside the door with no clothes on, even if we may want to find them standing inside the bedroom with no clothes on. Where the rules are widely agreed, they are hardly even noticed, but where the rules are opposed by a significant minority, even a majority, the censor is unlikely to be able to find a rational argument to justify their position. As Bertrand Russell wrote in another of his 'Sceptical Essays' ('Recrudescence of Puritanism'): 'It is obvious that "obscenity" is not a term capable of exact legal definition; in the practice of the Courts, it means "anything that shocks the magistrate".'

Is pop music good or evil?

When the writer Nick Hornby sampled the ten top-selling pop groups in the USA for the year 2001, he found the experience, as he put it 'dispiriting'. D12's entreaties to their audience to 'show them their mammaries and shut their mouths' unless they were taking part in some bizarre sexual ritual involving their parents (hey, if you want to untangle that lyric better go out and get the album!), sat alongside a 'skit' about how one gang member's attempts to have sex with another one's girlfriend is thwarted by uncontrollable (*hilarious*) farting noises. That is to leave undiscussed the scatological rap poetry of Puff Daddy, Eminem, Blink 82 and so on.

Hornby was following up an exercise by Gore Vidal in 1973, when that author had attempted to 'understand' popular taste. Vidal was shocked at the depths that scribblers such as Alexander Solzhenitsyn had sunk to. Hornby sadly concludes: 'I shall, when I have recovered my strength, creep back to my private Top 10, which consists of penniless artists such as the Pernice Brothers and Joe Henry and Shuggie Otis and Olu Dara, who make music full of thoughtful, polite ironies and carefully articulated cynicism. . . . But I won't kid myself that it's pop music – not any more.' Where did we go wrong? 'We should have seen this coming', says Hornby, 'our mistake was to imagine ourselves hipper than our parents'.

These problems are adapted from the celebrated 'board games' developed in the USA for use by large multinational companies. Probably the one best-known was developed by Citicorp and called, efficiently enough, *The Ethics Game*. It consisted of a number of imaginary scenarios, printed on cards, with multiple choice answers. The more ethical your answer, the faster you could move around the board, picking up rewards or forfeits as you did so. It was popular enough to spawn Spanish, French, German and Japanese versions, to mention just a few.

The Ethics Game was similar to *Scruples*, a card game. But in *Scruples* there is no board and no pieces to move – just lots of cards, describing situations in which someone might be tempted to break some implied social rule or convention. The way to win is to correctly predict the answer ('Yes', 'No' or 'Depends') of another player. You don't need to enter into discussion of the answer, although people often did want to – that was part of the fun. Anyway, all the games owe something to a much older board game called *The New Game of Virtue Rewarded and Vice Punished*. Produced in Britain in 1810, this one featured edifying images of 'The Stocks' and 'The House of Correction', as well as 'Faith' and 'Prudence'.

The approach was taken further by the industrial behemoth Lockheed Martin,* whose ethics game they called *Gray Matters*. So-called, as it is supposed to recognise that ethical issues are not straightforward matters of 'black and white'. Or indeed, 'right and wrong'. Which just goes to show that an ethics game in which there is no right and no wrong is a very funny sort of ethics game indeed. But to make matters more confusing, Lockheed Martin designed it not so much to make the employees better at dealing with ethical issues, but to make them better at following company policy. And policies are, of course, very 'black and white', if not clearly right or wrong.

So the perspective of ethics games like these has to be seen not so much as a moral one, but as a business one – a strategy. Lockheed Martin's interest in such matters, we might recall, was awoken only after it had been prosecuted under the Foreign Corrupt Practices Act for attempting to bribe foreign legislators to secure new orders

* So called after the merger of Lockheed and Martin Marietta. The original game has now been adapted for use by over a hundred individual companies and colleges.

for military transport planes. At the time, an unrepentant Lockheed argued that their behaviour was not unethical, as they were acting with the interests of their employees at heart (who might otherwise be made unemployed). This piece of practical utilitarianism fell on stony ground, and the company was fined US$25 million.

And so *The Ethics Game* is played according to very strict rules. Although, in a spirit of 'greyness', in most cases it allows that there may be several acceptable answers, it also suggests there are some totally unacceptable ones. Allowing employees to address each other with endearments is one such example, meriting in the original game a penalty double the normal one for a 'wrong' answer. 'Stealing from the government' comes out more black than grey too. And the employee who 'learns' that any answer involving making a report to their supervisor or the ethics office is 'good', is also learning something which is not really ethics, but simply pragmatics. The employees are encouraged to accept company rules and company procedures as ethically pure. Something sometimes hard to square with the reality.

Dilemma 40
The short memos by the pirate

The question of whether it is wrong to copy software is not actually so straightforward as its owners would have us believe. First, nothing physically goes missing or is taken, and second, the software company may not lose any sales by the activity – indeed, there is some evidence that even organised software piracy only helps establish the 'brand' in the marketplace. So plenty of scope for someone to try to produce a rationalisation of the theft, and having done so, join in themselves.

But it is still against the law, and that normally is enough to make it wrong in most people's eyes. Certainly the ethics office will take this line. If a company were to be reported for slack supervision of its software resources, it might even face substantial fines. It is in the company's interests that people suspected of such activity be reported immediately, and that is the 'correct' answer offered by the ethics games. The company may punish Sandra – as a common thief.

Software softies might feel that there is some sort of trust too between employees, and that, at least, Jackie should raise the matter with Sandra before reporting her.

(One of the things about ethics, in whatever context, is the creation of trust, and one hurtful thing about 'unethical' behaviour is often the intangible loss or betrayal of that trust.) She might be mistaken in her suspicions, and Sandra might be trying to make up time lost at work apparently slacking, by a little extra memo-writing at home. It would be a shame to make a censorious report in such a company-spirited case, wouldn't it? And if she does sound out her colleague, as a last resort, Sandra might claim, like Clovis to Mrs Eggleby, in the Saki story, to have 'forgotten' that it was wrong. To which Jackie might enjoy exclaiming with Eggelbelian incredulity, 'Forgotten the difference between right and wrong!'

Dilemma 41
The blaring radio

The correct answer (we are assured) is to play different music periodically. A certain sort of practical utilitarianism is employed, although if the new choice of music irritates everyone else, then perhaps (on the felicific calculus) the situation gets worse, not better. Going further than this and imposing your judgement of acceptable music in the style of a Platonic Guardian, would be an attempt to reach the 'right' decision irrespective of people's untutored views. But such judgements are hard to make. In one dialogue, the *Euthydemus*, Plato asks what is the 'specialised knowledge' (the Greek word used is *techne*, from which we get our words 'technology' and 'technical') that can enable bosses to achieve this desirable general preponderance of pleasure over pain? Plato concludes that while those in positions of power, like our machine-shop supervisor, have an obligation to make people prosperous (and protect their freedom), the task of making them wise is altogether too great. On that basis, the supervisor should ignore protests and put on whatever increases productivity – even *Gardeners' Question Time* if need be.

On the other hand, supervisors with sterner views on musical quality who consider themselves duty-bound to impose the noblest sounds might take encouragement from a story related by the excellent J. D. Mabbott about the master of an Oxford college during the First World War. The master would oblige himself to enjoy a cold bath every morning with the words 'Come along now, Phelps, be a man, Phelps, in you go!' thereby illustrating that other moral phenomenon whereby people can try to persuade themselves they like things if they believe they 'ought' to. Should people, perhaps, listen to classical music in the same spirit?

Dilemma 42
The infectious disease

Discrimination against people with AIDS – or simply 'HIV-positive' (and note how Bob's status swiftly switches between the two!) – is an ethics book in itself. The issues surrounding HIV sufferers are legion: in many countries they are the new lepers. When identified, they may be publicly shunned, banned from public baths, restaurants, cafés, libraries, buses . . . everywhere. Thrown out of jobs, or schools, forced out of homes – even attacked in the street. At the turn of the millennium, the UN calculated that there were nearly 35 million HIV-positive people worldwide – and that just under half of these were women.

According to the social scientists, Alec Irwin and Joyce Miller, this makes AIDS 'the most devastating communicable disease in history' (*Global AIDS: Myths and Facts*, 2002) and one whose effects are magnifying the toll from poverty all over the 'poor world' (as they rather inelegantly put it) or at least in 'marginalised communities' within wealthy countries. And AIDS is not just a disease, but a symptom – of a wider malaise in the global village. But what of our business scenario: what should you do in a situation where someone is carrying out a job where there is a, perhaps small but real, risk of infecting others, but may have failed to declare the reality of their infection and the associated risk?

The US Center for Disease Control (with over 1 million HIV-positive people in the country) has opted for a policy which protects sufferers, saying that despite campaigns, for example, to stop parents sending 'infected' children to school, that such children do have a right to be taught in an 'unrestricted setting' and that the number of people 'aware of the child's condition' should be kept to a minimum. Surgeons and dentists who are HIV-positive may also ask for the protection of the cloak of anonymity – and they may need it not because there is a significant risk of them infecting their patients but because patients may think otherwise. Hospitals which protect their surgeons' ability to carry on their jobs will need to do so at the expense of individual patients' freedom to exercise their prejudices. They will also be aware that if a patient does claim to have contracted HIV through the hospital, it will cost them dearly both in terms of money and in terms of reputation. So there is an understandable tendency in organisations to 'take the easy option' ('Thank you, Jackie!') and 'reach for the phone'. But this is not to say it is the ethical approach.

Yet AIDS is actually one of the *least* contagious diseases. (Jackie's coffee mug concern is part of the myth-making of AIDS.) There is still no consensus over many aspects of the disease, which takes many different forms, but it seems it can be spread as a result of sexual intercourse, and as a side effect of drug abuse. By whichever mechanism, in the West it has been associated with homosexual life styles and dubbed the 'Gay Plague' by newspapers. So, as far as spreading the illness, 'macho' cultural norms have been held to exact a more than usual toll on families and communities. Surely Bob's partners – male or female – are entitled to know the risks? The partners of those who have slept with Bob, particularly if unprotected, may also need to be alerted? In these cases his preference for privacy does need to be balanced against the concerns of others. Some 'communitarian' philosophers, notably Amitai Etzioni, argue that concern about supposed invasions of 'privacy' are merely sideshoots of what they call a 'freemarket liberal individualism' that is in itself socially destructive. Etzioni specifically gives the example of attempting to protect people with AIDS from ostracism, even at the risk of the disease being spread more widely.

But clearly in the memo business, the ability of Bob to carry out his job is not affected by the virus, and the reaction of others is irrational and prejudiced. 'Option B' – let alone the 'reach for the phone' one – is a shameful response, even if one not so far from everyday reality. It seems therefore appropriate, for once, to agree with the 'Leader's Guide' and set in motion some staff training.

Dilemma 43
The witness

The positive actions of 'Option A' are seen as 'responsible' and ethical here. Refusing to testify is drummed out as rather immoral, and anyway, it is hard to see what the company would gain by such a policy of covering up problems. To try not to get involved, we are reminded in the ethics game, is 'a cop-out' and 'a cop-out seldom gets points'. But is saying that to elevate a sin of omission to equal condemnation as that of actively refusing to testify?

This scenario, being devised by business ethicists, imagines a situation in which love of the company rates very highly, and so is not really thinking of the self-interest that might also provoke a reluctance to testify. In this sense, it is suggesting a conflict of 'duties'. So, what do you do, when you face two real but conflicting duties? Existentialists, like Jean-Paul Sartre, have made such moments central to their approach to ethics. Sartre rejects all rules and statements about goodness or duty, but retains instead values like 'engagement'. (Søren Kierkegaard speaks of 'commitment' similarly, as a moral goal.) Sartre gives the example of a young man torn between his mother (who clings to her only son in the absence of her husband) and the call of the Free French Army. Sartre concludes that it is only after he makes his choice that the value attached to filial duty versus patriotic becomes both clear and real. Actual choices determine our values.

What of situations where both self-interest and the company's interests coincide – but not the public interest? Cases like Enron, WorldCom and Arthur Andersen Accountants, for example, where a culture of disguising financial realties had become out-and-out fraud? In 2002, in a final futile splurge of memo-shredding, these pillars of corporate America toppled and fell, guilty of inflating profits with the aquiesence of the accountants. Of course, as George Soros (the billionaire financial wizard) has pointed out, artificially inflating profits *is* what the successful business executive is hired for – there are even 'off the shelf' accounting scams (called SPEs – Special Purpose Entities) for 'hiding' aspects of the business that make less pleasing reading for potential investors.

In these cases, 'whistle-blowers' are destroying not only their companies and the livelihoods of their colleagues, but their own jobs too – and only the most principled employee would still speak out, perhaps concerned for the many thousands of investors (particularly pension holders) in the company's shares. Here only the 'safety valve' of individual conscience – not the well-oiled machinery of corporate ethics – protected the general interest.

Dilemma 44
The Devil's chemists

In the Nüremberg trials at the end of the Second World War, civilians and soldiers alike *were* held to be under a higher obligation to the 'eternal' moral law than the prevailing civil one. In the extreme circumstances of experimenting on concentration camp prisoners that does not seem too controversial, some people will even say there is 'no dilemma' at all! Yet the chemists illustrate how upright citizens can do things that we consider to be very evil – as did so many others from camp guards to railwaymen. Yet on their own terms they were all upstanding members of 'the community', observing current practice.

And in general all businesses share one thing: they need to make money. If they do not make money, they cannot generate employment and pretty soon they cannot afford to make anything either. Business already obeys two laws: the secular one of the local administration, and the global law of the market. What need they of a third law – the moral law? After all the law of the market is: the weak go to the wall, and the strong survive. Why not:

- pay as little as possible to those who supply the raw materials;
- pay as little as possible, under the minimum necessary arrangements, to those who convert the materials into the 'products' – that is their employees;
- spend as little as possible on cleaning up afterwards.

Then, of course, there are the additional stages. There is the development and testing of products – this again can be very expensive unless you either cut corners or use dubious methods. (The IG managers must have been very pleased with the savings reflected in the memos.) Above all, there is the vexatious possibility of competition undermining both the eventual price and the volume of sales. At least in the short-term, the most profitable company has no competition – it has a monopoly instead. (Outside the long-term, the company is likely to stagnate and miss out on opportunities.) This leads to a fourth important 'unethical business' fundamental:

- manipulate the market in your favour.

Fortunately, 'the market' seems to be quite a shrewd judge of most issues. 'As little as possible' may still be enough. And it may pay too to take into account the negative effects on the 'bottom line' of bad publicity (witness the recent 'green campaigns' against oil companies, or the old boycotts of apartheid South Africa's goods). But the pressure is always there – to set up a sweatshop, to use child slavery, to dump waste, to buy cheap from unsustainable sources.

The economist J. K. Galbraith has described how big business controls the market through control of people's minds – creating unnecessary fashions and desires with the skill and detail of master puppeteers. All business decisions have ethical aspects, a director of a company may take decisions that directly affect tens or even hundreds of thousands of people – as employees, suppliers and subcontractors, and millions of people as consumers. Yet this power is often exercised in an entirely amoral way – profit is the sole criterion. As the prosecutor at Nüremberg went on to say: 'These are terrible charges, no man should underwrite them frivolously or vengefully, or without deep and humble awareness of the responsibility which he thereby shoulders. There is no laughter in this case, neither is there any hate.' Often for businesspeople who today launch the campaigns for baby milk in the African subcontinent, or order the logging of the forests that are 'unfortunately' the only home of some voiceless communities (let alone species), 'there is no hate'. But the consequences are just as bad.

The verdicts on the 'Devil's chemists' were mixed. On the one hand, twelve of the executives served prison sentences for slavery and mistreatment of prisoners. On the other hand, by the end of the 1950s, two of the convicted war criminals were back serving as directors in large companies. Nonetheless, the trial serves as a reminder to business people who have power over lives today to never underestimate the ethical dimensions of their decisions.

Dilemma 45
The unfruitful tree

The 'unfruitful' assistant might have done better to have taken the money and lived it up for a while. Then at least the option of repenting his selfishness would have been open to him. Indeed, in the parable of the prodigal son, two sons who share an inheritance behave like the rich man's assistants. One stays at home and uses the money wisely; the other goes off and has a good time – until the money runs out. At which point, the naughty boy returns home. And he (we are told) is now sorry. The family are delighted to see their errant son return, and use up the money the good son has been accumulating for everyone on a great celebratory banquet.

In the original Biblical story 'The Unfruitful Tree', the 'coins' mentioned here are 'talents', that is an ancient Eastern sum of money equivalent to many months' work. But in any case, they are really only metaphorical talents standing in for personal skills: powers and opportunities for doing good, for that is, of course, God's (the merchant's) work.

Yet the story also seems to be making the case for wealth generation. The moral then becomes, invest your money wisely – avoid internet stocks and the like.

According to Max Weber and other sociologists, the Protestant interpretation of this sort of Bible story made possible the whole capitalist transformation of society. Wealth became equated with God's approval, and with virtue. And although, it is true, I have fiddled with the original text somewhat, the reader may be assured, the speech endorsing, at the very least, putting the money in the bank to earn interest is flatly stated there in the original, and is in that respect very different from Islam, where usury is one of the greatest of sins.

Finally, the story is condemning someone again (yes, the outer darkness!) for what is really a sin of omission, not a sin of commission.

Dilemma 46
Job's lot

> Let the stars of the twilight be dark, let it look for light, but have none, neither let it see the dawning of the day. Because it shut not up the doors of mother's womb nor hid sorrow from mine eyes. Why died I not from the womb? Why did I not give up the ghost when I came out of the belly? . . . Wherefore is light given to him that is in misery, and the life unto the bitter in soul; which longs for death, but it cometh not; and dig for it more than for hidden treasures. . . . When I lie down, I say, when shall I arise and the night be gone? And I am full of tossings to and fro unto the dawning of that day. My flesh is clothed with worms and clods of dust, my skin is broken and become loathsome, my days are swifter than a weaver's' shuttle, and are spent without hope. . . . Man that is born of a woman is of few days, and full of trouble. He cometh forth like a flower, and is cut down: he fleeth also as a shadow, and continueth not.

So says Job. His story contains some of the most powerful images in the Bible, and contributes in large part to what might be called the 'founding myths' of Western society. But it also contains one of the most persistent philosophical challenges to Christian belief: the problem of evil. How is it that an all-powerful Being who is also completely benevolent allows so much suffering and evil in the world?

> My face is foul with weeping, and on my eyelids is the shadow of death; nor for any injustice in mine hands: also my prayer is pure. O earth, cover not thou my blood, and let my cry have no place. What is the Almighty, that we should serve him? And what profit should we have if we pray unto him? . . .

[Even so] all the while my breath is in me, and the spirit of God is in my nostrils, my lips shall not speak wickedness, nor my tongue utter deceit. . . . Let thistles grow instead of wheat, and cockle instead of barley, the words of Job are ended.

Then, we are told, God answered Job 'out of the whirlwind'.

> Then came there unto him all his brethren, and all his sisters, and all they that had been of his acquaintance before, and did eat bread with him in his houses and they bemoaned him and comforted him over all the evil that the Lord had brought upon him: every man also gave him a piece of money, and every one an earring of gold. So the Lord blessed the latter end of Job more than his beginning: for he had fourteen thousand sheep and six thousand camels, and a thousand yoke of oxen, and a thousand she asses. . . . After this Job lived one hundred and forty years, and saw his sons, and his sons' sons, even four generations. So Job died, being old and full of days.

It's a happy ending, and for Job, at least, the problem of evil is shunted into the sidings. But for those who, unlike Job, find suffering continues – even through 'no fault' of their own – the problem remains.

Dilemma 47
The sacrificial lamb

As far as religious direction goes, the idea that God wants us to do certain things is all very well, and cannot be argued with. (It is beyond rationality.) But the idea that we ought to do What God Wants is firmly in the realm of human decision making. It is not any help to say 'God wants us to do what God wants' either: this is the so-called 'Eythyphro Dilemma', after the character in Plato's *Dialogue* who insists that what is virtuous is whatever the gods approve of. To which Socrates (*en route* to his execution) just has time to say, but do the gods approve of things because they are virtuous – or are they virtuous only because the gods approve of them? Bertrand Russell, a confirmed religious sceptic, recounts how on the occasion of his arrival in prison (for peacemongering) he was asked by the warder to give his religion. 'Agnostic', the great philosopher replied. 'And how do you spell that?' queried the warder, before adding more tolerantly: 'Well, there are many religions, but I suppose they all worship the same God.' Russell's conviction, unlike Abraham, is that if we abandon our own reason, and are content to rely on authority, there will be trouble. After all, which authority? The Old Testament? The New Testament? The Koran? In practice, Russell says, people choose the book considered sacred by the community in which they are born, and 'out of that book they choose the parts they like, ignoring the others. At one time, the most influential text in the Bible was: "Thou shalt not suffer a witch to live."' Russell recalls, in the doubting spirit of Descartes, that if the forces of evil have a certain share of power, they may try to deceive us into accepting as Scripture what is really their work. This was indeed, he notes, the view of the Gnostics, who thought that the Old Testament was the work of an evil spirit. As for those who, like Spinoza, take God's omnipotence seriously, then they must abandon the notion of 'sin' too. This leads to frightful results, says Russell. As Spinoza's contemporaries asked: was it not wicked of Nero to murder his mother? Was it not wicked of Adam to eat the apple? Spinoza has no answer.

Søren Kierkegaard (1813–55) sees the story of Abraham as showing the limitations of ethics, with a paradox because we are asked to accept that it is right to do what generally is considered wrong, as long as God tells us to. Kierkegaard concludes that logical rules cannot guide actions, and instead we must reclaim responsibility for our 'existence' and actions. Otherwise all ethical systems are made void by a religious instruction. And Kierkegaard, himself a strict Lutheran Protestant, holds that the word of God is directly obtainable for individuals without the need to get confirmation of their understanding from anyone else, such as society in general or a priest.

Pierre-Joseph Proudhon might have seen less of a paradox, however, as he always maintained (along with 'property is theft') that 'God is evil'. Perhaps Abraham should search his conscience a bit harder after all, and judge the likelihood of the God of goodness asking for the sacrifice of an innocent in the interests of the faith of the rest. But then, perhaps he would conclude that this was very much God's way – after all, of course, it is the central Christian belief that He is supposed to have sacrificed His own son.

Again, this story is supposed to be literally true, rather than just a 'parable'. The conventional line on it is that although Abraham could not know how killing his son would be 'the right thing', his faith sufficed to convince him that it must. The story is important in the Bible as it stresses that Christianity is about faith, and not about blood. The book of Matthew spells out to the Jewish people that they will not be 'saved' by virtue of who they are, but only by following the trusting example of Abraham. The moral is: killing people is all right if God tells you to.

Dilemma 48
The modern day Good Samaritan

Stop, of course. Someone needs help. Our Good Samaritan stops and offers some. The driver pulls out a gun, shoots him, and steals his car. The Good Samaritan is no more. Was that the wrong call, Good Samaritan?

Although of course there are many happier stories of altruistic individuals like the Samaritan, who have taken great personal risks for others, there are also recent cases when their efforts have been ill-received. The US example is rather extreme, but even in the original story, there are costs to the Samaritan in helping. Then again, perhaps people have got worse?

Discussions

Consider the traditional story in Islamic cultures of 'the bad neighbour'. Here, a family is bothered by some nasty neighbours who (let us modernise it slightly) grow a very high Leylandii hedge, watch noisy telly all day, and play disco music all night long. The nice family ask the nasty neighbours once, twice – three times – to show some consideration and each time they are insulted and their requests treated contemptuously. So the family seek the prophet's advice. 'Next time they show so little consideration, take out all your furniture and put in the the street.' But how will that help? 'People will see it there and ask why – and then explain that because of the neighbour you can no longer live happily in your home. The neighbour will be so ashamed that the furniture will not be out there by the night.'

In the traditional tale, indeed the nasty neighbour is first out, begging the family to bring their furniture back in, and apologising profusely. A charming scenario which, however, rings completely untrue today. Perhaps in traditional societies with much stronger communities, it would be the case. Today, in most modern cities, chances are the furniture would not stay there overnight – it would be stolen. Or maybe just smashed up. And how the nasty neighbour would laugh at that!

David Hume, like both his great friend Adam Smith and Jean-Jacques Rousseau (and all completely unlike Thomas Hobbes, but that's still 3:1) believed that people are generally disposed favourably towards their fellows. Although each human is born not only with some self-love (which is very important and necessary) but there is also love for others. It is this compassion (or 'sympathy' as Smith calls it) that makes society possible. Conversely, 'evil is the absence of empathy', as G. M. Gilbert, a psychologist in the Nüremburg trials, put it. But empathy can be a weak force compared with self-interest, as the original parable demonstrates. Not to forget that third ethical force, between empathy and sympathy: apathy. As Helen Keller wrote in *My Religion* (1927), although 'science may have found a cure for most evils . . . it has found no remedy for the worst of them all – the apathy of human beings'.

Actually, Hume believed there to be, in fact, no differences between right and wrong, just different emotional responses to acts. These determine our actions. For example, we may be worried by the sight of an injured person lying in the road – or frightened – or just indifferent. Or we may be angered to hear of the latest bombing, or we may celebrate another blow for 'the cause'. But perhaps if we see the lifeless bodies and hear the tearful cries of the relatives, our 'emotional' response may be both more fundamental and appear more ethical.

Hume was not the first, nor would he be the last to debunk moral objectivity. This great toppling of the secular god is always being re-enacted, and hailed as a novelty. It underwent a particular resurgence in the early twentieth century as part of the rejection of 'Victorian values'. Edward Westermarck, in *The Origin and Development of Moral Ideas* (1906), summed up a view of society as a kind of school in which 'men learn to distinguish between right and wrong' and where 'the headmaster is custom, and the lessons are the same for all'. The 'presumed objectivity' of moral judgements (he said) is a 'chimera' and there is no such thing as 'moral truth' at all. 'The ultimate reason for this is that the moral concepts are based upon emotions, and that the contents of an emotion fall entirely outside the category of truth', he explained. As Wittgenstein offered:

> to write or talk Ethics or religion [is] . . . to run against the boundaries of language. This running against the walls of our cage is perfectly, absolutely hopeless. Ethics so far as it springs from the desire to say something about the ultimate meaning of life, the absolute good, the absolutely valuable, can be no science. What it says does not add to our knowledge in any sense.

Even if (as Wittgenstein, adopting an unusual and uncomfortable-looking posture, adds): 'it is a document of a tendency in the human mind which I personally cannot help respecting deeply and I would not for my life ridicule it'.

247

Dilemma 49
Lazarus the beggar

I like this story – it has, as do most religious stories, a very harsh flavour. How many unpleasant people have we encountered (or heard about) who we would like to think will at least be punished *eternally*?* On the other hand, how many times have we passed beggars by without the slightest intention of stopping to help? And now we find *we* will face eternal torment. Certainly, it gives a different perspective to the 'lifeboat' problem, clearly putting cuddly Peter Singer and hungry little Third World children in Abraham's' arms and short-sighted Mr Hardin in the flames.

Actually, the ethical force of the example relies on the beggar being, as he very obviously is, an extremely helpless and pitiful case. And clearly the 'rich man' has the resources to help. So in that sense it is not a true 'lifeboat scenario' after all.

A better modern day equivalent (as well as being another parallel to the tale of the Samaritan?) is the bigger lifeboat problem of asylum seekers. In 2001, a boatload of such unfortunates was sinking in the South Pacific, and a Norwegian ship responded to their SOS by picking the people up. The refugees insisted they did not want to go back to Indonesia (which they had just set off from) but only to nearby Christmas Island where, being on Australian territory, they would then be able to seek asylum. When the Aussie Prime Minister heard this, he ordered the navy to step in and prevent the boat going anywhere near the island, declaring that Australia had more than enough asylum seekers already. He suggested Norway should accept responsibility – but the Norwegian government pointed out that this would make it very impractical for anyone to rescue people at sea in the future. The injured, sick and in all cases miserable asylum seekers were left amongst the crates on the freighter instead, tormented by the flames of the hot Pacific sun, with hardly a drop of water to dip their fingers in, and cool their tongues. Whether their tormentors will one day swap places is, of course, the great unknown.

And the moral is? Virtue is not its own reward.

* 'In order that the happiness of the saints will be more delightful . . . they are permitted perfectly to behold the sufferings of the damned . . . the saints will rejoice in the punishment of the damned . . . which will fill them with joy' (St Thomas Aquinas).

Dilemmas 50 and 51
Monkey business

Democritus (once) said it was ridiculous to claim the superiority of man over animals when, in all important respects, the animals are our teachers. The spider is the tutor for weaving, the swallow that for architecture, the nightingale that for singing . . . However, it was only comparatively recently, perhaps after the contemporary philosophers Peter Singer and Paolo Cavalieri launched 'The Great Apes Project' (1993), that the notion of animals having in some sense 'rights' was moved up the philosophical agenda, if not so much the social and political one. (Although New Zealand came close to enshrining animal rights in law.) More recently, another contemporary American, Stephen Wise, himself a lecturer on Animal Rights and (most importantly) a lawyer, actually took a case to court arguing that chimpanzees and their smaller cousins, bonobos, should have the same basic legal rights as human beings. Together with Jane Goodall, a chimpanzee specialist who travels the world setting up sanctuaries and the like, he argued that these animals at least are not only capable of emotional reactions but are also rational thinkers. These creatures remind us that, as Darwin himself originally put it, any difference between animals and man is 'certainly one of degree and not kind'.

In fact, we share more than 99 per cent of the same genetic inheritance with chimpanzees – perhaps a few hundred genes differentiate us out of tens or hundreds of thousands. (We also share most of our genes with earthworms, fish and even plants.) And chimps can learn to navigate mazes using computer screens, play at looking after dolls or (again playfully) make faces at themselves in mirrors. They may use tools – such as sticks, to extract honey from bees' nests – which seems to show a certain amount of forward planning. One research group claimed to have taught bonobos some 3,000 words. Bonobos share with humans another unusual characteristic: they make recreational love, including kissing.

Stephen Wise's case is that since chimps have similar capabilities to small children, or severely disabled adults (who similarly cannot speak), then they should be entitled if not to 'full liberty rights', at least to 'dignity rights', including within that, the 'right to choose' their surroundings. Chimps should not be reduced to the non-status of 'objects'. Actually Darwin went further:

> The following proposition seems to me in a high degree probable – namely, that any animal whatever, endowed with well-marked social instincts, the

parental and filial instincts being here included, would inevitably acquire a moral sense or conscience . . . the limit being only one of intellect. Sympathy, not language, is the key element in acquiring this sociable aspect. And the form that morals take will be decided by the needs of the group as evolutionary biology has determined.

And many animals exhibit social behaviour. Baboons like to eat insects that live under stones and rocks. Several of them together will help to turn over large ones and share the pickings. Travellers have described seeing pelicans feeding older, blind pelicans; fish and other species of bird have been known to do the same. Horses and cows will nibble or lick each other's coats to remove ticks and the like. Monkeys will pick out thorns from each other's fur.

But in practice the key factor in excluding animals from our moral world seems to be their inability to speak. Certainly chimps have learnt to use simple language, but it is unlikely that the example given could ever arise – at least not the 'impassioned' final speech of Albert! But the reason to imagine it anyway is to ask: what *would* the appropriate response be if a chimpanzee *did* make its case so? Could the comfortable distinction between 'us' humans, and 'them' – animals – still be used as *carte blanche* to cover up all manner of abuses?

At the moment, chimps and bonobos are shot, kidnapped, eaten. In the USA, they can still be used in laboratories and still vivisected. At least in the UK, that has been illegal since 1996.

Dilemma 52
Life's not fair

Well, Thomas may think so, but so-called 'virtue theorists' have taken Aristotle's later discussion of it very seriously. On the other hand, if he read on, Thomas would see that Socrates actually disagrees with Meno. For a start (and again at odds with Aristotle's later version), Socrates says that he is *not* interested in different virtues, he is looking for the common feature of all of them, the defining characteristic that makes them virtues in the first place.

Some to-ing and fro-ing between Socrates and Meno leaves Meno bamboozled and admitting he does not know anything about 'virtue' after all. Socrates then takes the lead and offers the observation that if 'virtue' is a kind of special skill or knowledge, it should be possible to teach it. Since it appears no one can teach it, Socrates concludes, then no one seems to have it.

But Socrates has some ideas, which he then offers in unusually direct form. First of all, he states that virtue involves knowledge of the mean. Indeed, Plato's account has Socrates explaining that courage in excess is foolhardiness, a dangerous overconfidence, and that taken to excess, all virtues become vices. Instead they all need to be guided by wisdom. 'In short, everything that the human spirit undertakes will lead to happiness when it is guided by wisdom, but to the opposite, when guided by folly. . . . In short, virtue, to be something advantageous, must be a kind of wisdom.' So doing the right thing is, indeed, the *highest* form of wisdom.

Socrates then concludes the discussion by claiming that although some people have enough knowledge to appear wise and to be successful in some respects, they are only like those who have learnt a solution to a problem without truly understanding how it was arrived at. They appear knowledgeable, and may often be successful, but they do not truly know what is the essence of goodness.

Just like James, Samantha and even Brains!

Dilemma 53
Infantile ethical egotism

Thomas's bit of Latin is making the same point again, that Mrs Cook has already assumed the 'wrongness' of what she is supposedly proving should be condemned – a common enough fault in ethical debates to be sure. But Thomas is really interested in Kant (his favourite bedtime reading at the moment, having finished all the Hairy Poppers and Frederick the Pirate books). If all his special reasons are taken into account, surely everyone 'in the universe' would agree it is all right for him to take the sweets? If anyone else was in exactly the same situation, he would not object if they took some. (Fortunately, no one seems to be and it seems a very remote possibility.) His idea is that it is quite possible to make any way of behaving into a 'universal', as long as you define 'universal' very precisely, in fact, to mean whatever you want. As he mutters under his breath, in the disgraced children's corner of the classroom, 'It's not fair – there just *isn't* any distinction between act and rule utilitarianism!'*

He does not know or care that he is displaying what the philosopher, James Rachels, called mere 'me-ism', something which is not good, even a form of discrimination.

A bit of Thomas's educational philosophy – or is it Bollards?

Some philosophers, notably Jean Piaget (1896–1980), have identified various stages in children's development. For example, at a certain 'pre-logical' stage, they will watch water being poured from a tall thin glass into a bigger, fatter one, and insist that there is now less water – that some has disappeared. But young children will also exhibit irrationality in ethical decisions too. If Samantha accidentally loses her satchel full of her books on the way to school, whilst 'Brains' deliberately throws away his maths book – many children will give the firm opinion that Samantha has done the worse thing – as she has lost more books. They are interested in results, not intentions. But how irrational is that? Perhaps they have picked up the attitude from their parents, after report time.

Jean Piaget found that young children thought rules in games had a mystical quality, and were unchangeable and unchallengeable. (Although young children do not mind ignoring the rules themselves in their own interests.) At these ages, the child measures the rightness and wrongness of actions by a very utilitarian measure of the consequences – it is worse to drop the whole tea tray by accident than it is to deliberately smash a single cup in a moment of temper. And a 'big' wrong action – say dropping the whole tea tray, should be punished severely. The young child is quite happy for the punishment to be 'divine' – Sophie can be eaten up by a dog, if she is not burnt to death by the matches. In fact, the more awful the punishment, the more the young child feels reassured.

As they grow a little older, they see the rules are essentially human-made, and open to negotiation. However, they value everyone agreeing and at this stage, are

* *Rule* utilitarianism is that schoolroom-sounding policy of trying to choose 'the rules' 'for everyone's benefit'; *act* utilitarianism is the anarchic-sounding policy of allowing the maximisation of pleasure to be the sole criterion.

scrupulous in their application of the rules, even to themselves. The older child considers intentions to be important too, not just effects. And the older child will see punishment as having a constructive, reforming role: the punishment should be proportionate and appropriate to the crime.

Another psychologist, Lawrence Kohlberg, made up grisly stories to investigate children's moral development. One story is about a man whose wife is dying of cancer. The man has tried everything he can to obtain the drugs that will save her, and now, in desperation, he plans to steal them. Is that justified? Kohlberg says children go through certain stages. There is a pre-moral period, when actions are simply determined by avoiding punishment, followed by a 'hedonistic' period in which actions are justified by the pleasure they bring to the individual. Next, there is a period which Kohlberg calls the 'good boy' period, when behaviour is dictated by the desire to please others. This is later refined to doing what is 'expected' by others – a kind of sense of duty. At the fifth stage, individuals follow the dictates of conscience, and at the sixth, they have 'universalisable moral principles'. *A very good exercise for primary age children is to* classify moral philosophers into Kohlberg's types, based on their moral positions. Of course, Peter Singer is at the bottom, Kant at the top.

Dilemma 54
The rich man's dilemma

The problem of how to spend money when you are fabulously rich is a real one. George Soros, the billionaire financier famous for speculating against the British pound, certainly found it so. He only ever wanted to write a philosophy book: 'the real me is the contemplative one', he wistfully noted. All that lovely money was nothing but a burden for him. Soros's solution was to set up a network of trusts and foundations to give the money away: to the citizens of Sarajevo while their city was under siege by the Serbs; to the fledgling republics of the former Soviet Union; to philosophy postgraduates (in return for listening to his theories). But then, he was not really a philosopher. If he had been, the words of the economist Thorsten Veblen written at the very end of the nineteenth century might have given him pause for further thought. In a learned account, entitled 'The Theory of the Leisure Class', Veblen revealed that, for the very rich, it was never enough to merely *spend* money – money had to be not just used up but *wasted*.

Veblen's new term for that, *conspicuous consumption*, is what poor Mr Megabucks is struggling with. In simpler times, after all, people were impressed with conspicuously useless purchases like 800 pairs of gloves (the Emperor Charlemagne) or the English aristocrats wiping their bottoms with hand-cut parchment and serving their dogs dinner in silver bowls. But for today's rich, once yachts and private jets and islands have all been purchased, such little fripperies would not even use up the tea money, let alone rate an inch in the gossip columns.

Which is why burning it may be the sensible thing. And if someone says that's wrong, well, who shall cast the first stone, anyway? Many of us spend more on keeping our car in shiny paintwork and providing it with a snug garage to live in, than other families spend on survival. The UN calculated that Westerners spend five times more on *each cow* than most of the world's people have. (And that's not even to keep the cows happy!) Meanwhile, we keep ourselves busy making useless purchases but yet insisting that they *are* necessary.

All of which may seem perfectly obvious, but we might still like to think that *if* someone had too much money then they could easily work out a way of using the spare cash to help others, whether or not very few of them (us) even seem to be capable of realising that they are in that happy position.

Perhaps Megabucks *could* provide free musical instruments to schools, or set up academies for deprived talented musicians, or return his profits to his own company and employ a hundred more people. Or pay for the old records to be ground up into pieces and made into garden chairs – or *something*! Yet if Megabucks prefers to waste a bit of money, so do we all. If he treats himself to a flowery extravagance, then again, so do we all have some extravagances. If such things are banned (as some societies have indeed attempted to do) then the sum of human happiness seems to drop, not increase. If nothing else, the sight of rich people enjoying wealth may give others something to aspire to – *to envy*.

The conventional morality of sharing out wealth, to help those 'in need' or, if basic needs are already being met, simply to promote equality, is not as straightforward as some philosophers would have us believe. Peter Singer, for example, argues that it is both possible and necessary to calculate the maximisation of happiness. He says it is just laziness and weakness that results in people failing to follow through the results of that calculation. But, perversely, even on the most utilitarian system for maximising happiness, we may need a general rule that still allows people the freedom to spend their money on themselves in a selfish and irresponsible way. (Or in less obviously irresponsible ways, such as lavishing a fortune to keep a close relative alive – as Singer found himself doing, contrary to his own ethical system.)

John Stuart Mill wrote in the nineteenth century against the easy simplicities of welfarism. 'In all cases of helping, there are two consequences to be considered,' he says, 'the consequences of the assistance, and the consequences of relying on the assistance. The former are generally beneficial, but the latter, for the most part, injurious, so much so, in many cases, as greatly to outweigh the value of the benefits.' Like Mr Megabucks, Mill has a low opinion of the work of charities: 'In the first place, charity almost always does too much or too little; it lavishes bounty in one place and leaves people to starve in another.' Even so, 'the State has a duty to provide a safety net for those unable to fend for themselves. This is just a matter of logic.' How so? 'Since the State must necessarily provide subsistence for the criminal poor while undergoing punishment, not to do the same for the poor who have not offended is to give a premium on crime.'

So does Megabucks have any obligation to use his money to help others? Although for Mill, 'duty is a thing that may be exacted from a person, as one exacts a debt', there is no debt here. Mill insists no one has a moral right to our generosity or benevolence, because we are not morally bound to practise these virtues towards any given individual.

> If a moralist attempts to make out that mankind generally though not any given individual have a right to all the good we can do them, he at once by that thesis includes generosity and beneficence within the category of justice. He is obliged to say that our utmost exertions are due to our fellow creatures, thus assimilating them a debt.

Mill instead allows a general need to *respect* the value of all people, by increasing their autonomy and ensuring that there are ways and means for them to achieve their goals for themselves (which is why he is very popular with wishy-washy 'third way' social democrats today). But Mill, like most politicians, claims to have the interests of all at heart. There are those who would go a lot further and deny any social obligation. Friedrich Nietzsche of course derides what he sees as hand-wringing morality, saying that it is only part of an attempt by the weak and inferior to impose their will on the successful and strong. In his writings he instead celebrates the irresponsible individual, who far from feeling an obligation to the 'bungled and the botched', as he calls them, exploits, humiliates and enslaves the weak, taking 'joy in destruction', and has nothing but contempt for other's pain.

So perhaps the Megabucks flower festival isn't such a bad idea really.

Dilemma 55
The beauty trap

In the United States, more money is spent on so-called 'beauty' than on education or on social services. In countries like Brazil, the army of 'Avon' ladies selling make-up is larger and more numerous than the usual ugly assemblage of military types. 'Beauty' openly makes or breaks products via advertising, and decides success or failure in films, television newscasts, popular music and increasingly 'real world' activities such as politics, sport and business too.

Yet, in societies influenced by Christian ethics, there is great resistance to what has been called the 'manifest injustice' of beauty, and the way it appears to ride roughshod over more progressive notions of virtue and the dignity of the individual. Perhaps, instead, the values reflected in ranking people by appearance are genetic in origin, as Birdy mumbles, something to do with subconscious calculations of fecundity? Nancy Etcoff, in the pithily entitled *Survival of the Prettiest*, argues that 'beauty' is more than in the eye of the beholder – it is a cross-cultural reality. She illustrates this with a number of studies showing how people from different races and cultures nonetheless will rank other people unerringly in order of attractiveness.

The reason people do this is that they have been programmed by millennia of evolution to identify the most 'fertile' partner. Men look for women who have the 'hourglass' shape because this maximises the chance of the woman being old enough to bear children, but young enough not to be either pregnant already or breast-feeding (in which case she is not fertile.) Etcoff says 'Big John' is not a rotter at all. After all, women, equally, look for square-jawed, tall, dark and handsome men, who thereby illustrate not only their masculinity but also their ability to help bring up children.

Etcoff does not actually say 'the most beautiful of all women are blonde Americans', but she comes pretty close to it. She certainly does say 'gentlemen prefer blondes', and she does say men are programmed to prefer paler skin to darker skin. She says men do not like 'hairy' women, and without going into details here (!) she is again pointing at the 'Playboy' blonde and away from the classical brunette, let alone the African, Asian or South American racial types. Similarly, she insists that the lithe, muscular body is a natural preference – in the face of the evidence she herself cites (think of all those Renaissance 'picnic in Arcadia' scenes!) that for most places and most periods, women who were plump and evidently more leisured have been considered the more lovely to behold. Beauty is essential to social and political life, not only a kind of evolutionary mechanism, she says. To ignore its power, as the Plains are attempting to, is to order the tide itself to 'go back' and obey our will. Instead, 'How to live with beauty and bring it back into the realm of pleasure is a task for 21st century civilisation', she writes.

But perhaps the objection to Nancy Etcoff and perhaps the best hope for Birdy and Wolfie, is that being attractive is not the same thing as being beautiful. There is a degree of crossover obviously, but to treat the two terms as interchangeable is unscientific, not to say unphilosophical. Nancy Etcoff is not a philosopher, for her sins. She is a 'clinical psychologist', and perhaps her argument involves a little sleight-of-hand – she exchanges 'beauty' for 'attractive' and then substitutes for this 'most fertile-looking'.

The reason women wear make-up and are constantly dieting is that they have been taken in by a kind of cult religion – the cult being that of the body beautiful. And men are also victims, not only in their recent search for the 'elusive six-pack', but in that they are unable to relate to women as they really are. (Women who think they are really men, and men who think they are really women are at the extreme end of this 'trapped in their body' scale.) Just as Wolfie in the dilemma describes her discovery that she is unable to be herself, whilst imprisoned in her beautiful body.

Merleau-Ponty, in the *Primacy of Perception* (1976), places 'bodily self-image' firmly at the centre of his philosophy, arguing that the body 'forms our point of view on the world', and is 'the visible form of our intentions'. When this self-image goes awry the consequences are profound: anorexia, anxiety, stress, low self-esteem, sexual harassment, incest, even rape. Naomi Wolf, who has presumably influenced Mrs Plain, even in naming her children, describes, in *The Beauty Myth*, how historically several types of beauty have been esteemed, and how 'the qualities that a given period calls beautiful in a woman are merely symbols of the female behaviour that that period considers desirable'. We need to: 're-establish the roots of the mind in its body and in its world, going against the doctrines which treat perception as a simple result of the action of external thinking on our body'. So some support there for Wolfie and Birdy's manipulations.

But is there something underlying beauty that is timeless, that is fundamental? Of course, like the form of beauty described by the female philosopher Diotima to Socrates, it will not be peculiar to the human female, but a quality to be found in males, and indeed all of nature too. In the *Symposium*, Socrates, for once, is found to be on the receiving end of the philosophical cleverness, as Diotima demolishes his assumption that if you are not beautiful, then you must be ugly, demonstrating that it is possible sometimes to be 'inbetween'. She reminds Socrates that it is possible to believe something is true, and be correct in your belief, but still not really know it for sure. Such a person is neither ignorant nor knowledgeable, but something inbetween.

Dilemma 56
The good life

A middle way had to be found, decided Siddhartha, better known as Buddha (for it is he!). The 'middle way' is that of accepting the world as it is, but not striving-for-thingswithin-it. And Sid writes out his 'Four Noble Truths':

1   Life is full of suffering.
2   Suffering is caused by worry and craving for things.
3   When craving stops, suffering disappears.
4   You can defeat your cravings by following the 'Noble Eightfold Path'.

Of which last, enough to be said is that it is a sort of 'virtue ethics' programme, full of exhortations on 'right thinking', 'right speaking', 'right effort'. But at the end of it is a distinctive new prize, which gives Buddhism its mystical character: *Nirvana*. That is the state of mind in which men achieve perfect serenity, peace and insight.

For Buddhism is supposed to be less of a 'religion' than a practical philosophy of living. There are many parallels in the thinking to both Greek and Chinese philosophy, and, after all, these schools all flowered at approximately the same time in human history. Modern day Buddhists stress that the 'precepts' should be followed less as rules (with an external authority) and more as a kind of programme of mental exercises. Sangharakshita, one such, writes that morality is

> as much a matter of intelligence and insight as one of good intentions and good feelings . . . the moral life becomes a question of acting from what is best within us: acting from our deepest understanding and insight, our widest and most comprehensive love and compassion.

The worst thing about life, for Buddhists, otherwise, is that it is not even possible to look forward to its end. For Siddhartha warned that we are eternally reincarnated, going up and down the 'levels' of both human society and the animal kingdom, depending on the ethical value of our activities in the last life. Buddhists, like Pythagoras, see in the plight of the animals, the sufferings of their ancestors. Only if a man can achieve *Nirvana*, is he at last set free in the realm of truth and beauty.

Unfortunately, in line with the attitudes of the East, the highest things are reserved only for men. *Nirvana* is not for women. Although if a woman works very hard, she can hope to be reincarnated as a man at which point she can try again. One egalitarian concession is made to the female half of the human race: their suffering is considered to be the same sort of thing that men experience – a slightly improved status. And of course, animals obtain a *significantly* improved ethical status.

There are echoes in Buddhism of Plato's quest for the world of the 'Forms', of Socrates' intellectual contempt for the things of the material world, of Aristotle's advice on virtuous living, and indeed the entire life style of the Greek Stoics. Stoics such as Zeno and Chrysippus who considered virtue to be the only thing that is truly 'good' and worth having – everything else people might think they would like being morally irrelevant, and so should instead be regarded with complete indifference (*adiaphora*).

The Roman philosopher Marcus Aurelius (AD 121–80), who was a keen follower of the Stoics, summed up the approach like this:

> Everything that troubles you depends only on attitude. Change your attitude, and then, as a ship entering harbour, you shall find calm. All things become safe and steadying a tranquil bay protected from storm and tempest where you may rest in peace.

Whether Buddhism offers a practical insight into living is another matter.

Dilemmas 57–59
Flight 999 to Shangri-La

The 'cruise ship' scenario looks rather like the 'lifeboat' scenario described earlier but it is actually rather different as there is no intention to make political comparisons with the 'poor world'.

Nonetheless, it is similar in that the passengers might think that they are merely exercising their right of self-preservation rather than committing any particular act. Their sin is one of 'omission' – they did not help the weaker passenger, they did not 'sacrifice' themselves (shame on the captain!) *et cetera et cetera* – not of 'commission'.

As for the crashed plane, as with other supposedly 'rational' calculations in trolley dilemmas, we might want to dispute the inevitability of the injured boy dying. It involves a prediction about the future – how can anyone know that the rescuers won't turn up? Or even a friendly Yeti? The 'calculation' that the two others need to kill the boy, rather than (say) wait until he dies anyway and then eat him, is surely a rather fine one. But objections to eating crashed survivors rest more on an emotional, 'yuk' factor element in them than these careful calculations of utility. And verily emotional and aesthetic responses will change when you are dying in the snows of the Himalayas, or drowning in the seas of the Caribbean.

Dangerous nibbles

Why does it matter whether Sam is 'a bright, chirpy' bargirl? I don't suppose it does, but clearly it is harder for such people to take these decisions than it is for cold-blooded philosophers. They would say we can very easily save lots of innocent people by stopping someone (evidently very nasty) doing something that is in any case illegal. Going to the police (the barmaid might also reasonably expect) would NOT be so effective! On the other hand, in the 'real world' she might have got the whole situation wrong and it would be unfortunate to have made the young man very ill on the basis of a little misunderstanding. She could be forgiven for deciding instead to leave the nasty man to face a different sort of justice.

The terrorist

Actually, the most interesting thing about this scenario is not the ticking bomb which has become rather a worn-out 'ethical scenario', even as it becomes much more a plausible one, but the notion that someone could be considered a 'future terrorist'? If decent folk don't kill children today, that is not to say the prohibition has a long history. The slaughtering of children is explicitly recommended in the Bible for the enemies of the 'chosen people'. The Americans used the tactic in 'pacifying' the villages of Vietnam. But whatever the politics of it, at the time the children are surely innocent. To allow people to be injured or even killed on the basis of what our guess is about the future is really to remove all limits on human cruelty.

What the experts say (having brought a machine into the room to settle things)

There are hundreds, nay thousands of scenarios involving not just runaway trolleys and other railway paraphernalia, but crashed planes and sinking boats, terrorists and of course Nazis too. Although they are all supposed to be 'possible', they are not matters of very immediate concern, in a world full of 'real' dilemmas, and difficult decisions. However, at least according to their proponents (the would-be 'ethical experts' from the departments of philosophy, psychology and occasionally economics) they are supposed to be worth thinking about because they reveal something about how we 'solve' dilemmas – about how we think ethically.

But in another way, the responses are all a bit obvious. People don't like eating other people, especially not children. They will tend to 'turn a blind eye' to very serious bad effects, if they can be put at one remove. Philosophers do this too (as we saw in the earlier trolley dilemmas), inventing that special term for it, the 'Doctrine of Double Effect'. According to which, no one is responsible for bad consequences if their 'motives' are good. For example, if you drop a bomb as part of a war on 'terrorism' your motive is considered good, and the bad effect of killing bystanders is shunted like a naughty runaway trolley off on its own. But if someone plants a bomb in a block of flats, intending to kill the residents, say as part of a campaign to 'liberate' the country, the philosophers say they are very much responsible for the deaths. Even though, with perhaps only a little bit of pushing and prodding, the two situations can be seen as equivalent. The first bomb has only a very general aim of reducing 'terrorism', and the second bomb could be said to have the direct aim of 'liberation' with no particular victims in mind.

The US economists Daniel Kahneman and Amos Tversky similarly found that when people are asked to make 'difficult decisions', difficult for whatever reason, where relevant information is uncertain or perplexing, they fall back on quick rules of thumb instead, rules that frequently mislead them. The evergreen example of this regrettable public tendency is the 'gambler's fallacy' where the gambler expects to get a good hand in poker 'because' the last 100 hands have been awful. Mathematicians point out that paper cards neither know of nor care about previous rounds in the game, and so the probability of a good hand or a bad hand must be considered to stay the same.

Another aspect that seems to show that we are all fundamentally irrational is that in the words of the psychologist, Philip Johnson-Laird, 'people apply general and background knowledge to reasoning tasks'. This shameful finding, he says, was, in his academic terms, 'mildly embarrassing' to those who said we reason using formal rules of inference, because such rules should be blind to content. The well-known tendency of people to make judgements about each other, for example, in employment interviews, in milliseconds on the basis of anything but the official rules for assessment, is one of the consequences of this tendency. Another is the ability to get simple maths wrong.

For example, the Cruel Professors made people try this problem.

A bat and a ball together cost $1.10. The bat costs $1 more than the ball. How much does the ball cost?

Most people thought the ball cost 10 cents, but (already my brain is hurting!) in fact it doesn't.

What's more, people tend to be more interested in 'positives' than in 'negatives'. In money, they concentrate on possible profits and neglect possible losses; in medical ethics they focus on who will be saved and neglect who will perish, and even in mathematical problems, they focus on information about what 'is' the case, rather than adopt potentially more useful strategies involving information about what is known NOT to be the case.

Unveiling their latest technology, the brainscanners, the researchers found that people used the wrong part of their brains, 'the areas in the right hemispheres used for spatial representation', instead of the areas in the left-brain concerned with language processing.

Now look, is all this getting us anywhere?

Well, maybe not. The assumptions of the social scientists are a little like the assumptions of the Ancients, with their elevation of philosophical contemplation over feeling. For example, to say that because the problems caused by the runaway trolleys, the crashed planes and sinking ships and so forth *can* be treated as mathematical calculations does not mean that they *should* be. It is quite a leap to claim that 'illogical' thinking reveals a 'weakness' in the way people deal with issues, whereas it might really indicate that people think in a way that is more subtle and more sophisticated than the mathematical models can accommodate.

Nibbles, anyone?

Being democrats, the Democratian ministers have to weigh up the cost in terms of personal privacy, against the social gains from improved law enforcement and security, and indeed the smoother workings of the market. It's a perpetual dilemma: if the price of freedom is said to be vigilance, then it's also true that the price of vigilance is paid for in freedoms.

The philosopher who advanced surveillance as the tool for a well-run society was Jeremy Bentham, often called the 'father' of utilitarianism. Bentham it was who drew up detailed plans for the construction of circular buildings where the actions of many could be watched and controlled by just one – 'the Inspector'. Bentham thinks his invention is particularly suitable for prisoners, but the 'Panopticons', or 'Inspection Houses' are also, as the title page of Bentham's account makes it clear, applicable to any sort of establishment where people need to be kept 'under inspection'. Such as, he suggests:

> HOUSES OF INDUSTRY, WORK-HOUSES, POOR-HOUSES, LAZARETTOS, MANUFACTORIES, HOSPITALS, MAD-HOUSES, and SCHOOLS.

(And what is a Lazaretto anyway? Sounds fun – and saucy fun at that!)

The rewards from using 'the inspective force', as Bentham puts it, are far more general too:

> Morals reformed • health preserved • industry invigorated • instruction diffused • public burthens lightened • Economy seated, as it were, upon a rock • the Gordian knot of the Poor-Laws . . . not cut, but untied!

Bentham works it all out in enthusiastic detail.

> To save the troublesome exertion of voice that might otherwise be necessary, and to prevent one prisoner from knowing that the inspector was occupied by another prisoner at a distance, *a small tin tube* might reach from each cell to the *inspector's lodge*, passing across the area, and so in at the side of the correspondent window of the lodge. By means of this implement, *the slightest whisper* of the one might be heard by the other, especially if he had proper notice to apply his ear to the tube.

> *(Letter II)*

Discussions

The greater chance there is

> of a given person's being at a given time actually under inspection, the more strong will be the persuasion – the more intense, if I may say so, the feeling, he has of his being so. How little turn soever the greater number of persons so circumstanced may be supposed to have for calculation, some rough sort of calculation can scarcely, under such circumstances, avoid forcing itself upon the rudest mind. Experiment, venturing first upon slight transgressions, and so on, in proportion to success, upon more and more considerable ones, will not fail to teach him the difference between a loose inspection and a strict one.

(Letter V)

Clearly, given this sort of philosophical endorsement, the Cabinet should have no further qualms . . .

Dilemma 60
The Panopticon

Ever since George Orwell described the totalitarian despotism of Big Brother in his allegorical novel (of life under Stalin), *1984*, state surveillance has had a bit of a bad name. Prior to that, it was less controversial: Elizabeth I of England and Napoleon used it and were much admired for doing so. Now scarcely a month goes by without some new power being developed by governments and fiercely resisted by civil liberty groups. Even if today, two generations after Orwell was writing, the tide of opinion has begun to move back firmly in favour of state power and away from concern about private lives.

'Democratia' is not entirely a fictional scenario. In Britain, for example, there are 1.5 million closed circuit cameras, some visible, some hidden. That's one camera for every eight families. As for letter opening, an automated global system, *Echelon*, is operated already by the USA, Britain, Australasia and Canada to sift the billions of items of traffic on the internet for information. Under the *Regulation of Investigatory Powers Act*, each day's haul is also stored for future reference in special 'data warehouses' for years to come.

Mind you, there is one entirely fictional part. Our story says the watching works. At the turn of the millennium, Britain had more people (proportionately) in prison than say China, Saudi Arabia or Turkey – countries often considered laggards in respect for individual liberty, so clearly the deterrence effect has not really cut in yet.

Dilemma 61
The Panopticon: second section

A peculiar thing about privacy and surveillance is that what is very good for people in general is very bad for people in government. Governments hate people to watch *them*. Although access to government information is one of the great achievements of the USA Constitution, more generally openness and freedom of information are just 'goals' that unfortunately can't be achieved yet, sorry. (Come back maybe in thirty years.) Too many decisions need to be kept confidential, too many techniques, debates and arguments. Trials are best held 'in camera', government documents and witnesses shielded, maybe appearing as 'Mr X' behind a screen. Newspapers and television are kept on short leashes, overstepping the mark is punished routinely under various types of 'official secrets' laws. Now philosophers hate inconsistency, and this – the rights of the agents of the state to watch, but not be watched – seems a sharp example of it.

Dilemma 62
The Panopticon: third section

Bentham again:

> After applying the inspection principle, first to prisons, and then through mad-houses, bringing it down to hospitals, will the parental feeling endure my applying it at last to schools? Will the observation of its efficacy in preventing the irregular application of undue hardship even to the guilty, be sufficient to dispel the apprehension of its tendency to introduce tyranny into *the abodes of innocence and youth*?

> Applied to these, you will find it capable of two very distinguishable degrees of extension: It may be confined to the hours of study; or it may be made to fill the whole circle of time, including the hours of repose, and refreshment, and recreation.

> To the first of these applications the most cautious timidity, I think, could hardly fancy an objection: concerning the hours of study, there can, I think, be but one wish, that they should be employed in study. It is scarce necessary to

observe that gratings, bars, and bolts, and every circumstance from which an Inspection House can derive a terrific character, have nothing to do here. *All play, all chattering – in short, all distraction of every kind, is effectually banished* by the central and covered situation of the master, seconded by partitions or screens between the scholars, as slight as you please . . . whether the liberal spirit and energy of a free citizen would not be exchanged for the mechanical discipline of a soldier, or the austerity of a monk? – and whether the result of this high-wrought contrivance might not be constructing a set of machines under the similitude of men?

To give a satisfactory answer to all these queries, which are mighty fine, but do not any of them come home to the point, it would be necessary to recur at once to the end of education. Would happiness be most likely to be increased or diminished by this discipline? – Call them soldiers, call them monks, call them machines: so they were but happy ones, I should not care. Wars and storms are best to read of, but peace and calms are better to enjoy.

Dilemma 63
The Panopticon: final section

Bentham distinguishes firmly between that type of surveillance which he calls 'Dionysius' ear', which is ideally unknown to those being watched, and true 'inspection' where the nature of the activity demands publicity. Similarly, many closed circuit TV cameras proclaim their presence with notices, but the access of shops to your spending history will be more discreet. Bentham would certainly be hostile to privacy – it encourages shameful behaviour – of the sort favoured by Godless folk in fact. Because, of course, surveillance is only necessary in Godless societies – in a community of believers it is superfluous, as the Lord sees everything all the time, anyway. In any case, tidy theoretical distinctions – between government and private business, between collecting data and creating data – blur and eventually disappear, faced with the new realities of contemporary electronic surveillance.

Dilemma 64
Plutarch's uncongenial fare

Plutarch was a Greek priest at Delphi, and one of the few writers in the ancient world to advocate vegetarianism for reasons other than those involving the rather mystical notion of reincarnation. His essay 'On Eating Flesh' is considered a literary, if not so much a philosophical, classic. Plutarch challenges the 'flesh-eaters', who insist that nature has intended them to be predators, in that case to kill their meals for themselves – and eat the raw meat uncooked, with their bare hands. Perhaps eating like a wild beast is better than eating with a knife and fork. Dr Livingstone describes, in *Missionary Travels*, the effects of being killed by a 'big cat', which don't sound so uncivilised.

> it causes a kind of dreaminess, in which there was no sense of pain or feeling of terror. It was like what patients under chloroform describe who see all the operation but do not feel the knife. . . . This peculiar state is probably produced in all animals killed by carnivores; and, if so, is a merciful provision of our benevolent creator for lessening the pain of death.

Of course, we are all now used to the idea of humans eating meat, but that is not to say the activity is in evolutionary terms a very old one. One of the most famous anatomists, Baron Cuvier, wrote:

> The natural food of man, judging from his structure, appears to consist principally of the fruits, roots, and other succulent parts of vegetables. His hands afford every facility for gathering them; his short but moderately strong jaws on the other hand, and his canines being equal only in length to the other teeth, together with his tuberculated molars on the other, would scarcely permit him either to masticate herbage, or to devour flesh, were these condiments not previously prepared by cooking.

Indeed, it has been pointed out that horses have frequently been trained to eat meat, and sheep have been so accustomed to it as to refuse grass. 'Oh, my fellow men!' exclaimed Pythagoras:

> Do not defile your bodies with sinful foods. We have corn. We have apples bending down the branches with their weight, and grapes swelling on the vines. There are sweet flavoured herbs and vegetables which can be cooked and softened over the fire. Nor are you denied milk or thyme-scented honey. The earth affords you a lavish supply of riches, of innocent foods, and offers you banquets that involve no bloodshed or slaughter.

A dentist adds:

Proponents of the theory that humans should be classified as omnivores note that human beings do, in fact, possess a modified form of canine teeth. However, these so-called 'canine teeth' are much more prominent in animals that traditionally never eat flesh, such as the frugivores (gorillas, some chimpanzees and other primates) or camels, and male musk deer. It has also been noted that the shape, length and hardness of these so-called 'canine teeth' is quite different to those of true carnivorous animals.

Dilemma 65
The beast

The argument that it is 'natural' to eat meat justifies hunting. The Native Americans, the Inuit, Australian Aboriginals and other hunter-gatherer groups have traditionally lived more harmoniously with their environment than modern man achieves with urban civilisation.

Take the Australian native peoples, for example. For 40,000 years – that's longer than anyone else on Earth – they lived in a sophisticated harmony with nature. They hunted, for sure, but they were also custodians of the land, not owners let alone destroyers. The land was shared with the animals, the plants – and the spirits too. The land gave them their cultural identity, their collective stories, their myths, legends and their moral codes.

The swamp oaks were sustainably harvested for *kambio* – a kind of small mollusc. Paths were cleared along particularly important routes, and circular clearings maintained for important ceremonial occasions. Fire was used to clear areas for grass, to attract the likes of kangaroos for hunting. And fire breaks too were created, for example, to protect the *bunya bunya* tree. These trees, with their cones full of juicy nuts inside, were described by one nineteenth-century explorer as 'remarkable mountain brushes out of which the *bunya bunya* lift their heads, like the pillars of the blue vault of heaven'. The indigenous people revered them to such an extent that everyone born was assigned a tree. They became its guardians and the right to its fruit was matched also by a duty. If necessary, the guardian would be prepared to die to protect the tree.

When the white man arrived to log the forest, the sacred trees went too, and anyone who tried to protect them was beaten back by force of arms. The 'clearing' of the land – not only its trees and other plants, but animals too – went hand-in-hand with the 'clearing' of the native peoples. Although early settlers often treated the indigenous peoples with respect, learning their languages and recording their customs and folklore, later settlers destroyed both, forcing the remnants of the indigenous peoples either into reserves or to adopt European codes and ways of behaving. In fact, once driven off the land, people had no alternative, for the land was central to culture and consciousness. Aboriginals that were not killed in the battle for possession of land were lucky if they were then employed as labourers – and paid in alcohol and opium. The moral is: first, that throughout history the attitude towards nature and the production of food has very direct consequences for human rights, and, second, that to say eating meat is 'natural' is really a bit meaningless, if the act of eating meat is taken out of context.

And today's meat eaters, or more precisely meat producers, are the number one industrial polluters, contributing to half the water pollution in the USA, responsible for the poisoning of rivers all over the world and even the slow death of the seas as wetlands disappear and poisons accumulate. The water that goes into a large bull could float a destroyer. It takes 25 gallons of water to produce a pound of wheat, but 2,500 gallons to produce a pound of meat. Remarkably, the livestock population of the USA alone today consumes enough grain and soya beans to feed over five times the entire human population. American cows, pigs, chicken, sheep and so on, eat up 90 per cent of the country's wheat, 80 per cent of the corn, and 95 per cent of the oats. Less than half of the harvested agricultural acreage in the USA is for human consumption. Most of it is used to grow livestock feed. How natural is that?

Dilemma 66
Plutarch's response

(And George's last point is surely an argument for those who say it is inconsistent of people who eat sheep and cows to object to others who eat cats and dogs.)

In his second argument, Plutarch seems to link the slaughter of animals to capital punishment, observing that the first man put to death in Athens was 'the most degraded amongst knaves', but later the victims included the philosophers themselves. He concludes that killing animals is a bloodthirsty and savage practice which only inclines the mind towards more brutality.

An economic link between flesh-eating and war can also be found in Plato's *Republic*. Plato records a dialogue between Socrates and Glaucon in which Socrates extols the peace and happiness that come to people eating a vegetarian diet. The citizens, Socrates says, will feast upon barley meal and wheat flour, making 'noble cakes', as well as salt, olives, and cheese, 'for relish', all served on a mat of reeds. For dessert, some roasted myrtle berries or acorns, even boiled figs and roots. These are the foods of peace and good health: 'And with such a diet they may be expected to live in peace and health to a good old age, and bequeath a similar life to their children after them.'

The Yellow Emperor would agree, but Glaucon does not believe people will be satisfied with such fare. He insists that people will desire the 'ordinary conveniences of life', including animal flesh. He says such a diet might be all very well for a community made up entirely of philosophers, but scarcely appealing to anyone else. Socrates responds: 'I believe the true state to be the one we have described – the healthy state, as it were. But if it is your pleasure that we also contemplate a fevered state, there is nothing to hinder that.' Socrates then proceeds to stock the once ideal state with swineherds, huntsmen, and 'cattle in great number'. The dialogue continues:

SOCRATES: And there will be animals of many other kinds, if people eat them?
GLAUCON: Certainly.
SOCRATES: And living in this way we shall have much greater need of physicians than before?
GLAUCON: Much greater.
SOCRATES: And the country which was enough to support the original inhabitants will be too small now, and not enough?
GLAUCON: Quite true.
SOCRATES: Then a slice of our neighbour's land will be wanted by us for pasture and tillage, and they will want a slice of ours, if, like ourselves, they exceed the limit of necessity, and give themselves up to the unlimited accumulation of wealth?
GLAUCON: That, Socrates, will be inevitable.
SOCRATES: And so we shall go to war, Glaucon. Shall we not?

'Most certainly,' replies Glaucon. Critics of Plato who complain that his 'ideal' society is apparently also a militaristic or fascist state, with censorship and a rigidly controlled economy – not ideal at all – might be surprised to find Plato happy to agree with them: what they have failed to take into account is that the republic he describes is not his ideal one – it is merely the necessary result of Glaucon's (in the name of the citizens) demand for meat, a constitutional error (so to speak) which Socrates himself avoids.

Dilemma 67
St Paul's view

On the other hand, God also said (Genesis 1:29):

> Kill neither men, nor beasts, nor yet your food which goes into your mouth. For if you eat living food, the same will quicken you, but if you kill your food, the dead food will kill you also. For life comes only from life, and death comes always from death. For everything which kills your food, kills your bodies also. . . . And your bodies become what your foods are, even as your spirits, likewise, become what your thoughts are.

The early church fathers record that the Ebionites rejected Paul as both a false prophet and an apostate from Judaism. But Paul was clearly a very moral person. After all, he variously condemned wickedness, immorality, depravity, greed, envy, murder, quarrelling, deceit, malignity, gossip, slander, insolence, pride, drunkenness, carousing, debauchery and jealousy. Sensuality, magic arts, animosities, bad temper, and selfishness were not much approved of either. Not to forget dissension, envy and greediness, foul speech, anger, clamour, abusive language, malice and dishonesty. And then there's the scourges of materialism, conceit, avarice, boasting and treachery. In the eighteenth century, the English philosopher Lord Bolingbroke (1678–1751) saw two completely different moralities, if not creeds, in the New Testament, that of Jesus and that of Paul.

There is in fact a strong element of vegetarianism in the Bible. It is only after Eve defies God and eats the apple that killing animals for food is recorded in the Old Testament and Jesus appears to eat only fish, famously multiplying five barley loaves and two fish for over 5,000 people to eat. (And after all, many of the disciples *were* fishermen.)

Fish lovers will recall, however, that one Franciscan monk, the saintly Anthony of Padua (1195–1231), is said to have attracted a group of fish that came to hear him

272

preach. (It is clearly unethical to eat your congregation – even if they will go to heaven.) St Francis himself was once given a fish, and, on another occasion, a waterfowl to eat, but so moved was he by the natural beauty of the creatures that he chose to set them free. Given a wild pheasant to eat, he chose of course instead to keep it as a companion. 'Dearly beloved!' said Francis beginning a sermon after a period of illness, 'I have to confess to God and you that . . . I have eaten cakes made with lard.'

Dilemma 68
Chrysostom's warning

Perhaps Chrysostom would have been happier in the Bible Christian Church, a nineteenth-century movement teaching vegetarianism, the evils of alcohol and the virtues of compassion for animals. The church was founded in England in 1800, asking all its members to take vows of abstinence from meat and wine. One of its converts, Sylvester Graham (1794–1851), a Presbyterian minister, had apparently healed himself through a vegetarian diet and now advocated the use of unrefined, whole-wheat 'Graham' crackers. He also wrote lectures on sexual chastity, warning that spices and rich foods heighten sexual desire. (Which is a BAD thing.)

In Philosophy Heaven, however, no one was quite sure whose side Chrysostom was on anyway. The trouble with vegetarianism is that some of its adherents are too extreme. Is it *really* wrong to eat meat in all circumstances? What about those (maybe only a few left and those constantly under attack but still important counter-examples) native peoples living as a harmonious part of a general ecosystem? Is it always wrong for humans to catch and eat animals? If it's *that* bad, what about animals – should they be trained not to eat each other? What about protecting the little insects? What about the milk products, and eggs? If we grow any crops, how can we live with the knowledge that animals have lost their homes?

On the other hand, if eating animals is really as straightforward as Paul and some of the others would have, how can it be 'wrong' to kill animals for other reasons? In the first year of the new millennium, the British government slaughtered 6,000,000 healthy animals in a mass cull. The army had to be used as the job was too big for anyone else, although (predictably) the fox hunters volunteered to help. The bodies were piled up in quarries before being set alight. The stench travelled for miles. Afterwards, scientists like Professor Fred Brown went so far as to claim 'the barbaric conduct in Britain last year was a disgrace to humanity'! Similarly, the Australians offer farmers an annual mass cull of several million kangaroos.

As long as animal life is considered of so little moral significance that uncounted numbers of animals are slaughtered, be it for culinary reasons, for fun, for economic advantage or for 'research' data, it is hard to see how other rules protecting their welfare can ultimately be anything but conventional and arbitrary. Unless they're there solely to protect the moral health of human beings, not the animals, after all . . .

Dilemma 69
The Frog-King

Yes indeed. That is one of the basic principles of social life. It's important to keep promises, in the same way as you ought to obey the law. It's a sort of social contract.

Immanuel Kant (1724–1804, which is around the time of the most popular version of this story) felt so strongly about it, that he made it irrational (which for him was *very* bad) to break your promise – because you couldn't really have a situation where some people can break their promises, without thereby destroying the whole institution of promising. But frogs aren't people. Or so the naughty princess might reply. Then again, frogs don't usually talk and in so doing enter into arrangements of an obligatory nature either. Certainly our frog seems very rational, which in Kant's eyes should admit him into the kingdom of morally significant 'ends'. (As a matter of fact, Kant didn't seem all that keen to admit women into this hallowed world – considering them too often inclined to be 'irrational'. So the princess had better watch out.)

But there is also some textual support for the flippant attitude of the princess. Rumpelstiltskin, we learn, fulfilled his side of a bargain but perished – after showing that other great moral quality, compassion, and allowing the queen a kind of 'escape clause' in her contract with him. The miller's daughter, in the same story, breaks her side of the 'bargain' – and is handsomely rewarded.

David Hume (1711–76) cuts through all this by disputing the whole basis of promising, and demanding: '*Why* should we observe our promises?' Far from being 'rational', he thinks promises are totally irrational. Indeed, 'promises are, absolutely considered, an evil, and stand in opposition to the genuine and wholesome exercise of an intellectual nature'. This is because if you promise to do something which it is desirable should be done, then the promise is entirely superfluous. If you promise to do something that it is not desirable should be done, then it remains undesirable to do it, whether you promised or not. 'Nor can it with much cogency be alleged in this argument that promises may at least assume an empire over things indifferent. There is nothing which is truly indifferent.'

The naughty princess can tell herself as she runs away that, in Hume's terms, 'promises and compacts are in no sense the foundation of morality'.

The story continues

And therein lies one answer to the mystery of how the frog turned into the prince. Not so much magic as a matter of logic.

The overt message is that the King is evidently a Kantian, a promise must be kept. But there is a more subtle message too. It is only after the princess has defied the King and violently hurled her partner across the room that the miraculous transformation can take place, as the prince is released from the enchantment by the sudden passion of the princess.

A lot of people will know the story of 'The Frog Prince', even if they know one of the sanitised versions in which a kiss features, entirely inappropriately, as causing the happy transformation. And stories matter. 'Little Red Riding Hood' is a story warning against being fooled by people disguising their true nature; as is 'Hansel and Gretel', both typical 'fairy stories' full of (deep) folk imagery and values. Mary Shelley's *Frankenstein* has echoes of the moral tale of the Golem – a traditional Jewish story in Eastern Europe, in which a rabbi makes an artificial man out of clay that day by day, grows stronger, until soon the rabbi is unable to control him. 'Sleeping Beauty', 'Cinderella' and 'Beauty and the Beast' are other examples of transformative moral tales.

J. R. R. Tolkein, the scholarly author of *The Lord of the Rings*, and a strict Catholic who even ventured so far as to say that the Bible is a collection of fairy stories, wrote:

> about Fairy, that is *Faërie*, the realm or state in which fairies have their
> being. *Faërie* contains many things besides elves and frays, and besides

dwarfs, witches, trolls, giants, or dragons: it holds the seas, the sun, the moon, the sky; and the earth, and all the things that are in it: tree and bird, water and stone, wine and bread, and ourselves, mortal men, when we are enchanted.

For all the dryness of modern day academic writing, philosophy too has its quota of important stories, allegories and images: Plato's theory of the truth of ideas is also the story of the 'cavemen' watching shadows on the wall; his theory of motivation and of the 'trinity' of reason directing the will, which in turn controls the desires, is captured in the image of a 'carriage' with two horses and a driver. Most compelling of all of Zeno's Paradoxes is the famous story of how Achilles failed to catch up with the tortoise.

Recent philosophy offers a few tasty titbits. too. The tale of how Bertrand Russell's 'barber' became puzzled (as part of the paradox of set-theory) is one; the problem posed by the discovery of one black swan after the many white ones (for Popper's 'falsificationism') another, whilst political theory offers several imaginary stories to help explain the origins of social life and indeed of right and wrong.

Indeed, a whole new branch of philosophy, narrative theory, has appeared. In *After Virtue* (1981), the dry Alasdair MacIntyre claims the West has become morally lost because it has no 'founding stories' any more, and so we cannot place our lives in a meaningful, temporal context. As individuals, as much as for whole communities and cultures, we need our memory of what we were, what we are trying to do at the moment, and what we hope to one day become.

> Man is in his actions and practice, as well as in his fictions, essentially a story telling animal . . . I can only answer the question 'What am I to do' if I can answer the prior question 'Of what stories do I find myself a part?'

But these are fairy stories, and they have their own strengths and weaknesses. Although the term 'fairy tale' may come from the French – *conte de fées*, coined in the seventeenth century for the short stories that were then very fashionable amongst adults – and although the style was always of stories for children, in fact they are really subtle works of propaganda covering the whole range of issues and life. But this one is rather nice, when you consider that it may really be a subtle attack on the practice of arranged marriages current then.

'The Juniper Tree' is one of the most powerful of all fairy tales. It is widespread across European folklore; some say there are several hundred versions of it. It inspired a verse in Faust, and more than a few in J. R. R. Tolkein. It is especially rich in life experiences: it starts with a 'stirring tableau' of death bringing forth life, before moving through – in swift succession – child abuse, murder and savage revenge. The Grimms wrote in the introduction to *Nursery and Household Tales* that whilst folk tales were not there to convey lessons, nevertheless: 'a moral grows out of them, just as good fruit develops from healthy blossoms without help from man'. And fairy tales are moral magnets, as Maria Tatar has put it, picking up bits and pieces of value systems, if never the whole thing.

Charles Dickens thought they were a very powerful tool for conveying values:

> It would be hard to estimate the amount of gentleness and mercy that has made its way among us through these slight channels. Forbearance, courtesy, consideration for the poor and aged, kind treatment of animals, the love of nature, abhorrence of tyranny and brute force – many such good things have been first nourished in the child's heart by this powerful aid.

The contemporary American philosopher Martha Nussbaum looked at the emotional force of narratives in her book, *Love's Knowledge*, and concluded that the stories are actually quite rational. Disappointment, hate, grief, gratitude – occasionally even love – can all be rational, reasonable responses to complex situations such as require decisions in life. Why do we feel anger? Because we believe someone has done something wrong – either to us or to someone we care about. There is some sort of lurking logic, even if on examination it falls apart. Why does some behaviour disgust us? Or seem noble, or somehow just? Even when the first behaviour may fit some supposed moral rule, and the latter flout it? These kinds of emotional response reveal our values and access to our inner selves. They are important, and the way to access them is through stories – the structures of emotion.

Nussbaum believes there was a time when philosophers understood the value of narrative. Even Aristotle believed that watching a story or drama unfold has many hidden ethical aspects, and that poetry was more philosophical than the study of facts, being 'concerned with universal truths'. There are lessons in stories about the way to live, about virtue, and life itself in general. There are messages about emotions and the importance of the appropriate feelings at the appropriate time. But Western philosophy in general has pursued a resolutely unemotional, ostensibly 'higher' path of dispassionate reason.

Another branch

Why a millstone, for goodness sake? But it is a traditional image of retribution – even there in the Bible as part of a warning against bringing children into sin. And the story is very much child-centred. It is not just in the ridiculous subterfuge adopted by the evil stepmum, or even the naivety of the father, but in the plot outline. Marilena and her brother both suffer and the children carry out the important acts following the stepmother's evil one. ('Hansel and Gretel', 'Snow White' and 'Cinderella' tell a similar story too.) And we are firmly on the side of the children against the adults, who are shown, even in the case of the father, to be just ever so slightly foolish. Not to mention the bizarre approval of the black puddings, which would no doubt make more sense to the Callatians or even the Hairlanders (of Dilemma 73).

Some have said the story is a metaphor for the reorientation of children from the omnipresent, all-controlling mother to the distant, remote father figure, but, Freudian or not, there is a powerful sense of poetic justice at work in the piece. The evil of the stepmum (they always get these roles in fairy tales) is fittingly undone, with the innocent saved, and the guilty punished. The symmetry of birth and death is repeated at the end.

Dilemma 71
A cautionary tale

Well certainly not for just playing with matches, anyway.

The Duchess of Wonderland observes that 'everything has got a moral – if only you can find it'. George Cruickshank, Dicken's illustrator, went through the fairy tale books and found, to his horror, that the moral had somehow inadvertently been left out, and so introduced a few himself. He enthusiastically rewrote the fairy tales to make them much more moral – out went 'vulgarity', as he reported to a dismayed Dickens, in came 'temperance truths'. At Cinderella's wedding, for example, a well-intentioned plan to have fountains of wine in every square to celebrate is scrapped at royal insistence, in the interests of avoiding 'ill health, misery and crime'. A great bonfire of all the wine and spirits is made instead. In the story of the naughty girl who played with matches there is little danger of losing the moral: it is pretty much thrust upon us not as a true fairy tale, just a cautionary tale.

In fact, most fairy tales that have survived are now 'cautionary tales'. Losing some of the depth, the charm and indeed the power of the originals in the process. But a lot of ethical baggage is added on. This story conveys not only the apparently uncontroversial message about not 'playing with matches', but also the general one about not disobeying your parents. (And that means your social superiors too.)

So Pauline's error, that here requires her to pay the ultimate penalty, is not so much the literal 'playing with fire' as the metaphorical 'playing with fire' of disobeying authority. Like 'the little fish that would not do as it were bid' (and gets caught by the fisherman), of another rhyme, she should have listened to her mother. In the world of the cautionary tale, disobedience has two roots: curiosity and stubbornness. These are both bad traits

– indeed, vices. Pauline exhibits both. Conversely, the virtues are the 'three h's' – hard work, honesty, and humility.

In cautionary tales, children often die for their sins, but then so do the villains. Around the time these tales were most popular, death was also a matter for public policy, with Calvin advocating capital punishment for (literally) naughty children, and New England even implementing the policy for some unfortunates. And, of course, many children were imprisoned or even executed at this time for more conventional misdeeds, such as stealing apples and the like. Those not in prison might be taken to the prison yard to see 'real criminals' being executed.

So there is a harsh reality to the mock world of the rhymes – perhaps, the reality may be what the parents wanted to warn their children of so vigorously. Ironically, the sheer viciousness of the tales makes them less threatening – the range is from the boy who sucks his thumbs (they are cut off) to the 'girl who stood on the loaf'. (She is covered in snakes, flies and slime.)

The tales also reflect another unedifying social reality. In them, it is not only the children who must obey, it is the daughters and wives. Many tales depict the range of fates available to women of independent outlook – and they are all bad. Just as independence is a characteristic to be ground out of the child, so for the women in fairy tales. There is no command that is too outrageous for the moral onus to be on the young princess, wife or daughter obeying. Which in a way brings us back to the story of the frog, and so, perhaps, time for bed.

Dilemma 72
The Illegals: a modern fairy tale

In *real-politik* politics, the bottom line is that people who die outside your country's territory are not your responsibility. (Even if they are only outside it because you have prevented them entering.) And then there is the other type of 'relativism', which basically is the belief that other people are so different from us that different standards apply and it really doesn't matter much what happens to them anyway. But in our Biggles-type scenario (and yes, it *is* a little like a certain very English children's book hero) something philosophers like those nasty post-modernists have raised as a general issue for all ethical stories is made pretty blatant. What *are* the sort of 'hidden' rules and assumptions governing the 'narrative'? What alternative viewpoints are excluded? With refugee tales, there are the alternative stories of the 'migrants' with their alien ways trying to trick and lie their way in, contrasted irreconcilably with the tales of innocent people fleeing persecution and enduring much hardship finally to arrive where they find sanctuary.

Actually, Biggles stories themselves are very moral, at least in a sort of 'white man's burden', kind of way. Our heroes are scrupulously fair towards the stereotype foreigners. These fall into two categories: the majority are the harmless if obviously rather simple 'natives', as contrasted with the small but dangerous minority of 'treacherous scoundrels'. At the end of each story, these last are of course – thank goodness! – eventually despatched. But not so much for being foreign, that is just incidental, as for being morally deficient.

In a typical incident (*The Case of the Remarkable Perfume*), Biggles hears that a 'half-caste' employed by an English explorer, Mr Cotter, in search of rare orchids, has tried to rush back to the 'find' and grab them for himself. Asked to intervene, Biggles ruminates: 'For moral reasons alone the rascal shouldn't be allowed to get away with it. I'm all against rogues prospering.' His boss, the Air Commodore, elaborates for the reader's benefit on the vexed issue of intellectual property rights:

'After all, this fellow Ramon was employed by Mr Cotter. He broke his contract. The treacherous scoundrel has stolen something, and has sold it. In my opinion, stealing the fruits of the expedition makes him just as much a thief as if he had made off with a piece of equipment.'

Biggles intervenes to ensure the profits from the orchids do not go to the natives (in the form of the rascally Ramon), but abroad to the English. Such stories illustrate why much of the world considers Western ethics to be just another form of imperialism, if not actually racism.

But back to the 'illegal boats'. How realistic is our dilemma? During the 1970s, many people were fleeing parts of Southeast Asia, often in extremely unseaworthy craft, and merchant shipping initially picked them up following the usual law of the sea about rescuing people. But they soon found it impossible to disembark the passengers, despite the centuries old convention that ships be allowed to offload those rescued at the next port of call. As a result, ships changed their routes to avoid being near the refugee ships. No one knows how many people drowned.

In the 1980s, a British ship that rescued 900 boat people *en route* to Hong Kong was refused permission to offload them by Mrs Thatcher, causing an uproar in the British Parliament. Perhaps the most notorious case of unwanted 'boat people' of all was that of the Jewish refugees who fled on the *SS St Louis* from Nazi Germany in 1938. Arriving at Havana, the US coastguard drove them away, back to Britain, who followed suit, sending them on to Belgium, and in due course, to the concentration camps.

In our tale, we start by assuming, without being really conscious of it, that Wiggles is going to 'do the right thing' (after all, the central characters of tales should be heroes!) and then are torn by the increasingly outrageous requirements of the text between this and our own judgement. Unfortunately, in 'real life', as it were, the official narrative is less often challenged. A story which assumes asylum seekers are invaders, cheats, drug-dealers, criminals, terrorists – anyway, too many of them – to be locked up in prison camps or left to drown in the seas, finds many uncritical listeners who make no comparison with any underlying set of principles. Faced with some ill-defined but politically powerful 'threat' from asylum seekers, or from the homeless or the mad, Western countries' generosity and tolerance has not grown in proportion to their capacities and wealth, perhaps the reverse.

The language of the tale is important too, just as the language of our everyday tales is. If the author of the Biggles stories, 'Captain' W. E. Johns, uses terms like 'merchants', 'half-castes' and 'scoundrels' with cheerful indifference to the implications concealed within them, the language of the Australian government in telling its version of the refugee tale is much more calculated, and of course much more prejudicial. Refugee boats boarded at gunpoint and the terrified families being incarcerated for years in prison camps become dashing tales of coastal patrols apprehending 'SIEVs' (without an 'e', but just as leaky) or 'Suspected Illegal Entry Vehicles'. If a SIEV is boarded (but not by 'Mad Harry'), then there's the 'Pacific Solution', of placing the 'queue jumpers' in 'secure centres'. Over it all is the substituting for the sympathetic-sounding term *refugees* the coldly prejudicial jargon 'illegals'.

Humpty Dumpty's point on this – as recorded by Lewis Carroll (and indeed cited in many heavyweight articles on semantics) rings true. Suggests Humpty, with language, it is the powerful who dictate meanings. 'There's glory for you!' Humpty observes in *Through the Looking-Glass*, with Alice failing to understand – as well she might.

Discussions

'I don't know what you mean by "glory,"' Alice said. Humpty Dumpty smiled contemptuously. 'Of course you don't – 'till I tell you. I meant "there's a nice knock-down argument for you!"' 'But "glory" doesn't mean "a nice knock-down argument,"' Alice objected. 'When I use a word,' Humpty Dumpty said in rather a scornful tone, 'it means just what I choose it to mean – neither more nor less.' 'The question is,' said Alice, 'whether you can make words mean so many different things.' 'The question is,' said Humpty Dumpty, 'which is to be master – that's all.'[6]

Dilemma 73
The Baldies of Hairland

The reader may say such a society seems unlikely. Why would anyone want to distinguish between people on the basis of irrelevant, trivial physical differences? But once put that way, it no longer seems so implausible. Human societies revolve around such distinctions, and where the physical differences are not clear, religious or other social criteria will be used. In modern day Japan, for example, 3 million

[6] The contemporary French philosopher Jacques Derrida is very like Humpty but says 'paleonomy' instead. This is where he takes an 'old' word and 'puts a new meaning on it'.

Burakumin are systematically discriminated against, in the manner of the 'Baldies'. *Burakumin* are supposedly descendants of people who worked in 'unclean' professions, such as cobblers or butchers. In 1975, light was briefly shed on the practice when the high-tech *zaibatsus* that make up Japan's industrial base admitted to using *buraku chimel sokan* – lists of *Burakumin* names and geographical districts to weed out possible applicants. What defines these inferior people? Not racial, religious, or physical identifiers – just traditions.

But the question here is not to challenge the logical basis of the Hairlandic culture – does anyone challenge the *logical basis* for the treatment of women in most of the world, so often considered not worth educating or training – or the persecution of racially defined minorities in so many lands? Not the relativists, anyway. One of the standard-bearers (if that's not a contradiction in terms) for whom is Ruth Benedict (1857–1948), an anthropologist who worked amongst the Northwest Coast American Indians. Benedict wrote an influential paper describing how for these people it was customary to view a natural death in the tribe as an affront requiring a 'war-party'. On one occasion, the chief of one tribe lost both his sister and her daughter in a drowning accident, and so a group from the tribe was assembled and set out looking for Indians from any other tribe to kill. Coming soon upon seven men and two children, by good fortune, as it were, asleep – they killed them. On returning home, all the tribespeople joined in the celebration.

In Western ethics, if not politics, we usually make the bold assumption that all people are of equal value, irrespective of physical attributes. So how then to explain the acceptance of so much social policy in other lands that goes contrary to this supposedly universal value?

The philosophical underpinning for this is the doctrine of relativism. Which says, in effect, that what is right for us, is not necessarily right for everyone else. In fact, it suggests it would be quite 'inappropriate' to try to impose one culture's way of doing things on another. This is partly a response to 'cultural imperialism', where groups attempt to impose their own values and customs, in ignorance of and contempt for other societies. Jean-Jacques Rousseau's story of the 'noble savage', who runs away leaving the foolish white sailor standing helpless after offering to help carry his bag of sugar, was also a reaction against this ethnocentricity.

Certainly rules and social values vary. Anthropologists remember that the Kaffir people were shocked when they were told that in some countries people formed sexual partnerships – even married for goodness sake – out of love! The behaviour, the Kaffir mocked, 'of a cat'. Today, in America, Massachusetts law still states that dogs must have their hind legs tied together in April (to stop misbehaviour), and that it is illegal to go to bed without a bath. Famously, in the Netherlands it is okay to smoke dope in cafés. While in parts of Africa, girls may be forced to undergo dangerous and painful circumcision. In many parts of the Middle East it is normal to prevent women going in many public buildings, driving cars or working in most jobs. Yes, yes, yes, the reader will say, so what? So in many respects, in most of the world, custom really is king. The relativists are right. *Bon appetit!*

Dilemma 74
The Baldies of Hairland II

In ethics, there are really only two possible positions. Either you think something is right, or it's wrong, or you don't, or you're not sure. Or both. Or neither, or a bit of both or a bit of neither. Call it eight main positions. Of course, philosophers have delighted in creating extra terms, so that there are many subtly different types of each position. For example, there are those who definitely believe there is no difference between 'right and wrong', who are called 'moral nihilists', although they may as well be lumped together with moral 'subjectivists', who say that calling things 'good' is only announcing that you like them, and that therefore a 'moral viewpoint is valid only for the person who holds it' – which is really no sort of morality at all.

That already may be enough for another couple of main positions. But, similar to the subjectivists, are the ethical relativists who say that moral viewpoints are 'valid' between groups of individuals at particular times and places, but never universally, nor for all time. This more specific 'cultural relativism' is the point being fought over in the example of Hairland.

Mind you, if we thought the same things can be right in some *circumstances* and wrong in others, then we might still be 'moral absolutists' albeit rather more sophisticated ones. What is right for one person may not be right for another living in a different culture because their situation is different.

Then there are those (sometimes called moral sceptics) who think there may be moral truths, but that no one knows them, or those who think there are differences between right and wrong but you can only tell *intuitively*. Those, like Plato, who think that some things are really right and some are definitely wrong, are sometimes subdivided into two groups: those who think that it is not so much particular actions but the values underlying the actions that have moral significance, and those who think that there is one set of rules, a moral code, which everyone can be expected to obey. The former are sometimes called 'soft universalists' by philosophers, and the latter 'hard universalists' or 'moral absolutists'. Religious codes are all examples of the latter. They have to be, it makes no sense to believe them otherwise, even if today many religions 'allow' non-believers to break the code, preferably discreetly, perhaps on the grounds that they are all going to hell anyway.

Of course, we must also distinguish between normative and descriptive theories, and intrinsic and instrumental values and prescriptivists, distributivists . . . But that's plenty of positions already for the Relatavian delegates to entertain their hosts with . . .

Dilemma 75
Just desserts

One of the most celebrated examples of the variety of moral perspectives, goes back to the Greek philosopher Herodotus (*c*.484–431 BC) who related the curious tale of King Darius and an Indian tribe called the Callatians. Darius had heard that some peoples felt it right and proper to eat their fathers after they died. Intrigued, and conducting an early piece of anthropological 'action' research (filial piety was particularly important to the Greeks), Darius sent a messenger to the Callatians to enquire how much it would take to persuade them to instead burn their dead, as was the Greek custom. At the same time, he asked a Greek village if they would instead adopt the Callatian method of disposing the recently demised.

Herodotus records that both groups were shocked and would not for a moment countenance such changes, insisting that their policy was the only possible one. The moral? That 'custom is king', as Ruth Benedict 'rediscovered' so many centuries later. Neither Herodotus nor Benedict actually proved that right and wrong were, so to speak, a moveable feast, that is interchangeable. What they found was that people's opinions of right and wrong vary, and that indeed was

285

often only as circumstances varied. In any case, it might be said that the only moral issue to be found in dealing with the dead is that it should be done respectfully, as they would want to be treated. Of course, if any of the Callatians that Darius invited to Greece ended up marrying and living there, then there might be some tricky decisions later, when someone dies.

Some peculiar tales of Herodotus (c.484–431 BC)

One peculiar custom related by Herodotus in his famous *Histories* is that of the Persians. These are the people who believe it best to 'deliberate upon affairs of weight when drunk' before, bizarrely, reconsidering the decision the next morning when sober (albeit with a headache). If it still seems like a good idea, they then act upon it. 'Sometimes, however, they are sober at their first deliberation, but in this case they always reconsider the matter under the influence of wine', Herodotus adds (Book I, 133).

Another Persian credo provides a very useful measure of nations and other peoples: 'the further they are removed, the less the esteem in which they hold them'. Like the English (who Herodotus luckily never visited), 'the reason is, that they look upon themselves as very greatly superior in all respects to the rest of mankind' (Book I, 133). At least the Persians, like so many devout Immanuel Kants, believed that the 'most disgraceful thing in the world' was to tell a lie, and 'the next worst, to owe a debt: because, among other reasons, the debtor is obliged to tell lies' (Book I, 139).

Babylonian customs reflected a more sociable nature. Once in her life, every Babylonian woman was obliged to go to the temple of Aphrodite, and there to sit and wait patiently until 'released by a stranger' (a man), who did this by tossing a silver coin into her lap, beckoning and taking her with him 'beyond the holy ground' for the activity associated with Aphrodite. The woman had to accept the first man and reject no one. 'Such of the women who are tall and beautiful are soon released, but others who are ugly have to stay a long time until they can fulfil the law. Some have waited three or four years in the temple', Herodotus would relate, no doubt to much male merriment (Book II, 199).

As the Babylonians had no physicians, when a man became ill, they laid him in the public square, 'and the passers-by come up to him, and if they have ever had his disease themselves or have known any one who has suffered from it, they give him advice'. Suffering doubly, as it were, in this way, those capable of recovery doubtless would do so quickly and return to work (Book II, 197).

Still sociable, but perhaps less contemporary, were the customs of the Massagatae, the famous tribe who held very special suppers for old people. Herodotus recounts their ways:

> when a man grows very old, all his kinfolk collect together and offer him up in sacrifice; offering at the same time some cattle also. After the sacrifice they boil the flesh and feast on it and those who end their days thus are reckoned the happiest.

Other of their customs are harder for us to swallow, indeed quite repugnant . . . 'If a man dies of disease they do not eat him but bury him in the ground, bewailing his ill fortune' (Book II, 216).

At least the Padaeans, a wandering tribe, were more tolerant of the frail. Perhaps because they actually lived off raw flesh, they also ate the sick. If one of their number should fall ill, far from forcing them to listen to home remedies all day, they would speedily put the patient to death, because, they considered, the 'flesh would be spoilt for them if he pined and wasted away'. At the same time conscious of etiquette, the Padaean men ate the males, and the women the females (Book II, 99).

The Scythians unfortunately had a number of bloodthirsty customs too grisly to detail anywhere other than a Penny Dreadful, and certainly not here in a serious work of philosophy. So perhaps we can only say that they favoured scalping and skinning all those they killed in battle, and using their bodies for ingenious and devious purposes. For instance, the skulls – 'not indeed of all, but of those they most detested' might be used for a drinking vessel, whilst a number of scalps sewn together made a special cloak (Book IV, 64 and 65).

The Tauri had other uses for their victims' skulls. Anyone unlucky enough to fall into their hands would have their head cut off, and this would then be proudly carried home, fixed it up on a tall pole, 'most commonly over the chimney'. Far from being rather bad *feng shui* as we might say today, the reason was, Herodotus goes on helpfully, 'in order that the whole house may be under their protection' (Book IV, 103).

Last but not least, to the Trausi of Thracia and their very sensible approach to marking the arrival of a new baby. 'When a child is born', Herodotus offers,

> all its kindred sit round about it in a circle and weep for the woes it will have to undergo now that it is come into the world; making mention of every ill that falls to the lot of humankind. When, on the other hand, a man has died, they bury him with laughter and rejoicings.

(Book V, 4)

From the translation of *Herodotus' Histories* by George Rawlinson, Wordsworth edition 1996

Dilemma 76
Another problem with the relatives

That's a bit of a tricky question, really. Some readers, not being Relatavians, may find this dilemma hard to follow. A bit 'topsy-turvy' even. They may think there must be some 'universal' right to life which the Jones have violated. But if so, they will have to be prepared to face the charge of imposing their own cultural values. For in at least twenty countries of the world, the practice of 'honour killings' is very much the 'norm', and very much alive and well. At the turn of the millennium, for example, even a vaguely termed UN resolution regretting the continuing toll – 2,000 recorded deaths in Pakistan, Yemen, Egypt, Lebanon, the Palestinian territories – just the tip of the iceberg – found twenty member states not prepared to sign up.

A proposal to increase the civil penalties in Jordan (where half of all 'homicides' are in the name of family honour) was resoundingly defeated by a parliament furious at being 'lectured by the USA'. And their display of independence comes cheap, as the West is quite happy to turn a tolerant eye to the practice, to keep the trade-flows of cash and goods going (preferring instead to concentrate on human rights issues that just happen to involve conflict with its political enemies).

Some of the countries do indeed lay claim to higher moral ground, and say their stand on this matter is ultimately one 'of conscience'. They say theirs is a tradition of Islam, and refer to a version of 'Sharia law' which compels those couples caught 'in the act' of committing adultery to be publicly killed. But grim though the code is, it does not authorise killing for single people conducting 'unauthorised' relationships, as in the example, and as in many of the so-called 'honour killings'. Nor does it sanction killing for victims of rape, as many other cases involve, usually by members of the same family. It stipulates 'eighty lashes' instead.

The practice of 'honour killing' really comes from the older 'moral' code of Hammurabi* – the Assyrian laws of 1200 BC which make daughters, but not sons, the property of the family. This is a very old but very prevalent cultural attitude. The Christian church marriage ceremony physically depicts the transfer of 'ownership' from the father to the husband, as the bride's hand is released by the one and taken up by the other. (Lévi-Strauss in the *Elementary Structures of Kinship* points out that the incest taboo, which Freud sees as the key to the development of social life, also exists primarily as part of a system where the woman is kept 'pure' ready to be given away. Once the taboo is violated, the woman is no longer suitable for being given away, hence the response of the 'honour killing'.)

The status of women, of course, is the not-so-hidden agenda here: not religion, or traditional values. Rather it's about the power assumed by male over female, and if the positions were reversed, as in the dilemma, perhaps the issue would be rather higher up the moral agenda.

Dilemma 77
The good fight

Britain and the USA bombed small towns in Germany during the final stages of the Second World War. The picture shows the devastation that 'conventional' warfare had become capable of.

These towns were not military bases, and were known not to be. Instead, as documents recently released in Britain show, the criteria were that the towns:

- should be easy for the bombers to locate, and
- should burn easily.

* The Law of Hammurabi, that wise king, for example, offers (rules 209 and 210) that if a man's daughter is struck by another man such that she miscarries, the man must pay ten shekels of silver in compensation for the lost baby. If additionally the woman dies, then the man must be punished more severely. *His daughter* must be 'put to death'.

Dresden was completely razed in February 1945: an estimated 30,000 people died. These were almost entirely civilians, many of whom had only just arrived there after fleeing the advancing Russian armies. An American Air Force general commenting on the bombing raids noted that they would not shorten the war, but he hoped rather that the results would 'be passed on from father to son, thence to grandson, [so] that a deterrent for the initiation of future wars will definitely result'. Which is as clear a 'utilitarian' position as you could hope to get, justifying the killing of large numbers of civilians now to save lives in the future . . . maybe.

More definitely, the German and Japanese people, taken as a whole, presented a very real threat to the British and Allied bombers. It was 'total war', and these raids were believed to undermine the morale of the enemy. The approach came to its most dreadful conclusion with the US bombing of Hiroshima and Nagasaki. Again, these were targets selected for their ease and convenience, selected to send a message to the wider population about the inadvisability of aggression. Again, men, women and children perished in their thousands, whether or not they had any support for or say in their country's policies.

The bombing of civilians (Cambodia, Vietnam, Colombia, the Philippines, East Timor, Chechnya, and Palestine to name just a few) continues to be seen not as a 'war crime' but a *legitimate* part of military operations. The victims are reduced to being 'collateral damage'. Rebel forces themselves target civilians: in Ireland, Spain, Italy, Germany, Sri Lanka, the Philippines, Israel – the list goes on.

Cyprian, Bishop of Carthage, denounced the hypocrisy of war, writing:

> The whole earth is drenched in adversaries' blood, and if murder is committed, privately it is a crime, but if it happens with State authority, courage is the name for it: not the goodness of the cause, but the greatness of the cruelty makes the abominations blameless.

Dilemma 78
Just some wars

Certainly, philosophers like to call upon the warriors in their own preferred activity – to defend and uphold human rights. (Even if they are not very clear at identifying individual cases which are actually suitable.) Rights like the ones President Roosevelt called at the end of the Second World War the Four Freedoms: Freedom from Want, Freedom from Fear, Freedom of Speech, Freedom of Religion. The carnage of the Second World War, like the one before it, was fought by the Allies 'to preserve human rights and justice in their own lands as well as other lands'.

That's why, at the Yalta Conference, rather than pledge to not have any more wars, the Allies promised to set up a 'United Nations' Organisation prepared to 'take effective collective measures for the prevention and removal of threats to the peace and for the suppression of acts of aggression or other breaches of the peace'. The UN would wage 'just' wars.

Yet, in one of Plato's dialogues, Socrates convinces Cephalus that it is impossible that harming other people can also be the act of the 'just'. But Socrates was not typical. Most of the Ancients thought that – at the very least – wars provided the forum for developing manly virtues such as 'courage'. Hegel too favoured war in itself as providing timely reminders of the 'transitory nature' of human existence.

As to manly virtues and warriors, Erasmus wrote of them: 'Military idiots, thick-headed lords . . . not even human except in appearance'. As to the ethics of those who dispatch the armies – war merely served rulers as a mask behind which they could carry out actions that would otherwise be unthinkable – not only to the enemy – but to their own people.

The writer Bruce Chatwin recalls a 'Vietnam vet' who defines the professional soldier as the man who for thirty years is employed to kill other men. And after that? 'He prunes the roses'. He notes that the Middle English *wargus*, meaning 'stranger', is also the word for 'wolf', and contains the implication that both are dangerous beasts to be driven out – or killed. And so war propaganda aims to degrade the enemy into something 'bestial, infidel or cancerous'. Or alternatively, to change its own side into beasts.

Homer, after all, distinguishes two quite different kinds of killing behaviour. One, which Odysseus shows in the story of the *Iliad* during the execution of the suitors, is cold-blooded – this the Greeks called *menos*. The other, though, is a wolfish rage, a frenzy of blood-fuelled slaughter, a rage such as Hector experiences on the battlefield. To be in the throes of *lysa* is to be no longer human, and no longer bound by any rules.

Likewise, in one of his most powerful passages, Sigmund Freud describes human nature rather cruelly:

> Men are not gentle, friendly creatures wishing for love, who simply defend themselves if they are attacked, but that a powerful measure of aggression has to be reckoned as part of their instinctual endowment. The result is that their neighbour is to them not only a possible helper or sexual object, but also a temptation to them to gratify their aggressiveness on him, to exploit his capacity for work without recompense, to use him sexually without his consent, to seize his possessions, to humiliate him, to cause him pain, to torture and to kill him. *Homo homini lupus*; who has the courage to dispute it in the face of all the evidence in his own life and in history?

Discussions

Many philosophers have a high opinion of human beings. In *Perpetual Peace* (1795) Kant opines that the 'sanction of the citizens is necessary to decide whether there shall be a war or not', and that if they were consulted, 'nothing is more natural than that they would think long before beginning such a terrible game'. Even so, Kant, like Thomas Hobbes with his famous 'Warre of all on all', saw the natural state of humankind as one of either active or threatened conflict. But eternal peace was undoubtedly the goal, indeed this quest was 'the entire end and purpose of a theory of rights within the limits of pure reason'.

Meanwhile, Jeremy Bentham busied himself in his study, before emerging with a *Plan for Universal and Perpetual Peace* (1789). Undeterred by the lukewarm reception to his 'Panopticon', the plan is the same principle writ large, essentially relying on a supranational 'eye' to police the world – not by force of course, but by the free exchange of information, shaming any transgressor nations into line.

'Globalisation' was another route identified by philosophers for reaching Kant's dream. Adam Smith offered the profit motive as the antidote to the warrior impulse: 'If commerce were permitted to act to the universal extent it is capable, it would extirpate the system of war and produce a revolution in the uncivilised state of governments.' In 1848, John Stuart Mill wrote that:

It is commerce which is rapidly rendering war obsolete, by strengthening and multiplying the personal interests which act in natural opposition to it. And it may be said without exaggeration that the great extent and rapid increase of international trade, in being the principle guarantee of the peace of the world, is the great permanent security for the uninterrupted progress of the ideas, the institutions, and the character of the human race.

(*Principles of Political Economy*)

Unfortunately, as global trade increased in the nineteenth century, so did global wars.

So is war good? Or bad? Or maybe? Quite obviously war is not bad – people are.

Just some wars?

In *East Timor* – to save the indigenous peoples from genocidal killing by Indonesian militias.

In *Afghanistan* – to protect the Western way of life from Islamic fundamentalism. (Oh yes, and to liberate the Afghans.)

In *Sierra Leone* – to prop up democratic government against criminal militias intent on destabilisation including random killings and massacres.

In *Cambodia* – to remove the murderous Khmer Rouge regime that set about eliminating the 'educated classes' and starting the country again at 'Year Zero'.

In the *Balkans* – to prevent the 'ethnic cleansing' of the region by the Serbian demagogue Slobodan Milosevic, intent on recreating a mythical 'Serbian Empire'.

In *Rwanda* – to stop the slaughter of Tutsi people by the Hutu militias, which had left the rivers running with blood and fields covered in bones.

Dilemma 79
The unjustified false belief

Well, he certainly didn't *know* that he knew it.

But then, politicians – like the rhetoricians that aroused Plato's ire – rely on all the illegitimate tactics, especially equivocation, ambiguity, of course, but also that 'nuclear bomb' tactic in argumentation: the downright lie. Misleading responses are the bread and butter of political debate, indeed, the ancient art of rhetoric, so that has long been accepted as 'not lying'.

One well known example, at the time of the US–Iraq war, is that the US President felt able to reassure television viewers that US troops would never abuse prisoners but always respect the law in interrogations – without adding that he had just signed a memorandum changing the law to allow interrogation techniques leading to prolonged pain, 'organ loss' and death!

Then there is the promise uttered in good faith, which changes with circumstances. Many times politicians have pledged 'no new taxes' only to announce shortly after being elected some . . . 'new taxes'. This apparent reversal, they say apologetically, is not a 'lie' because when they made the pledge, they believed the economic circumstances et cetera et cetera were better than they turned out to be straight after the election.

But what of the particular case where a politician claims to 'know' something, citing evidence that turns out not to support his position? Is that a lie – or not?

Tony Blair, Britain's Prime Minister through much of the 1990s and the opening years of the twenty-first century, occasionally dubbed in the British press 'Tony Bliar', was often accused of a steady stream of little fibs; indeed there were books written in a vain attempt to expose them. The studies delved into the pledges to reform voting systems that never happened; there were the announcements of new money for hospitals and schools that turned out to be merely re-announcements of old budget plans; and most famously of all, there was the personal guarantee that Saddam Hussein had nuclear, chemical and biological weapons primed and ready to strike. Weapons, that is, that he had secret evidence of, yet . . . turned out eventually not to exist.

Neither the parliamentary opposition nor the journalists could ever pin him down. But could philosophical techniques have shed any light on this sort of debate? After the war in Iraq (in which many tens of thousands of bystanders died) the suggestion was made in the British Parliament that 'an inquiry' was needed to find out what the Prime Minster really knew about these 'weapons, of mass destruction'. However, using a kind of Socratic or 'dialectical' reasoning they could already have deduced quite a lot:

- Either the Prime Minister believed there were weapons of mass destruction in Iraq, or he did not. If he did not, then he was a liar and should have resigned.
- If he believed there were such weapons then either he had secret evidence for it, or he did not. If he did not, then he was lying.
- But even if he had evidence for the existence of the weapons, then the weapons must either have been destroyed at the outset of war, or the secret evidence was wrong. If the weapons had been destroyed it would have been immediately possible to demonstrate this. But it had not in fact been demonstrated; in which case, the secret evidence must have been wrong.
- But if the secret 'evidence' was wrong (perhaps taken from information found on the internet), then the Prime Minister would have had no reason to keep expecting the weapons to turn up, as he maintained repeatedly he did expect. Unless he was a barefaced liar and wanted to avoid having to resign, of course.

There is a notion in philosophy that we cannot say we know something unless we believe it to be so, we have a good, relevant reason for believing it, and (finally) that it really is so. This is sometimes called 'knowledge as justified true belief'.

As there weren't any of the weapons, and there was no 'reason' to think there would be any, Mr Blair appeared to fall down on two of the three requirements for 'knowledge', leaving open only the possibility that he 'believed' what he was saying at the moment he said it. This is sometimes called knowledge too, albeit as 'unjustified false belief', and only by Mr Blair.

This standard clears up many problems. He could have 'believed' there were weapons, as long as he 'believed' he had evidence for it. But it is also a dangerous tactic, which if considered legitimate, tends to destroy the distinction between truth and falsity itself.

In fact, it might be better if politicians lied more.

Dilemma 80
The deterrents

Are the Meanies and Ingrates rational? They want the rest of the drinkers in the pub to believe that they are, that they have not set up their booby traps as mere violence, but rather as Clausewitz, the great philosopher of war, described in *On War* as 'disciplined statecraft'. Politics by other means, in fact.

Perhaps Phil the barman is stuck with the thought that if either neighbour did ever set off the explosives, the damage would seem to be both terrible and out of all proportion to any conceivable 'victory'. Certainly, in relation to nuclear war, the US war planner, Bernard Brodie, says an exchange cannot be considered rational if it could not take place without resulting in a scale of destruction that would be unacceptable to any rational person. The same would apply to our warring neighbours – no 'rational person' would detonate the explosives – but how about just threatening to?

Discussions

As a term, deterrence appears in the 1820 *Oxford English Dictionary*, meaning 'to frighten from'. But as a concept it dates back at least to the time of the ever warring city-states of Ancient Greece. And as a theory, deterrence relies on the kind of thinking favoured by philosophers – abstract, rational judgements of self-interest. The 'Prisoners Dilemma' writ large (see, for example, my *101 Philosophy Problems* [Routledge, 2007]). The so-called 'Colonel's fallacy', which is to look at the other side's military capabilities, and take for granted the intention to use them all against you, is central to this kind of thinking. The Colonel sits in his bunker calculating:

- effectiveness of his missiles in destroying enemy missiles
- *plus* effectiveness of his missiles in destroying enemy targets
- *plus* rate of fire of his missiles
- *plus* time his missiles might have to cause damage before enemy response
- *minus* effectiveness of enemy missiles in destroying his missiles
- *minus* how many casualties would need to be sustained before the enemy surrenders or is annihilated
- *and* how many casualties could be sustained before he has to surrender – or is annihilated.

(Did Mr Meanie sit in the outside loo calculating how many pounds of explosive would cause unacceptable damage to the Ingrates' hedge?)

Shortly after the end of the Second World War, with the mushroom clouds over Hiroshima and Nagasaki still settling into the world's consciousness, Einstein wrote: 'Unless [world government] prevails, and unless by common struggle we are capable of new ways of thinking, mankind is doomed'. And Brodie summed up the paradox of nuclear weapons: 'Thus far, the chief purpose of our military establishment has been to win wars. From now on, its chief purpose must be to avert them.'

Brodie notes that since the atom bomb, the old economics of war no longer applied: there could be no gains from the war, only losses. 'Everything about the atomic bomb is overshadowed by the twin facts that it exists and that its destructive power is fantastically great'. But as far as 'deterrence' goes, Brodie recognised that it is not necessary that there should be any use for the weapons, only that both sides should live in fear of at least the possibility of some such possibility. The more likely aggression might result in nuclear war, the stronger the deterrent effect. As Clausewitz said, war has its own language, but not its own logic – military might must still remain a tool of rational judgement.

And once one side has the ability to entirely destroy the other, more weapons should be of little significance.

But if it is nuclear war we are thinking of, there has never been any shortage of other military experts to argue that on the contrary, nuclear war is both thinkable and 'winnable'. Another influential advisor to the US government, William Border, predicted that it was inevitable and would be manifested as a sort of 'aerial duel' in which the missiles of each side fought it out, leaving the cities to the last. By the 1970s, it was his kind of view that had come to the ascendent, at least in the USA. The Secretary of Defense, James Schlesinger, announced the junking of the old theory of 'Mutual Assured Destruction' in favour of strategies designed to help the US 'prevail' in the event of a nuclear exchange. Under both the 'dovish' President Carter and the 'Star Wars' President Reagan, the US military expanded its list of strike targets to include not only 200 Soviet cities (enough to kill nearly everyone in the continent) but *also* missile silos. The plan was said to be to 'force the Soviet Union to seek the termination of hostilities on terms favourable to the US' – that is to focus not merely on preventing a war, but winning one. And if you can win a war, then the prospects of having one don't seem nearly so bad. (At least, not if you live in a bunker.)

In fact, the new policy, known officially since 1983 as the 'Strategic Defence Initiative' and unofficially as 'Star Wars', was specifically promoted as *more moral* and *more ethical* than the old policy – of MAD. Of course, peaceniks everywhere were appalled at the new thinking. Yet even the idea that you can 'win' a nuclear war is in a way supposed to enhance deterrence. Similarly, protecting your missile silos perhaps through a 'Star Wars' system is in theory going to put off the enemy from attacking. On the other hand, protecting yourself makes the chances of your launching an attack a lot more likely.

And deterrence requires continual propaganda to ensure there is both a public will to blow up the 'enemy' – and that this hostility is evident to the other side. (Again, the drawback is that although it might help deter attack, this policy makes the chance of your own side launching an attack much greater.)

But back to our neighbours. The 'nuclear balance' did not deter non-nuclear war. Korea (1950–53), Vietnam (1961–73), Hungary (1956) and Czechoslovakia (1968) took place despite the ominous presence of the nuclear bomb. Likewise, the Meanies are likely to find their car tyres let down, and the Ingrates that the cat has been sprayed green. War, not annihilation, is the real threat. If averting the latter causes the former, then it is no solution at all.

Dilemma 81
The school for terror

Just one problem. The school is based at Fort Benning in the heart of the American South, and is directly funded by the US government. For over half a century it has trained its own brand of political warriors to take on the supposed enemies of the United States government, if not the people of the USA.

The sort of things it encouraged are illustrated by an incident in 1988 when a massive car bomb exploded in Beirut, killing eighty-five innocent passers-by (and missing an Islamic mullah – its intended target). The bombers were none other than Washington's own CIA operatives, in a covert operation funded by Saudi Arabia.

In 2000, Congress voted on a motion to close the school, but it was narrowly defeated and the House of Representatives instead adopted that very important ethical practice known as 'inventing-a-new-name-for-it'. The School of the

Americas, now unfortunately infamous as the 'SOA', became the much more respectable-sounding 'Western Hemisphere Institute for Security Co-operation'.

If knowing the US-link affects your view of the rightness or wrongness of condemning, let alone bombing the school, then you might need to make your decisions, as John Rawls puts it, from behind the 'veil of ignorance'. His idea is that it is only when we can look at issues dispassionately, not knowing quite who our decisions will harm and who they will benefit, that we will truly weigh up the factors and come to a just conclusion.

After several shocking and indiscriminate mass killings attributed to the shadowy 'al-Qaeda' organisation, culminating in the infamous September 11 suicide hijackings and the destruction of part of New York City in 2001, which seemed for a moment to provide a universal benchmark of unacceptable depravity, the President stated firmly: 'If any government sponsors the outlaws and killers of innocents, they have become outlaws and murderers themselves. And they will take that lonely path at their own peril.'

Wise words indeed.

Dilemma 82
The hate preacher

Although the story is made up, the quotes are real enough (references to the Shakir translation of the Koran). And the interest of the police (at least) in what goes on in Holy Places is certainly there. If the Koran speaks favourably of the 'churches and synagogues and mosques in which Allah's name is much remembered' (XXII:40), there is increasing suspicion in the West of what goes on 'under the minarets', especially the plastic ones. In 2005, a large squad of heavily armed police raided the mosque at London's Finsbury Park and bundled off one of its fiery imams – the one who had really 'fought in Afghanistan' and who really had a hook for a right hand. He was subsequently convicted of inciting terrorism and sentenced to many years of quiet reflection.

Doubtless this would include re-reading the passages in the Koran which counsel religious tolerance, warning followers to 'Be not unduly immoderate in your religion' (V:73).

Dilemma 83
The dodo's call

Dodos are just birds – how many of them do you need to have? Maybe just enough to keep the zoos going – next to the last few pandas and cuddly koala bears! Enough to provide something for future generations to look at – and if we ever got another planet, to even return to the wild. In which case maybe about thirty dodos would have been enough. Nowadays, scientists are keen to reduce this minimum level further by stockpiling DNA and the genetic codes of rare animals, then they can die out but always be resurrected later – if we want. In which case no dodos need be left, but plenty of test tube samples. But maybe we don't need any dodos while there are pigeons in Trafalgar Square. As Darwin himself remarks in the *Origin of Species*:

> Many years ago, when comparing, and seeing others compare, the birds from the separate islands of the Galapagos Archipelago, both one with another, and with those from the American mainland, I was much struck how entirely vague and arbitrary is the distinction between species and varieties.

Species, Darwin admits, are terms 'arbitrarily given for the sake of convenience' to what are in reality all unique creatures bearing more or less resemblance to each other.

Nonetheless, as Holmes Rolston, an environmental writer, has pointed out, our 'duties to endangered species' depend on these rather arbitrary distinctions.

For example, *betula lenta uber*, a kind of birch tree, is unusual in that the ends of its leaves are round. Originally, it attracted no significance, but in the 1960s a distinguished botanist announced that it qualified as a distinct species. As there are only two known places where it grows, both in Virginia, USA, it was clearly an endangered one at that, and the proud Virginians dutifully put sturdy fences around both of them. On the other hand, the endangered 'Mexican duck' became rather less worrisome when it was recently 'delisted' and became just another kind of common mallard. In one alarming case, on San Clemente Island, 2,000 wild goats woke up one day to find that they were down to be shot as part of a 'conservation' drive to protect 'rare grasses'. Fortunately fellow mammals rallied round to save them from the vegetables.

Scientists point out that we are actually in the middle of the 'sixth great extinction' as it is called. The last one was 65 million years ago and saw the disappearance of the dinosaurs. This time, we are losing all types of creatures, especially our fellow mammals. And the sixth age of extinction truly is not even a modern phenomenon. It began as the inevitable consequence of the success of one species, some 50,000 years ago, which began to multiply and spread across the face of the earth, killing and destroying as it did so. Alfred Russell Wallace, forgotten co-author of the theory of 'natural selection', wrote: 'we live in a zoologically impoverished world from which all the largest, and fiercest, and strangest forms have recently disappeared'. Creatures such as the flightless birds, of which the dodo is the only one we remember, are its victims, along with the woolly rhino, mammoth and elk, and giant varieties of kangaroos, sloths, goannas and even car-sized tortoises. Then there's pygmy hippos and elephants, despatched from the last few places in the Mediterranean where they had survived up to perhaps 10,000 years ago.

What we are living through, or more accurately, participating in, is a cyclical process of the reduction in biodiversity. Previous extinctions were due to climatic change, perhaps triggered by geological or celestial events. This one is just due to our own approach to nature – basically, like the Dutch sailor, destroying whatever we find for the immediate satisfaction of our own wants. When the large animals have disappeared, along with the medium and small ones and the forests and woodlands that sustained them, we may find the prospects for our own survival are not too good either. In which case, in answer to the question, how many dodos need to be left alive, the answer is more than you might think, and certainly more than the Dutch sailors imagined.

Dilemma 84
Killing the wolf

In this case, Leopold points to the role of wolves in keeping the deer population in check. There are no wolves in most of the world now, and often no deer either. But where deer are encouraged, they do, it is true, tend to take over, nibbling all the tasty green shoots. Similarly, rabbits multiply in the fox-free zones that farmers work so hard to create. In parts of Africa, elephants, the world's largest herbivores, eat forests to destruction.

Even if nature is 'out of balance', though, a new balance will soon emerge of its own accord, as food for the pesky herbivores runs out. But that is often less satisfactory for humans (and it's not much good for all the other animals either) so we find 'conservationists' arranging mass shootings or poisonings of animals. In the light of this, Leopold's description of the ecological value of the much-maligned wolf was both timely and influential. As a result, wolves are now being reintroduced into national parks in the USA (like Yosemite) and in Europe.

Dilemma 85
The Green Revolution

Aldo Leopold was sceptical of the 'green economics' approach; in *Round River* he wrote:

> The outstanding scientific discovery of the twentieth century is not television, or radio, but rather the complexity of the land organism. Only those who know the most about it can appreciate how little we know about it. The last word in ignorance is the man who says of an animal or plant: 'What good is it?' If the land mechanism as a whole is good, then every part is good, whether we understand it or not. If the biota, in the course of aeons, has built something we like but do not understand, then who but a fool would discard seemingly useless parts? To keep every cog and wheel is the first precaution of intelligent tinkering.

In *The Land Ethic*, published in 1949, he argues that the approach will fail to protect many species which do not have sufficient economic value. Instead, he offers a holistic or 'ecological' approach as old as philosophy itself. Plato uses one such in the *Republic*, where he speaks of the well-governed state as being like an organism, and says that there is 'no greater evil . . . than the thing that distracts it and makes it many instead of one'.

But, in his criticism of 'green economics', Leopold describes economists who put a low value on a species without considering the wider net of relationships of which that species is a part. If they had done, then an economic value may be found, and Leopold's objection evaporates somewhat, like the rain on forest leaves in the sunlight. Perhaps Leopold's real objection is that the economics mindset perpetuates the attitude of human beings as 'conquerors' of nature, rather than as citizens of the 'biotic community', and distracts people from remembering that they 'are only fellow voyagers with other creatures in the odyssey of evolution'. This second, 'deep green', objection may be true, but it is irrelevant, even on his own terms. For Leopold says that in environmental ethics: 'A thing is right when it tends to preserve the integrity, stability, and beauty of the biotic community. It is wrong otherwise.'

No mention there of the 'attitude' that prompted the actions. On Leopold's terms, in environmental ethics intentions are irrelevant, only consequences matter. And if the 'green economics' mindset, with its language of 'managing assets', results in greater preservation of the environment than what otherwise is essentially an appeal to altruism, then that approach is the one to promote.

'Deep Greens' imagine that by making a duty to the environment somehow separate from human interests, they adopt a more radical approach (hence the name of the movement) and take a step forward in understanding. But put that way, it becomes clear that what has become known as 'ecocentrism' is actually a step back, because by again separating the interests of the environment from the interests of *homo sapiens*, the 'ecocentrists' continue to promote the fallacy of Descartes – and reinvent human beings as fundamentally different and separate from the natural world.

And the moral is . . . Yes, direct action is justified to protect the environment, but you must still avoid hurting other members of the 'biotic community'.

In fact, it looks like it might be easier to find an economic argument against the new crops than to physically trample them. Some doubts centre on the dangers of 'mono-culture', which tend to reduce species diversity and be vulnerable to one large-scale disaster or disease, but, human nature being what it is, we have to wait for it to happen before anyone really cares. 'The Greenies' thought they had found a promising argument when it was discovered that monarch butterflies, if force-fed large quantities of the herbicide-resistant pollen of the new crops, became ill. However, it later emerged that 'real' monarch butterflies did not actually eat the pollen of the crops, so this argument was weakened somewhat. The general and often cited argument that 'tampering' with plants opens a biological 'Pandora's box' of mutant, Frankenstein strains, would have more substance if we did not already rely almost entirely on mutations for our sustenance. For thousands of years, selection, grafting and cross-pollination have ensured that new strains of life have appeared regularly on the planet without the say so of either 'nature' or 'God'.

But GM crops are part of a longer story about 'high yield' crops and a different type of 'green revolution'. (And now we have genetically engineered animals too.) New strains of rice were supposed to remove the scourge of global poverty, just as genetically modified ones are supposed to reduce the amount of chemicals used, and enhance flavour and texture of the food. As radical writers like Susan George have documented, the promise has historically been only partially fulfilled: yes, crop yields have gone up, but only at the expense (read profit) of increased dependence on fertilisers, herbicides, machinery and other agricultural equipment. The wider consequences have been ecological and social stresses on some of the poorest countries of the world, and ultimately less food for people. This 'green revolution' offered technological solutions to problems which were social in origin, and thereby exacerbated them.

In as much as it is desirable to reduce the spraying of chemical poisons on crops (and it is) then much more obvious solutions are available than fiddling around with the genetic structure of the plants and, for example, inserting toxins. Traditional and organic farming offer plenty of alternatives, the downside being a reduction in volume of harvest. But then, that is already a key element in the strategy of food producers worldwide, determined to maintain price levels. And they will have saved on herbicide.

Dilemma 86
Pain is good

Joel Feinberg wrote that

> the question 'What's wrong with pain anyway?' is never allowed to arise. I shall raise it. I herewith declare in all soberness that I see nothing wrong with pain. It is a marvellous method, honed by the evolutionary process, of conveying important organic information.

Darwin would certainly say that pain and anxiety are part of life, and cannot be removed, any more than death can, without destroying the whole natural system. If nature as a whole is good, then death and pain are good too. In a way, this brings us back to Garrett Hardin's unattractive view of the correct approach to poor people. (Eradicate them – pests!)

However, Feinberg himself thinks that because pain is generally considered (at least by others) to be 'an intrinsic evil' then anyone who 'causes pain' in 'a being that can experience it' should show that it is both necessary and done for a good reason. And he recalls the words too of Alan Watts who, when asked if he thought there was too much pain in the world, replied: 'No, I think there is just enough.'

Dilemma 87
Greed is good

It seems that they should all try to make as much money as possible. As Smith puts it in his *Inquiry into the Nature and Causes of the Wealth of Nations*, published in 1776, the year of American Independence, and consumed avidly by a world intent not only on discovering the nature of money, but also how to make more of it:

> It is not from the *benevolence* of the butcher, the brewer, or the baker, that we expect our dinner, but from their regard to their own self-interest. We address ourselves not to their humanity but to their self-love, and never talk to them of our own necessities but of their advantage.

After all, 'nobody but a beggar chooses to depend chiefly upon the benevolence of his fellow citizens'. And:

> Even a beggar does not depend upon it entirely. . . . The greater part of his occasional wants are supported in the same manner as those of other people, by treaty, by barter and by purchase: with the money which one man gives him he purchases food; the old cloaths which another bestows upon him he exchanges for other old cloaths which suit him better, or for lodging, or for good, or for money.

Or for drink, or for drugs, or whatever. No matter – at least our beggar is now back participating in the great 'wheel of circulation', the money-go-round of the modern economy.

It's not just Smith who thinks money is good. Aristotle too waves the flag of the rich. In his view, it is not only virtuous to *make* money, but simply to *have* money. On the other hand, Aristotle is rather keener on the spending of it than either Smith or the Protestants. Famously, his role model, 'Magnanimous Man', 'is one who will possess

Discussions

305

beautiful and profitless things rather than profitable and useful ones; for this is more proper to a character that suffices to itself'. And Aristotle explains in the *Nicomachean Ethics* that Magnanimous Man prides himself particularly on his parties:

> Great expenditure is becoming to those who have suitable means to start with, acquired by their own efforts or from ancestors or connexions, and to people of high birth or reputation, and so on; for all these things bring with them greatness and prestige. Primarily, then, the magnanimous man is of this sort, and *magnificence is shown in expenditures.*

Yet there are ethical considerations even in this display:

> the magnanimous man spends not on himself but on public objects, and gifts bear some resemblance to votive offerings. A magnanimous man will also furnish his house suitably to his wealth (for even a house is a sort of public ornament), and will spend by preference on those works that are lasting (for these are the most beautiful), and on every class of things he will spend what is becoming; for the same things are not suitable for gods and for men, nor in a temple and in a tomb.

Of course, as with all virtues, being rich must be done in a balanced sort of way:

> such, then, is the *magnanimous* man; the man who goes to excess and is *vulgar* exceeds, as has been said, by spending beyond what is right. For on small objects of expenditure he spends much and displays a tasteless showiness; for example, he gives a club dinner on the scale of a wedding banquet, and when he provides the chorus for a comedy he brings them on to the stage in purple, as they do at Megara. And all such things he will do not for honour's sake but to show off his wealth, and because he thinks he is admired for these things, and where he ought to spend much he spends little and where little, much. The *niggardly man* on the other hand will fall short in everything, and after spending the greatest sums will spoil the beauty of the result for a trifle, and whatever he is doing he will hesitate and consider how he may spend least, and lament even that, and think he is doing everything on a bigger scale than he ought.

Ironically, it would seem that Professor Smith, despite being money's greatest ever advocate, despite even raiding the sugar bowl at the Scottish Philosophical Society, is an example of *niggardly man.*

Discussions

So should people study money more than morality then? Well, most of the philosophers, including Smith, agree at least on one thing: that it is in the origins of societies that we find the origins of both laws and moral codes. In fact, in his *Theory of Justice* (1972) John Rawls recognises the intimate connections between economic structures and morality. There he notes that the

> nature of the decision made by the legislator is not, therefore, materially different from that of an entrepreneur deciding how to maximise his profit by producing this or that commodity, or that of a consumer deciding how to maximise his satisfaction by the purchase of this or that collection of goods.

(Indeed, the whole edifice of 'utilitarianism' is constructed necessarily on the principle that each person is a consumer of happiness, of equal worth to each other: 'rights and duties are to be assigned and scarce means of satisfaction allocated in accordance with rules so as to give the greatest fulfilment of wants'.) Plato too, recognised the material basis of his ideal society, even whilst making it clear that true philosophers would have no need for such fripperies. And although we conventionally imagine laws to be based on 'right and wrong', in fact, they are based, as Thomas Hobbes so effectively put it in the seventeenth century, on self-interest.

In the *Leviathan* (1651), Hobbes explains that laws, 'the introduction of that restraint upon themselves', are accepted by people only in the 'foresight of their own preservation and of a more contented life thereby; that is to say, of getting themselves out of that miserable condition of War, which is necessarily consequent . . . to the natural passions of men'. This is the famous state of 'war' in which: 'nothing can be unjust. The notions of right and wrong, justice and injustice have no place. Where there is no common power, there is no law: where no law, no injustice'. Hobbes stops there. But it is only self-interest that stops people waging war. And there is nothing more self-interested than making money. A theory based on the virtue of the maximisation of money has quite considerable explanatory force. For example, killing people becomes wrong not because it cannot be universalised (it can) or because it does not maximise happiness (maybe it would?) but because it certainly would severely impair the making of money.

Plato would not want to have money as the key to the moral life, of course. In the *Republic* he briskly dismisses it as only a 'means to an end'. Well, Smith agrees:

it is chiefly from this regard to the sentiments of mankind that we pursue riches and avoid poverty. For to what purpose is all the toil and bustle of the world? What is the end of avarice and ambition, of the pursuit of wealth, of power, or preeminence? . . . To be observed, to be attended to, to be taken notice of with sympathy, complacency and approbation, are all the advantages which we can propose to derive from it. *It is the vanity, not the ease or the pleasure, which interests us.*

For money, as well as being the creation of self-interested action, can only be valuable in a social context. Equally though, Smith sets out the 'psychological' case for morality as being, like money, a by-product of social life, and peculiar to it, offering a kind of 'Robinson Crusoe' case:

Were it possible that a human creature could grow up to manhood in a solitary place, without any communication with his own species, he could no more think of his own character, or the propriety or demerit of his own sentiments and conduct, of the beauty or deformity of his own mind, than the beauty or deformity of his own face. . . . Bring him into society and he is immediately provided with the mirror.

Freud would later have it that moral behaviour is built up in the mind from the influence of such as parents, teachers, school chums (peer group) and society in general. However, where Freud would allow the unconscious mind to lead us astray, Smith supposes instead a mental 'impartial spectator', a reliable guide, perhaps more like what Freud called the 'super-ego', intent on leading us towards the light.

To judge your own behaviour requires you to, at least for a moment, divide into two people, and one be the spectator of the actions of the other. Nature has endowed each of us with a desire not only to be approved of, 'but with a desire of being what ought to be approved of' (which is rather harder).

And as Smith emphasises repeatedly, nothing is nobler than being rich, and more disgraceful than being poor.

A bit of interest to add to the account

The great question of what makes something right, right, has been converted into the equally great question of what gives money its value in the first place anyway.

After all, you can't just print it, although many people have tried. (It loses its 'value', even when governments do it.) 'Labour alone, never varying in its own value, is the ultimate and real standard by which the value of all commodities can at all times and places be estimated and compared. It is their real price; money is the nominal price only' is the answer both Adam Smith and, funnily enough, Karl Marx, give. And this is a very tidy answer. After all, labour is something very basic, and fundamental, very tangible, and also something very holistic, that unites not only all people, but people with the natural world. Perhaps the Protestants were right: virtue lies in hard work? Smith again:

> every individual necessarily labours to render the annual revenue of the
> society as great as he can. He generally, indeed, neither intends to promote
> the publick intent, nor knows how much he is promoting it . . . he intends only
> his own gain, and he is in this, as in many other cases, led by an invisible
> hand to promote an end which was no part of his intention.
>
> (*Wealth of Nations*)

That end is the 'utilitarian' one, of the maximum happiness. For by the wonders of 'trickle down' (as the economists put it):

> The rich consume little more than the poor, and in spite of their natural
> selfishness and rapacity, thought they mean only their own conveniency,
> though the sole end which they propose from the labours of all the thousands
> whom they employ be the gratification of their own vain and insatiable desires,
> they divide with the poor the produce of all their improvements, they are led
> by an invisible hand to make nearly the same distribution of the necessaries of
> life, which would have been made, had the earth been divided into equal
> portions among all its inhabitants.
>
> (*Theory of the Moral Sentiments*)

The great discovery that triggered the Industrial Revolution in Europe, rather than the mechanical ones of the steam engine or the printing press or some other technological innovation, was the theological one by a pastor in Germany. Martin Luther's Protestant work ethic freed entrepreneurs from the legacy of a disdain of worldly success that Plato had left, and gave them instead the assurance that their success was a mark of God's favour. Making money really *was* divine!

Or both. But not, assuredly, neither. During the great famines at the end of the nineteenth century Indians did in fact die. In their millions. The British record 1.3 million people died in 1877, another 3.75 million in the last fifteen years of the tax. (Curiously enough, the last person in charge of its collection became one of the founders of the Indian National Congress that would eventually end the tax.) Taxed on their meagre salt requirements, they either fell victim to a host of painful and often fatal diseases which lack of salt leads to – or starved.

Tax policy is rather a dry subject for an ethics book (already in itself quite dry enough). But taxes shape society, and society, as we have seen, shapes moral life. Anyway, of all the practical issues with an ethical dimension, taxation is perhaps the most all-pervading. Not that it normally gets much of a mention.

A few philosophers have recognised its importance though. John Stuart Mill was anxious that taxes be levied mainly on 'unearned' income, such as inherited wealth, which he believed was quite indefensible. Today corporations the size and might of countries can be passed from father to son (which is still how it usually is, inheritance tending to entrench male power). But it was Smith, not only a philosopher of money, but sometime Customs Commissioner, who advised that taxes should be:

- affordable
- anticipatable (not sprung on citizens as a surprise)
- proportionate (not used as a sort of punishment, for example on cigarettes and tobacco), and
- convenient (payment should be easy, not a matter of hiring an accountant).

We might add a fifth principle, that taxes should favour protection of the environment.

Yes, but why should I pay any *taxes?*

Marx and Engels had a different take on the matter. Far from redistributing private wealth, they wished to abolish it. Borrowing (without repaying) a phrase from the French anarchist Proudhon, their scandalous pamphlet, the *Communist Manifesto*, declared property was theft. Justice required a one-off 100 per cent taxation of everything and everybody, with the state sharing out its profits thereafter on the basis of need. In the absence of such wholesale restructuring of society, justice was just a ruling-class sham. Which it certainly was for those caught trying to sneak through the 'Great Hedge'.

So taxation may be the systematic exploitation of the rich by the poor (or vice versa) but you can't ask *why* you should pay taxes as the 'why' only exists as long as you continue to do so.

Dilemma 89
Rough justice

Well, this is what happened in the actual case of Messrs Spiggot and Phillips.

> The reading of this sentence producing no effect, they were ordered back to Newgate, there to be pressed to death; but, when they came to the press-room, Phillips begged to be taken back to plead; a favour that was granted, though it might have been denied to him: but Spiggot was put under the press, where he continued half an hour, with three hundred and fifty pounds weight on his body; but on the addition of fifty pounds more, he likewise begged to plead.

The evidence being clear and positive against them, they were speedily convicted and executed at Tyburn on 8 February 1720. Yet even while under sentence of death:

> Phillips behaved in the most hardened and abandoned manner; he paid no regard to any thing that the minister said to him, and swore or sung songs while the other prisoners were engaged in acts of devotion; and, towards the close of his life, when his companions became more serious, he grew still more wicked; and yet, when at the place of execution he said 'he did not fear to die, for he was in no doubt of going to heaven'.
>
> (*Newgate Calendar* vol. 1, 1824, 131–33)

Today for 'highway robbers', read 'terrorists', perhaps. And the much saluted values of justice are rapidly dismantled and put in storage in many countries when it is thought they might be interfering with the pursuit of these international outlaws. After the events of 11 September 2001, when several hijacked planes were flown into skyscrapers in the USA, the rooting-out of the feared global network of these self-appointed Nemesises was said to be a 'gloves off' exercise, with torture, assassination and even bombing of hide-outs all legitimate tools in this new world order. Human rights lawyers, used to the subtle fencing of legal niceties, watched in bewilderment as suspects were taken blindfolded, gagged, and bound hand and foot to Guantanamo Bay, a military base in Cuba, by the US Justice Department, there to be kept in cages pending 'interrogation'. (Of course, other countries make no bones about it – if you are arrested, you will be tortured, and maybe killed too, but then, these countries do not normally claim the moral high ground.)

Some people, and quite a few governments, would say that terrorists *should* be tortured because (unlike highway robbers) they may be part of a network planning more unspeakable outrages. (Better one crushed Spiggot than lots of robbed highways.) For those countries which do have some kind of moral principles governing, then the philosophy of punishment is quite straightforward, and torture does not fit in. This is because you are innocent until proved guilty and even then, there are conventionally only four ethical justifications for harming people. These are summed up as:

Discussions

RESTITUTION
RETRIBUTION
DETERRENCE
and
REFORM

(Father Abraham is using the first three elements in the case of Lazarus – Dilemma 49.) The first involves forcing the criminal to 'make amends' for the harm that they have done, to try to undo the damage and put things right again. It is not a very practical response to many crimes, even those involving damage to property or theft of goods or money, but it is certainly a minimal sort of justification for fines and community work orders or such like. Reform may be an unpleasant process too, but it is often the aim of punishments for younger offenders.

More serious crimes tend to be impossible to 'undo', just in terms of the emotional and psychological harm to the victims. However, a punishment which makes other people 'think twice' before repeating the crime is also justified under certain utilitarian measures. With 'retribution', society recognises the desire of law-abiding citizens to 'get their own back' on criminals. In nineteenth-century England, the system allowed a powerful sense of involvement, the public were allowed to sit in judgement on their fellows, ultimately with the power of life or death over them, and also to witness the executions.

Of course, at some point the general social desirability both of 'making an example' (deterring), and satisfying the need for retribution, has to be set against the individual rights of the prisoners. The 'Bloody Code', followed until the middle of the nineteenth century at prisons such as Newgate, demanded the death sentence for nearly 300 offences such as 'consorting with gypsies', 'impersonating a Chelsea pensioner' or (if you were a child) 'strong evidence of malice'. Even then, many offences were reclassified to avoid application of the ultimate penalty, perhaps because of the practicalities. In 1817, for example, the majority of nearly 14,000 prisoners held at Newgate alone were liable to be 'punished by death', which would have required a throughput on the famous gallows that would not be discreditable to a supermarket checkout. Public executions were eventually abolished in Britain in 1868, although gibbeting (where executed corpses were left suspended in cages for public satisfaction) was abandoned slightly earlier. Today about ninety countries of the world eschew the practice of capital punishment.

In our example, the torture is highly effective in modifying the behaviour of the 'accused', but we may feel some qualms over its ethical status. The *Newgate Calendar* itself records that in 1772, 'the Act becoming barbarous to Englishmen', it was instead determined that 'persons refusing to plead should be deemed *guilty*, as if convicted by a jury'. Which is a nice way of providing some sort of sop to the prison reformers, whilst keeping the public thirst for 'real punishments' satisfied.

Dilemma 90
Son of Sam

The day of Berkowitz's arrest, Sergeant Joe Coffey was called in to interview him. Calmly and candidly, David told him about each of the shootings and, at the close, politely wished him 'good night'. There was no doubt that Berkowitz was the Son of Sam. The details that he supplied about each assault were bits of information that only the killer would have known.

The defence psychiatrists classified David as a paranoid schizophrenic. They believed that his difficulties in relating to other people drove him further into isolation. The isolation was fertile ground for wild fantasies, such as that of the 'demon dogs' that he claimed haunted him. They were based on his neighbour's real dogs, from his various rented abodes, and one of them, a black labrador called Sam, was the 'master' demon, always howling for more blood. Eventually (the psychiatrists thought) the fantasies crowded out reality and David really lived in the twilight world his mind had created. In this world, tension grew and was only released when he successfully attacked someone. But inevitably, the tension would soon begin to increase again and the cycle repeat itself.

However, according to the prosecution, 'while the defendant shows paranoid traits, they do not interfere with his fitness to stand trial . . . the defendant is as normal as anyone else. Maybe a little neurotic'. When he was arrested, David remained calm and smiling. It appeared as though he was relieved at being caught. Perhaps he thought that finally in jail the demon dogs would stop howling for blood. In any case, David Berkowitz pleaded guilty and was sentenced to 365 years in jail. But not executed.

There is a footnote to all this. In 1979, a former FBI detective called Robert Ressler interviewed Berkowitz in Attica Prison. Berkowitz told him the demon story was to protect him so that when and if he was caught he could try to convince the authorities he was insane. According to Ressler, he admitted that his real reason for shooting women was out of resentment towards his own mother, and because of his inability to establish good relationships with women. He described in detail how he became sexually aroused in the stalking and shooting of women and liked to fantasise about it after it was over.

He told the detective that stalking women had become a nightly adventure for him. If he didn't find a victim, he would go back to the scenes of his earlier murders and try to recall them. He even wanted to go to the funerals of his victims but was afraid that the police would become suspicious. However, he did hang around 'diners' near the police stations hoping to overhear policemen talking about his crimes. He also tried (unsuccessfully) to find the graves of his victims.

He particularly cherished the newspaper attention the murders received. The idea of sending the letter to the police he obtained from a book on Jack the Ripper. After

314

the press started calling him 'Son of Sam', he adopted the nickname, and even designed a logo for it.

David Berkowitz is as bad as they get. But mad? Not so mad as not to know the advantages of sometimes appearing to be so. So, who to blame? I would blame David, otherwise, there would really be no one left to blame – and not much left to believe in either.

Dilemma 91
The Twinkies: not a normal act

Clarence Darrow, the infamous US 'Attorney of the Damned', is setting out the stall for determinism, if not indeed 'fatalism' in this influential case. This is the theory, popular then, that mental states are merely a function of physical behaviour, and have no real existence separately and that our 'behaviour' is simply a response to the stimulus of the environment. J. B. Watson and Burrhus Frederick Skinner were amongst the main academic proponents of the theory, the latter of whom is famous for demonstrating repeatedly how animals will respond to positive and negative stimuli (like being fed, or being electrocuted. Skinner gives his name to a device to do this).

Although Darrow says 'the boys' must be considered mad – abnormal – there is a school of thought which says that the boys are perfectly normal in wanting to kill other people. The British philosopher Herbert Spencer, for example, says we evolved as hunters and that unrelenting competition is a human survival mechanism. This is the view of so-called social Darwinism as opposed to social cooperation.

And Konrad Lorenz and Robert Ardrey went further, popularising the view of humans as fundamentally aggressive (the latter coining the phrase 'the territorial imperative'), and saying that evolution has made us into hunter-killers. Humans are beasts who will perish if we lose our aggressive instincts. Their theory echoes the words of Freud, who posited an inborn anti-social instinct he called *Thanatos*, or the Death Instinct. After witnessing the slaughter of the First World War, Freud wrote: 'we are descended from an endlessly long chain of murderers whose love of murder was in their blood as it is perhaps in our own'.

Did evolution really do that to us? Well, looking at the question that way, a ground-breaking study of the chimpanzees at Gombe by Jane Goodall indeed found that they, like humans, were aggressive, even capable of killing other chimps to take over their territory. But also that, like some of us, they cooperate too, they give food to other members of the community, and grieve when one dies. And some anthropologists say we evolved primarily as gatherers rather than as hunters, and that the invention of tools had more to do with the mundane needs of gathering than the dubious urge for weapons.

Dilemma 92
The Twinkies: the villain enters

The blame is with those who publish such filth.

Final curtain

Twinkies became a nickname for a certain kind of 'Insanity Defence' which led to a tightening of the criteria for claiming clients should be held responsible for their actions. It's the name of a sugary snack.

In a notorious murder trial that took place in San Francisco in 1979, a former police officer, Dan White, was accused of the murders of the Mayor and one of his assistants. That White did it was never in dispute, as he carried out the killings at midday inside City Hall. But when the case came to trial, he claimed to have been suffering from a mental lapse brought on by eating junk food – the famous Twinkies. Psychologists who testified for him postulated that even though he carried extra ammunition with him to City Hall and reloaded between killings he had been in such a depressed state that 'on the day of the crimes he really had no meaningful, rational capacity' to weigh up the considerations for and against his actions.

And White was indeed only convicted of manslaughter as a result, receiving a much lighter sentence. Riots followed in San Francisco's gay community. Eventually, the case also led to the abandonment of the legal notion of 'diminished capacity' in favour of a 'substantial capacity test'. In future, it was ruled, defendants would need to demonstrate either that they had been *propelled* in their action by 'an irresistible impulse', or that at the time they had been completely unable to distinguish between right and wrong. This last may seem easy enough to a philosopher, but we have already seen what Mrs Eggleby has to say about that.

Darrow's appeal, reproduced here, was not in fact against the *guilt* of the boys as against their responsibility, and hence the application of the death penalty. In his attempt to diminish their responsibility, he was successful. I do not know which of the grounds convinced the jury!

Dilemma 93
Diktatiaville City Square

In Diktatiaville, no one reoffends . . .

That is until the heatwave. And then over a period of three days public order breaks down – including hundreds of people who are later prosecuted for bathing in the fountains – and one of these is a 're-offender'.

Alberta, a single mum with two little infants, is the unfortunate, and she duly goes off to serve a year in the grim Diktatiaville gaol. By the time she is released, the children have developed what their teachers say are 'anxiety problems', her car has been repossessed, her boss says she is not wanted back at work, and her mother is in hospital with a nervous breakdown. All for bathing in the fountain during the heatwave!

This does seem a bit rough. Perhaps there is a problem of 'proportionality' . . . Some would say this is the case in the US with policies like the 'Three Strikes and then You're Out', which although media-friendly (the phrase is a baseball one) has consigned large numbers of young hooligans to jail 'forever' after committing three crimes which although usually nasty (such as the case of the hooligan who grabbed a youngster's pizza while they were waiting for a train) would not in themselves have been considered to merit especially heavy sentences.

Whether the US laws (like the death penalty itself) 'deter' offenders particularly is a statistical exercise, but the philosophical issue is whether, even if it did (as in Diktatiaville with the fountains law) have a very clear effect on 'reforming' behaviour, the price individuals and indeed 'bystanders' (like family members) pay for this general benefit is too high. If the offence is something more weighty, let us say, robbery with violence, then that tips the balance in favour of the 'three strikes'

317

law. If it is something that affects no one else anyway, say driving without your seatbelt on, then it surely tips the other way.

In our case, the law serves a general interest (the fountains look pretty on 'Victory Day', and residents are no longer shocked or alarmed by drunken antics – but what about the cost paid in terms of respect for individual rights?). To take a year out of Alberta's life, to part a mother from her children, to wreck a family's lives – surely that requires a greater justification than mere civic pride?

The case of the French hooligans

During the summer of 2006, thousands of French youths, from the outskirts of the big cities, went on a spree of vandalism, in particular torching parked cars. At the time, the newspapers all agreed (and found plenty of hooded rioters to confirm this) that the actions were a protest against the difficulties youths found in obtaining employment, difficulties aggravated by racism.

A study afterwards of who actually was arrested showed that almost all the rioters were under twenty (two children of nine and ten were caught trying to set a car on fire) and the great majority, 76 per cent, of them were either employed or at school or college. So why were they rioting, then? Family structures seemed to be a factor – half of those arrested came from what the police classified as large families – those with between six and sixteen children! Of more interest to the Diktatiaville case was the finding that half of the young rioters had already been caught and 'punished' four times or more. One had even been caught and punished thirty times . . .

Dilemma 94
Sanctuary Island

Of course, this is rather an unlikely story. For one thing, making a volcanic island into a golf course is just about possible, whereas, in the real world, clearing rainforest for cattle results only in land no use for anything except maybe as a landfill for rubbish. (And even that will backfire eventually as it pollutes the water supply.) And in the story, Sanctuary Island really is uninhabited, whereas most wilderness areas actually have small numbers of 'indigenous' people, who are then (like the animals) either driven out, or even killed. But the issue is the same one: doesn't land 'have to be developed' in the interests of the majority of people?

And, of those funny animals mentioned, in reality development has claimed several already. Not just the dodo, but the Great Auk and the thylacine (which died a lonely death in Hobart Zoo in 1936) are extinct, while the Toolache Wallaby, which used to be abundant in the swampy grasslands of south Australia, and the Desert Rat Kangaroo, now exist only in photo albums. And the Spotted-tailed Quoll, the Torrent Tree Frog, the Golden Bandicoot, the Woylie, the Double-eyed Fig Parrot and Boyd's Forest Dragon are all waiting in the last few shrinking remnants of their habitats for fires, chainsaws and bulldozers to catch up with them too.

The last Great Auk was thought to have been clubbed to death by Icelanders in 1844, and the dodo perished on the island of Mauritius. But all of the rest of these animals live (or lived) on that one large 'sanctuary island', Australia. In fact, half of all the mammal species that have become extinct worldwide in historical times have been there. In total, 126 species of plants and animals of existence in one country in just 200 years. Now extinction is part of the natural world. *But a rate like this would normally take a million years.*

Is there really so little space left on earth for other species? Aldo Leopold wrote of development:

> If in a city we had six vacant lots available to the youngsters of a certain neighbourhood for playing ball, it might be 'development' to build houses on the first, and the second, and the third, and the fourth, and even the fifth, but when we build houses on the last one, we forget what houses are for. The sixth house would not be development at all, but rather it would be mere short-sighted stupidity. 'Development' is like Shakespeare's virtue, 'which grown into a pleurisy, dies of its own too-much'.

Lara dreams of some 'reserves' and Crofter's man a mountain theme park. Only small concessions, but mitigation of environmental damage is often all that is on offer. McMoor rejects the 'replica' Black Mountain, just as environmentalists often reject re-routed rivers, or 'replanted' forests. Indeed copies often are not 'as good', certainly there is evidence that 'new growth' forest supports only a fraction of the number of species as ancient woodlands, and that the new straightened riverbed causes flooding. But as with pictures, just occasionally, the copies are worth appreciating on their own merits, and then it is harder to say just what the objection is. Even the slightly metaphysical difference between a 'forgery' and the 'real thing' was held to apply in the case of Fraser Island, off the coast of Queensland, Australia. It being an almost intact ecological sanctuary, industrialists had asked if they could just scoop out some minerals, before 'restoring' the land cover. The Inquiry Commissioners ruled that

> even if, contrary to the overwhelming weight of evidence before the Commission, successful rehabilitation of the flora after mining is found to be ecologically possible on all mined sites on the Island . . . the overall impression of a wild uncultivated island refuge will be destroyed forever by mining.

Mr Crofter's replica mountain sounds unlikely to convey that sort of impression either, but perhaps if it is put in a Glasgow City Square a use can be found for it.

Dilemma 95
Sanctuary Island II: the blackbirds

McMoor is remembering the words of St Francis of Assisi (1182–1226), perhaps. 'Not to hurt our humble brethren (the animals) is our first duty to them, but to stop there is not enough. We have a higher mission – to be of service to them whenever they require it.' Or perhaps he recalls the more recent writings of William Ralph Inge (1860–1954), who warned:

> We have enslaved the rest of animal creation, and have treated our distant cousins in fur and feathers so badly that beyond doubt, if they were to formulate a religion, they would depict the Devil in human form. . . . The great discovery of the nineteenth century, that we are of one blood with the lower animals, has created new ethical obligations which have not yet penetrated the public conscience.

The contemporary philosopher Mary Midgley, once asked whether if Robinson Crusoe set fire to his island on leaving, he would have breached his 'duty' to the land? On most views of 'duties', as there are no people there to be affected, the answer would be no. Similarly, John Rawls concludes *A Theory of Justice*, having just carefully worked out how society can be seen as a special kind of social contract, by saying that even so, 'Not only are many aspects of morality left aside . . . but no account can be given of right conduct in regard to animals and the rest of nature'.

Midgley blames the Roman philosopher, Grotius, for the problem, saying that by 'ditching' the classical notion of 'natural law' in which all species have rights, for a new system open only to human beings, he sent justice astray. But even with natural law, she goes on, the exceptions are manifold, and seem to undermine the whole basis of the system. What about the interests of:

- the dead (past generations)
- the unborn (future generations)
- the very young (infantile)
- the very old (senile)
- the insane, temporarily or more permanently, and the 'incapacitated' (on drugs? depressed?) or
- the severely mentally handicapped?

Midgley herself concludes that duties cannot be limited to 'rational' agents, and if we attempt to, the principle will be inadequate to govern behaviour – as too few actual 'real' cases will be covered. In the old days, however, and perhaps it is this that McMoor remembers, it was not the duty to our fellows that governed behaviour, but rather the one to God, and that duty covered many more cases. Indeed, it may even have included 'duties' towards plants, rocks, rivers and, of course, trees.

Tree rights

Now we're getting somewhere: tree rights?

In 1974, an American lawyer, Christopher Stone, wrote a paper entitled 'Should Trees Have Standing?', by which he meant legal standing or status, rather than any more obvious sort. This followed a court case in which some environmentalists, trying to protect Giant Redwoods, had been told that they hadn't sufficient interest in any particular case (tree). Christopher Stone drew from this the conclusion that the legal system had been too concerned with individual human behaviour. Unfortunately it is institutional

---

321

systems, particularly corporations, who nowadays are most in need of social control.

So, in answer to the question 'What sort of new controls can be, and must be adopted to control corporations?', to protect the environment, he suggests appointing legal guardians to natural objects. For example, a forest, perceived to be endangered, would have a guardian that was known to be a friend of that object, such as the US Sierra Club or the Natural Resources Defense Counsel. McMoor could have been a guardian for Black Mountain, if there was such a provision in Scottish law, which there isn't.

Guardians would have the right of inspecting the land's condition and bringing it to the court's attention, as well as carrying out tasks such as monitoring, and setting legal standards. (And, in the discussion of the *bunya bunya* trees in Dilemma 65, we recall that Aboriginals thought of this system a long time ago.)

> It is not inevitable, nor is it wise, that natural objects have no rights to seek redress in their own behalf. It is no answer to say that streams and forests cannot have standing because streams and forests cannot speak . . . One ought, I think, to handle the legal problems of natural objects as one does the problems of legal incompetents.

Under California law, lawyers are frequently assigned to speak for corporations, universities, states, even unborn children, so why not the environment? he asks. Of course 'Whenever it carves out "property" rights; the legal system is [also] engaged in the process of creating monetary worth. I am proposing that we do the same with eagles and wilderness areas.' The significance would be that you could start fining polluters because their behaviour is 'bad for nature', not just because of any effects on people.

Dilemma 96
Sanctuary Island III: the sourpuss

Steller's Sea Cow, as large as a bus and three times as heavy, was otherwise believed fished out by 1768. Economic usefulness certainly didn't help it then. So, can economics, which puts only human interests (and selfish ones, at that), into the balance, *really* come to the rescue of the environment?

Many so-called 'Deep Greens' would endorse Lara's strategy for wildlife conservation through hunting. Even the 'father' of radical ecology, Aldo Leopold, talks of 'bushmeat' and prefers a vision of the environment where hunting is the only sort of 'management' of the wildlife allowed (he abhors the domesticity of nature reserves, national parks and the like). In Leopold's phrase, the highest form of sustenance is 'meat from God', hunting down and killing *wild* animals, garnished with a few wild veg. Living off one's own organic farm is second best.

Against that is a perspective which sees hunting for fun as wrong in itself, irrespective of any ecological benefits. One of the most bitterly contested 'dilemmas' of conservation these days is whether to allow the shooting of elephants for their ivory. The argument is that to do so keeps the numbers of elephants down, in parks where the vegetarian beasts have begun to demolish entire forests, and that if the elephants need shooting, then it may as well be 'fun' – and profitable. There is the practical issue of legitimising ivory sales, which may undermine the effort to destroy the market in tusks, a market which in many parts of the world is responsible for the local extinctions of elephants.

The same approach lends itself to production of furs, or shells or whatever. It sees all animals as commodities, as part of a great natural farm. And the only principle is that of sound management. (Plants too may be valuable for as future genetic resources for medical or other purposes.) The oldest and most successful management of this kind was that of the Australian Aboriginals, before the arrival of the Europeans.

Moving beyond animals though, water meadows, wetlands and river systems are now recognised as being not only 'nice' to protect and preserve, but economically essential too. The errors of the twentieth century in ignoring nature have proved expensive. Studies have frequently found that the economic value of marshes is higher than the value of the land used for crops, and the value of forest is higher than that of grazing land for cattle. Marshes and coastal wetlands are a key part of the entire water cycle, crucial to fish life both in the rivers and in the seas. They host many of the world's bird species, and are a reservoir for aquatic plants. They are valuable as sea defences, and for recreation and tourism. Forests play a central role in climate: they absorb the heat of the sun, and protect the land from desertification. They trap and slowly release moisture and help prevent flash floods. They support not just one but three ecological systems: the canopy, shrub and ground layers, each of which can be sustainably harvested. Today, European countries are not building but bulldozing the dykes, rivers are not being straightened but allowed to meander and overflow again, and concrete sea defences are being replaced with sand dunes and salt marshes.

Similarly, destruction of forests for grazing, often justified as necessary for 'poor countries' to create logging income and arable farms for feeding their people, makes little economic sense, and often destroys the livelihoods of a hidden majority, in the interests of short-term profits for a few. In Australia, Malaysia and Indonesia, large transnational companies extract one-off profits from forest clearance, whilst indigenous people are forced from their traditional lands and homes. But it is not just these forgotten people who lose. The wider populations lose the greater economic value of sustainable forestry, of selective cropping, and of course tourism. They also lose the climatic functions of the forests in regulating the water and temperature cycles, and providing heat sinks for these equatorial lands. Not for nothing are the brave glittering new towers of these modern cities like Kuala Lumpur, Bangkok and Shanghai, to name just a few, swathed in choking acrid smogs much of the year.

Astonishingly, one third of China is now desert, and the sands are blowing round the streets of Beijing. Massive programmes of reforestation have failed, even as, in the name of economic necessity, work proceeds on river projects which are destined to destroy forests the size of whole countries. The examples of the former Soviet Union and Australia argue an economic case for conservation – but then economics contains more politics than it does economics. Holmes Rolston concludes:

> Several billion years' worth of creative toil, several million species of teeming life, have been handed over to the care of this late-coming species in which mind has flowered and morals have emerged. Ought not those of this sole moral species do something less self-interested than to count all the produce of an evolutionary ecosystem as rivets in their space ship, resources in their larder, laboratory materials, recreation for their ride? . . . If true to their specific epithet, ought not *Homo Sapiens* value this host of species as something with a claim to care in its own right? . . . There is something overspecialised about

an ethic held by the dominant class of *Homo Sapiens*, that regards the welfare of only one of several million species as an object of duty. If this requires a paradigm change about the sort of things to which duty can attach, so much the worse for those ethics no longer functioning in, nor suited to, their changing environment. The anthropocentrism associated with them was fiction anyway. There is something Newtonian, not yet Einsteinian, besides something morally naïve, about living in a reference frame where one species takes itself as absolute and values everything else relative to its utility.

Dilemma 97
B-movie openers

These ethical scenarios are both from a movie called *The Bombmaker*, made in 2000. The utilitarian judgement might be that the Irish housewife should not do the terrorists' bidding, as it is one life against many. Then again, on grounds of principle, she should not do it either as if she makes the bomb she is guilty of doing something very wrong, whereas if they kill her daughter the guilt is entirely theirs. Some consolation really, you might think. Funnily enough, in the movie, she decides that it is okay to build the bomb, which is a kind of emotivist theory. Perhaps she is influenced by the writing of A. J. Ayer, who as one of the 'Vienna circle' of 'logical positivists' announced that:

> in so far as statements of value are significant, they are ordinary 'scientific' statements; and in so far as they are not scientific, they are not in the literal sense significant, but are simply expressions of emotion which can be neither true nor false.

> (*Language, Truth and Logic*, 1936)

In fact, Ayer concludes on behalf of his fellow circular colleagues, 'we find that ethical philosophy consists simply in saying that ethical concepts are pseudo-concepts and therefore unanalysable'.

Or the housewife may just be thinking of the 'Little Prince' in the classic illustrated book, ostensibly for children, that:

> It is only with the heart that one can see rightly; what is essential is invisible to the eye.

> (Saint-Exupéry, *Le Petit Prince*, 1943)

325

Anyway, in the event, fortunately the SAS turn up and shoot everyone.

Now in Part 2, the situation is more suitable for a heated debate. Clearly, on the one hand, the little girl is under the moral duty to keep a promise, albeit one made under duress. Kant would say this was straightforward enough, she must not pick out the kidnapper or otherwise identify him. (Anyway, he's not so bad – he doesn't kill little girls, only helps in bomb plots.) But others might say that her duty is to the law and society at large, and she must identify the criminal.

In the film, the little girl actually lets the kidnapper get away with it. We are invited to forgive him. Which is a very nice Christian ethic in itself, of course.

Dilemma 98
The main feature

Discussions

Well, according to our resident movie ethics buff, Zev Barbue, it is. This is what Zev says is going on:

ZEV: The sex/violence theme expresses a strong claim put by man to extend his universe, to suspend any predefinition of his existence, to dislocate anything that has been located, to undo anything that has been done so as to make available everything in every place and at any time.

STUDENT 1: But Alex and the droogs also enjoy the violence, they have an insatiable appetite for more and more cruelties, and the pleasure of inflicting fear and humiliation!

STUDENT 2: (*dozed through most of film, anyway*): Why?

STUDENT 1: Don't ask why – they *consume* it, just as ordinary people consume goods and money. Alex is a true 'terrorist' – the creation of fear is the end, not just the means.

Does that make any difference?

ZEV: If you want to live for pleasure you have to put up with aggression, one man's meat is another man's poison; if you want a safe home, you have to accept Big Brother; if you want technology, you have to put up with mad scientists; if you want total individualism, you have to accept the law of the jungle; if you want the Welfare State, don't complain about hooligans and layabouts.

Towards the end of the film, Alex ends up in hospital, covered to the chin in plaster and reduced from being a symbol of independence, expressed in extreme aggression, to a symbol of complete, infantile dependence, as he is symbolically carried into the 'home' he had earlier on smashed his way into. Now the film warns that those who use violence will also suffer it.

A bit more about film ethics

Film ethics is quite the thing in philosophy departments, these days. It is after all, a very pleasant way for a tired student to pass the time. Its great advantage is it doesn't seem like doing ethics at all. Its great disadvantage is . . . it doesn't seem like doing ethics at all. Not only films, but television programmes are part of the 'course', and the inevitable baggage of philosophical theory can be reinterpreted as film analysis, so that's not too bad. These philosophers say that mass communications, such as films, are an essential tool for modern society, the ethical cement that used to be provided by the great myths and religions.

But what kind of cement are we using? Matthew Arnold, writing in *Culture and Anarchy* (1882), says the responsible author or artist 'tries not to make what each raw person may like, the rule by which he fashions himself, but to draw ever nearer to a sense of what is indeed beautiful, graceful and becoming, and to get the raw person to like that'.

Unfortunately, films like *A Clockwork Orange* are concerned with ugliness. Voyeurism of the most ungraceful kind, they legitimise sitting and watching someone being brutally raped, someone being tortured, someone being killed.

This brings us back, of course, to the debate over censorship. Amongst film makers it is sometimes said that if the use of music, the stylisation and the 'artistry' of the cinematography make the actual images acceptable, it is because there is some sort of 'distancing' of the audiences from the violence. This notion of 'distancing' is quite important outside films too; it clearly applies to all types of cruelty where people create special terms for what they are doing to whom – perhaps street talk, perhaps racist jargon, perhaps 'technical terms' of scientists

327

and administrators or politicians. We have hinted at the language of police and military 'élite' squads – all full of euphemism and opacity – in the exciting adventures of Wiggles and Illegals, whilst two very media-savvy nations, Israel and the USA, speak of assassinations of suspected subversives as 'focused prevention', or of 'collateral damage', in place of 'civilian casualties', for example.

Whether anyone can learn anything from watching films is a moot point. Many philosophers are sceptical enough about learning ethics from 'actual cases', much less imaginary ones. In a conventional ethical thought experiment for example, like Kant's friend who tries to borrow money despite knowing that he will not be able to pay it back, many philosophers would say we should allow such stories as a convenient 'illustration' of a logical statement, but certainly not as something to embellish. Movies that have so much 'incidental detail' and so little intellectual theory, seem, for these philosophers, to creep in last of all as methods for considering ethical dilemmas.

Yet it is this 'flow' of events that makes a story. And the good one will catch the reader up in the excitement and the anticipation too. As Martha Nussbaum puts it, film ethics is one of the very few times we can see the world as others may see it, to step into the shoes of others – with all the ethical significance that process has.

Special feature: six of the best from the film ethics pantheon

The Seven Samurai (1954) serves as an examination of one of the key virtues, namely 'honour'. It is quite a good yarn about some villagers in sixteenth-century Japan who hire some 'samurai' to protect them from the outlaws and warlords. The samurai emerge at the end with their virtue intact, but with no practical benefits – so what 'value' has courage anyway?

Those not sure are invited to spend another couple of hours watching that old favourite, *Star Wars* (1977) and in particular to consider whether Darth Vadar (that is, James Earl Jones, or at least the voice is) is a Nietzschean 'Superman' – or just a lost soul.

In *Rebel Without a Cause* (1956), Jim (James Dean) is seeking new moral values to replace the tarnished utilitarianism of his dad, and finds 'Kantian deontology' – or at least for movie ethics buffs he does.

In *Do the Right Thing* (1989), 'Mookie' (played by Spike Lee) is a disillusioned young black man who falls out with the local pizzeria (as one does), partly over a girl, partly over the usual selection of Italian celebrities on the walls – 'there ain't no blacks'. And then there's a riot, followed by some obscure references to Malcolm X and Martin Luther King by a white handicapped bloke. Cultural and ethical relativism and stuff.

In *Marnie* (1964) the great director Alfred Hitchock portrays a young woman (Tippi Hedren) who is a past master of fraud and deception, going from job to job cheating her bosses. We find out that she does it only to buy presents for her mum who does not love her. Another town, another job and – drama! – she is recognised by Sean Connery from one of her previous scams. Naturally, they have an affair and it becomes clear to Connery that there is a Freudian aspect to her story – Marnie feels a need to change identities all the time as she cannot come to terms with sexual commitment. Fortunately, a full and therapeutic discussion of all these matters at the end of the film removes the psychological block, and allows for a happy ending for the couple, and presumably ends Marnie's career of crime too. The film makes the case for getting to the psychological route of crime, which is usually (as we know from Dilemma 92) to do with your parents having too much money.

Finally, in *Network* (1976), we see a TV executive making a deal in which terrorists give interviews, tip off the network to their activities, and eventually even carry out their crimes to fit in with the network news requirements. (Naturally, governments are entitled to do this all the time, but then they are always acting in everyone's interests so it does not matter.) This is a good one not only for a film ethics course but for a media studies course or even a politics course. In fact it's only as a film that it's not much use.

Dilemma 99
100 Person Village

Well, someone seems to have done. The shrewd reader will not need telling that the figure of a 100 is just a convenient way to relate some of the well-documented and really rather disconcerting statistics about the present world we live in. Perhaps all the story really shows is that it is not really the same thing to compare the world to a village at all – after all, if it were true that we lived in a village like this, we might be more concerned about it. In ethics, a kind of 'proximity' factor comes into play in many such matters. David Hume summed it up very nicely with his epithet: 'it is not contrary to reason to prefer the destruction of the whole world to the scratching of my finger'.

Now chronically hungry people and the conditions that keep them that way are very dull subjects, as Susan George has rightly said, but the view that there are too many people in the world (and that is why some of them starve) is not only ethically dubious, but factually flawed. The 'Third World' is not even overcrowded – there is no relationship between population per arable acre and poverty – but there is a relationship between land ownership and poverty. Most of the world's population still live on the land. The catch is, most of the world's land doesn't belong to them.

The world food industry is run by the USA, with a bit of help from Canada and Western Europe. The aim of the business is to produce as cheaply as possible (that's where the rest of the world comes in), and to sell for as much as possible – which means selling to the overfed. Indeed the bulk of the world's food nowadays is fed to pigs and cows in preference to people, because the owners of the pigs and cows at least are able to pay. These factory farmed animals are then converted into beef burgers or bacon sandwiches for the 'rich six' at the village high table, who then need to try find a way of losing the excess fat by jogging.

If we return to our original 'lifeboat' metaphor, for a moment, it is as though a third of the lifeboat has been grabbed by one of the burly first-class passengers, squeezing out not one, but half-a-dozen of the economy grade types. The passenger has claimed ownership of the rations, citing their expensive ticket, and installed a large TV set amidships, which they watch whilst munching ship's biscuits and waiting to be rescued – and all around them figures are seen dismally losing the struggle against the waves.

It would surely be labouring the point to say what is 'ethically' wrong with such a lifeboat, nor yet such a village, suffice it to say that the management is not all that it might be. However, although Susan George seems to emphasise what might be called the malign power of 'agribusiness' (like Cargill in the USA, which sells amongst other things, grain, flour, corn, cotton, salt, juices, animal feed . . . perhaps the biggest private business in the world) we might instead emphasise the failure of certain ideas and values. John Maynard Keynes, summing up his General

330

Theory of Employment, in 1936 said 'I am sure that the power of vested interests is vastly exaggerated compared with the gradual encroachment of ideas' and that 'soon or late, it is ideas, not vested interests, which are dangerous for good or evil'. Which is where ethics comes in.

Our villagers might also learn from the experience of the 'rich peasants' of England who, under one Wat Tyler, marched on London in a just-slightly-ahead-of-its-time Marxist revolution (1381). Having burnt a few palaces, beheaded an archbishop and so on, they met the King of England who agreed to their revolutionary demand that every man in England be considered equal, 'beneath the king'. 'Are we not all sons and daughters of Adam and Eve?' Wat demanded. Working on the Lord's fields as bonded slaves was no longer on. To Wat's surprise, the King agreed. Our revolutionary hero drank a pint of ale to seal the deal, turned around to tell his followers the good news – and was killed by one of the King's men from behind. Not soon after, all the other revolutionaries were executed too.

And the moral of that story? Don't try stirring up global revolution – the bosses have the edge. But, at the same time, the fact is that the English peasants did achieve their aims in just a few generations. The 'hidden hand' of the market came to their aid. Even without a 'global revolution', the inequalities and injustices that are the norm in '100 Person Village', may not be the end of the story.

Dilemma 100
Voltaire's dilemma

Most of the 'philosophical' arguments against vivisection, that is experiments on animals by human beings for human reasons, are 'utilitarian'. It is therefore perhaps surprising to find that the 'father' of that school is firmly against such arguments. This is what Jeremy Bentham (1748–1832) has to say about it in *The Principles of Morals and Legislation*:

> The day may come, when the rest of the animal creation may acquire those rights which never could have been withholden from them but by the hand of tyranny. The French have already discovered that the blackness of the skin is no reason why a human being should be abandoned without redress to the caprice of a tormentor. It may come one day to be recognised, that the

number of the legs, the villosity of the skin, or the termination of the *os sacrum*, are reasons equally insufficient for abandoning a sensitive being to the same fate. What else is there that should trace the insuperable line? Is it the faculty of reason, or, perhaps the faculty of discourse? But a full-grown horse or dog is beyond comparison a more rational, as well as a more conversible animal than an infant of a day, or a week, or even a month old? But suppose the case were otherwise, what would it avail? The question is not, Can they reason? nor, Can they talk? but *Can they suffer*?

C. S. Lewis (1898–1963), the novelist and (overtly) Christian philosopher, broods that the debate is not in any case 'rational'. Something else is going on in our minds when we start from the position that nature (and animals) are 'out there', and separate from us, waiting for our decisions on whether to spare it – or not. (That long shadow of Descartes again.)

> Now I take it that when we understand a thing analytically and then dominate and use it for our own convenience we reduce it to the level of 'Nature' in the sense that we suspend our judgements of value about it, ignore its final cause (if any), and treat it in terms of quantity . . . something has to be overcome before we can cut up a dead man or a live animal in a dissecting room. . . . It is not the greatest of modern scientists who feel most sure that the object, stripped of its qualitative properties and reduced to mere quantity, is wholly real. Little scientists, and little unscientific followers of science may think so. The great minds know very well that the object, so treated, is an artificial abstraction, that something of its reality has been lost.
>
> (C. S. Lewis, *The Abolition of Man*)

George Bernard Shaw said that once you grant the ethics of the vivisectionist

> you not only sanction the experiment on the human subject, but make it the first duty of the vivisector. If a guinea pig may be sacrificed for the sake of the very little that can be learnt from it, shall not a man be sacrificed for the sake of the great deal that can be learnt from him? . . . You do not settle whether an experiment is justified or not by merely showing that it is of some use. The distinction is not between useful and useless experiments, but between barbarous and civilised behaviour . . . for vivisection is a social evil because if it advances human knowledge, it does so at the expense of human character.

332

Dilemma 101
The pragmatic response

Even if you were to adopt such an attitude of 'perfect indifference', many would
say the vivisector was still behaving with dubious 'rationality'. After all, 'results
from animal tests are not transferable between species, and therefore cannot
guarantee product safety for humans. . . . In reality these tests do not provide
protection for consumers from unsafe products, but rather they are used to protect
corporations from legal liability', to quote one Baltimore medic, Herbert
Gundersheimer (in 1988).

That's one opinion. But more important than the argument over 'the facts' is the
argument, as Shaw says, over the values. After all, as Rousseau wrote in his prize-
winning essay 'Discourse on the Origins of Inequality' (1755), to make sense of it
all we must first of all start by 'setting aside the facts, as they will not affect the
question'. But too often ethics is taken as handmaiden to a survey of the facts. Let
C. S. Lewis instead sum up the different kinds of 'morality' inherent in this final
debate, and the significance of society's selection, echoing Plutarch's (unheeded)
warnings 2,000 years before. It is about animals, yes, but it is also about
ourselves.

> It is the rarest thing in the world to hear a rational discussion of vivisection.
> Those who disapprove of it are commonly accused of 'sentimentality', and
> very often their arguments justify the accusation. They paint pictures of pretty
> little dogs on dissecting tables. But the other side lie open to exactly the same
> charge. They also often defend the practice by drawing pictures of suffering
> women and children whose pain can be relieved (we are assured) only by the
> fruits of vivisection. . . . Now vivisection can only be defended by showing it to
> be right that one species should suffer in order that another species should
> be happier . . .
>
> The victory of vivisection marks a great advance in *the triumph of ruthless,*
> *nonmoral utilitarianism over the old world of ethical law*; a triumph in which we,
> as well as animals, are already the victims, and of which Dachau and
> Hiroshima mark the more recent achievements. In justifying cruelty to animals
> we put ourselves on the animal level. We choose the jungle and must abide
> by our choice. . . . You will notice I have spent no time in discussing what
> actually goes on in the laboratories. We shall be told, of course, that there is

333

surprisingly little cruelty. That is a question with which, at present, I have nothing to do. *We must first decide what should be allowed*: after that it is for the police to discover what is already being done.

And let that also be the moral of our story too.

Glossary

Aristotle (384–322 BC) is often credited with being the true 'father' of Western philosophy, and nowhere does his name appear to be held in more reverence than in ethics courses. His views are set out in the Eudaemian and the Nicomachean Ethics where he wisely notes that 'without friends, no one would choose to live, though he had all other goods'. Other doctrines often attributed to Aristotle, notably the merit of fulfilling your 'function', of cultivating the 'virtues', and of the 'golden mean' between two undesirable extremes are, of course, all much older. Indeed **Plato** puts the ideas forward much more cogently.

Nonetheless, one important difference between Aristotle and Plato is there in the *Nicomachean Ethics*, where Aristotle starts with a survey of popular opinions on the subject of 'right and wrong', to find out how the terms are used, in the manner of our 'customary rules' (Dilemma 4). Plato makes very clear his contempt for such an approach. Thomas Hobbes said that it was this method that had led Aristotle astray, as by seeking to ground ethics in the 'appetites of men', he had chosen a measure by which (for Hobbes) correctly there is no law and no distinction between right and wrong.

Bentham (1748–1832) saw the world as torn between two great forces, the quest for pleasure, and the avoidance of pain. In *The Principles of Morals and Legislation* (1781) he writes that:

> Nature has placed mankind under the governance of two sovereign masters: *pain* and *pleasure*. It is for them alone to point out what we ought to do, as well as to determine what we shall do. On the one hand the standard of right and wrong, on the other the chain of causes and effects, are fastened to their throne. They govern us in all we do, in all we say, in all we think.

From this, he intuited that it would be better to maximise the former and minimise the latter, and that all other considerations are irrelevant. This became known as the 'principle of utility', and Jeremy Bentham's writings are a pure form of **utilitarianism**, a doctrine that allows no room for rights or duties, although Bentham allows that these may have socially desirable roles as convenient fictions.

Business ethics is big business, and that justifies its inclusion here, at least on the sort of thinking set out in Dilemmas 87 and 88 and attributed to **Adam Smith**. On one definition, if we might borrow some jargon from economics, *micro*-business ethics looks at the correct (the 'just') management and organisation of commercial enterprises: working practices, recruitment issues, management 'styles', financial accounting and so on, as well as the effects of these enterprises' individual decisions on suppliers and the environment. Then, what might be termed '*macro*-business ethics' needs to consider notions of free will and of rationality as well as the dictates of human rights, as perhaps contrasted with that form of **utilitarianism** known as *Pareto optimality* – which is the attempt to arrange the world so that as many people as possible are 'satisfied'.

Collateral damage and the Doctrine of Double Effect According to Robert Elias, a US professor of political science who recently seems to have 'disappeared', the list of US wars of liberation in the second half of the twentieth century caused considerable numbers of deaths, most of them civilians.

Glossary

Nicaragua: 30,000 dead
Brazil: 100,000 dead
Korea: 4 million dead
Guatemala: 200,000 dead
Honduras: 20,000 dead
El Salvador: 63,000 dead
Argentina: 40,000 dead
Bolivia: 10,000 dead
Uruguay:10,000 dead
Ecuador:10,000 dead
Peru: 10,000 dead
Iraq: 1.3 million dead
Iran: 30,000 dead
Sudan: 8–10,000 dead
Colombia: 50,000 dead
Panama: 5,000 dead
Japan: 140,000 dead
Afghanistan: 10,000 dead
Somalia: 5,000 dead
Philippines: 150,000 dead
Haiti: 100,000 dead

Dominican Republic: 10,000 dead
Libya: 500 dead
Macedonia: 1,000 dead
South Africa: 10,000 dead
Pakistan: 10,000 dead
Palestine: 40,000 dead
Indonesia: 1 million dead
Greece: 10,000 dead
Laos: 600,000 dead
Cambodia: 1 million dead
Angola: 300,000 dead
Grenada: 500 dead
Congo: 2 million dead
Egypt: 10,000 dead
Vietnam: 1.5 million dead
Chile: 50,000 dead

Recently the invasion of Iraq (2002) added an estimated 500,000 more to the list.

Descartes (1596–1650) warned against conventional thinking, and suggested instead a technique, 'the method of doubt', which should have great value for moral philosophers. His own doubts were assuaged by the manifest absurdity of imagining God not existing, as well as by his famous realisation: 'I think therefore I am'. From these humble beginnings, in no time at all, René Descartes not only convinced himself that there were two quite different things in the world – mind and matter, and that the former should investigate the latter using only means of rational deduction – but created many of our ethical dilemmas too.

Environmental ethics, or at least a conventional view of it, looks at changes caused by human beings to 'the environment', and at whether they are in human interests. Concerns such as 'climate change', 'depletion of the ozone layer', over-pollution of the rivers, the seas and the air, are all essentially human-centred. Concerns about our propensity for destroying habitats and with them animals and plant species, are also sometimes put in terms of the loss to humans – what if such and such a plant contained a cure for cancer? How will we feel if there are no more pandas to look at – even in cages? Other ethicists say self-interest, when it is fully understood, leads inexorably, in a sort of holistic way, to respect not only for other humans, but for all creation. Either way, much of environmental ethics still concerns the same sort of human self-interest as any other ethics.

The human perspective that taming of nature is 'good', and the dangerous or simply inconvenient activities of wild nature are 'bad' is what so-called 'Deep Ecologists' insist that we must move away from – and to accept that what is good for us is not necessarily good for nature, and that we should instead begin to apply values such as 'freedom and autonomy' to rivers and animals, and 'respect for others' to trees and mountains.

The first step in moving to a wider concern for the environment would be to consider the interests of animals, and that is one reason why so many of the problems here relate to animal rights. Pollution of habitats: perhaps rivers full of raw sewage, air full of toxic particles from industrial processes, seas dying from agricultural run-off, as well as many more subtle, harder-to-spot changes, will in the first place affect animals. Second, what we eat is both profound, pervasive and fundamental. Our attitudes and our whole approach to life stem from fulfilment of this basic need. 'There is nothing more intimate than eating, more symbolic of the connectedness of life, and more mysterious', as one 'Deep Green', Paul Callicott, put it.

Hippocrates (*c.*450 BC) was a physician who maintained early on that epilepsy and other illnesses were not the result of evil spirits or angry gods, but due to natural causes. He has been called the 'Father of Medicine', and the 'wisest and greatest practitioner of his art'. Hippocrates of Cos taught the sanctity of life and called other physicians to the highest ethical standards of conduct. The Oath of Hippocrates marked a turning point because for the first time it created a complete separation between curing and killing. The Oath says:

> I swear by Apollo Physician, by Asclepius . . . I will use treatment to help the sick according to my ability and judgement, but never with a view to injury and wrongdoing. I will neither administer a poison to anybody when asked to do so, nor will I suggest such a course.

No support there for euthanasia. And similarly, it continues, 'I will not give to a woman a pessary to cause abortion'. Nonetheless, under Hippocrates, medicine emerged as the prototype of the learned professions.

David Hume (1711–76) is a humbugger of ethics. ' 'Tis an object of feeling – not of reason!' he scoffs. And in his Treatise on Human Nature (1740) he warns: 'when you pronounce any action or character to be vicious, you mean nothing, but that from the constitution of your nature you have a feeling or sentiment of blame from the contemplation of it'. Vice and virtue are merely qualities which we see in things, just as we see colours. And Hume continues:

> I cannot forbear adding to these reasonings an observation which may, perhaps, be found of some importance. In every system of morality, which I have hitherto met with, I have always remark'd, that the author proceeds for some time in the ordinary way of reasoning, and establishes the being of a God, or makes observations concerning human affairs; when all of a sudden I am supriz'd to find, that instead of the usual copulations of propositions, *is* and *is not*, I meet with no proposition that is not connected with an *ought* or an *ought not*. This change is imperceptible; but is however of the last consequence.
> (Book III, 'Of Morals', Part I)

The *I Ching* or *Book of Changes* (*c*.3000 BC) is the oldest philosophical text in the world, and a deeply ethical one – essentially a guide to living. It consisted originally of eight (later sixty-four) 'hexagrams' which are randomly created by throwing either coins or yarrow sticks. It is believed to have first taken written form 3,000 years ago, and has been part of the decision making process for Chinese emperors, generals and 'statesmen' ever since. Confucius considered the Book of Changes to be one of the 'Five Classics', and this endorsement spared the text from the book burning of the third century BC when much other Chinese philosophy disappeared, albeit to reappear (disguised) amongst the Ancient Greeks.

Islam (AD 700 onwards) is a global faith. Nearly one person in seven – some 800 million people in over seventy-five countries – is a Muslim, and it is the fastest-growing religion in the world today. Within a century of its being introduced amongst the Arabs in the seventh century, Islam governed and regulated an empire larger than that of either Rome or (Aristotle's errant pupil) Alexander. The word 'Islam' means 'submission' – to God, and there is no God but Allah, of whom Mohammed is a messenger, as was Jesus too. A solemn recitation of faith is required of every Muslim every day, facing Mecca.

The *Koran* is revered by Muslims as the literal word of God, superseding all previous revelations, such as the Bible. It forbids gambling, the consumption of animal blood, foods offered to pagan gods and idols, pork and alcohol and the eating of carrion. It describes at length punishment in hell and reward in paradise. The 'Sharia', or Islamic law, is cruel and seems barbaric. The penalty for habitual thievery may be loss of a hand; for pre-marital sex it may be 100 lashes in public; for adultery it can be death. All this sits uncomfortably with stories of the prophet's own life such as that telling how, on awakening from his rest one afternoon, Mohammed found a small, sick cat sound asleep on the fringe of his cloak. The Prophet cut the corner off his garment, allowing the cat to sleep on undisturbed.

Islamic ethics is an all-embracing comprehensive approach to living, covering all aspects of both individual and social life. There is no distinction between material and spiritual, physical and mental, religious and political, and the most minute act is seen as being subject to guidance by ethical experts, who are by definition, religious leaders. Fortunately, for the practicality of such a totalitarian doctrine, Good (Hasan) and Bad (Qibih) are subdivided into imperative, recommended, allowed, and forbidden or disapproved of, with vagueness entering into many decisions. Almsgiving to the poor, aged and orphans is an obligation, as is a yearly 2.5 per cent *zakat* tax on your total assets. As for the treatment of women, the *Koran* is ambiguous.

Mohammed instructed his followers to respect those 'who have borne you as mothers' and gave Muslim women civil and property rights – still a revolutionary step in the Arab world. The practice of wearing a 'chador' or a veil is not mandated by the *Koran*; this practice appeared centuries after Mohammed. (Some scholars think that, ironically, 5000 years ago headscarves originally signified a temple priestess responsible for ritual sex as part of fertility rites.) Women are merely injuncted to dress 'modestly'. The role allowed for women is hard for Westerners to see as anything other than oppressive and second best, although there are female advocates of it, who say that it in fact provides a superior and honourable role for women.

Justice is traditionally at the heart of ethics, but not necessarily so, as the utilitarians rediscovered in the nineteenth century. Justice is usually summed up as 'to each his own' – you get what you deserve. But how do you decide what someone deserves? Anyway, people all seem to think they deserve better than they have, and at least some of them must be wrong! Lawyers are concerned with 'corrective' justice, which is punishment, but moral philosophers are usually more concerned with 'distributive' justice, which is that complicated calculation of laws, rights and happiness that is (evidently) so difficult to make.

Immanuel Kant (1724–1804) was one of the first salaried, academic philosophers, who churned out dry, dense treatises with tiring titles like *Groundwork of the Metaphysics of Morals* (the *Grundlegung*) which were intended to prop up the creaking edifice of conventional morality, based on 'duty', 'truth telling', 'promises', etc., etc., in an increasingly godless age, with a morality based on logic and 'reason'. But then, that is only what Plato was trying to do all those years ago. Like Plato too, he had no time for those who argued that 'consequences' had a place in the philosopher's calculations.

Aldo Leopold (1887–1948) developed an interest in ornithology and natural history, and graduated in forestry. Today, he is considered the father of wildlife conservation in America. His views are set out in several of the Dilemmas (especially 83–86) but can be summed up as man-eating wolves are good, and people are bad, although wolf-eating people are slightly less so. Appropriately or not, he died while helping his neighbours fight a grass fire.

Lying (Some more lying words for deceitful lovers.) The greatest advance in the philosophy of lying and promise-breaking in recent years has been the deconstruction of 'language' by Jacques Derrida and other so-called 'post-modernists'. Derrida claims that there is 'no transcendent logos', which is a waffly way of saying that there is no such thing as 'truth', let alone 'right and wrong'. This is a post-modern ethics; a 'value-free ethics' and is not really ethics at all.

But the value-free approach has found plenty of fertile ground. Academics in literature and history, for example, fell hungrily upon the theory, and devoured it whole. The debate about whether there is a distinction to be drawn between a history of events that 'actually happened' and one that the author has just made up as they go along, for example, still rages.

Aided by general cynicism towards 'politics', 'the media' and so on, surveys in the USA amongst college students have found that one-third felt it really was okay to cheat to pass exams and that half had stolen something in the past year. The students had justifications for their behaviour which included a rejection of the 'dominant' value system, often citing unsavoury aspects of it. Like the post-modern historians, they were refusing to allow one 'narrative' to dominate and displace theirs. Not that they would have put it quite like that, of course.

G. E. Moore (1873–1958) accused other philosophers of committing something he called the 'naturalistic fallacy', which is supposing that right and wrong exist in nature. Instead, Moore thought you had to derive moral values either by logic or by intuition. In nature, there is no 'right' or 'wrong' about it. This is all set out in his 1903 magnum opus, *Principia Ethica*, where he also declares that 'art' and 'love' must be the defining values of the non-natural world.

Myths Greek culture has been said to be about the supplanting of a mythic tradition with a supposedly straightforwardly rational one, although Paul Feyerabend, author of *Against Method*, says differently. Conventionally, though, when **Plato** and other philosophers return to myth, it is supposedly just by way of description, not as a way to advance the argument. Yet the themes of myths are eternal, concerning the boundary between people and gods, natural and supernatural. Boundaries are where philosophers are to be found, some might unkindly add, 'sitting on the fence'.

Friedrich Nietzsche (1844–1900) was against morality, considering it to be a rather nasty tendency, a sort of form of weakness. Instead he favoured what he called 'antimorality', as where a great man (and it had to be a man) enjoyed his power to the full, untrammelled by dreary notions of 'responsibility', 'duty' or 'pity', let alone (of all things) 'being "good" '. After all, as he puts it at the end of *Ecce Homo*:

> in the concept of the good man common cause [is] made with everything weak, sick, ill constituted, suffering from itself, all that which ought to perish – the law of selection crossed, an ideal made of opposition to the proud and well-constituted, to the affirmative man, to the man certain of the future and guaranteeing the future.

Yet Nietzsche was not really so original. His theory is really just an attack on Christian morality, and many others prior to him (not least Thomas Hobbes) had observed that 'might' is in some sense 'right'. His bizarre prose trumpeting that he at least had 'transcended' all other values, overstates his radicalism, as he had only reversed the conventional ones. Likewise, he promised that his own life would be a Dionysian orgy, with lots of killing and destruction, but of course, had to settle for one that was rather bleaker and less dynamic. Nonetheless, Nietzsche is useful to philosophers in providing an alternative position to the other rather sanctimonious 'smiley' view of ethics.

Paradoxes – moral In ethics there are countless discussions of 'puzzling' or 'paradoxical' cases, like our 'trolley dilemmas'. It is very much the bread and butter of ethical problems.

In particular, many 'dilemmas' can be recast as paradoxes, and it is this paradoxical element that attracts attention. Strictly speaking, a paradox is a kind of contradiction, a kind of logical impossibility, but even very dry logicians like Willard Quine have allowed that any apparently sensible argument that leads to an unacceptable conclusion can be considered paradoxical. (In the process he unfortunately then divides all the paradoxes up into three new types he specially invents: 'veridical', 'falsidical' and 'paradoxes of antinomy'.) Many other 'moral problems' are paradoxical in the sense that outcomes are so bad that doubts are thrown on the assumptions adopted at the outset.

However, the term 'dilemmas' is more familiar within the range of ethical puzzles as it concentrates on the aspects of human choice, choice being the essence of ethics. Judith Thompson's famous violinist, who requires the 'life support' of the unfortunate kidnapped passer-by, for example, can be seen as a paradox; the two conflicting views on the matter – yes, we should help save someone's life if we can, but no, no one should be forced to do things against their will in the interests of another – seem irresolvable. Or the 'lifeboat' scenario (Dilemmas 1 and 2) can be recast similarly as two conflicting views – or as a chain of 'apparently plausible reasoning that leads to an unacceptable conclusion'. For example,

The lifeboat has five people in it
The lifeboat will sink if it has more than four people in it
If the boat sinks everyone on board will drown
Everyone drowning is worse than just one person drowning
Therefore, one person must be thrown overboard

has been suggested as a suitable definition for 'moral paradoxes'.

Plato (427–347 BC) Plato's dialogues recording historical conversations between Socrates and various fellow citizens of Athens range far more widely than 'ethics' is normally allowed to. However, it is clear from his elevation of the 'Form of the

Good', and his metaphor of the Cave, (both in the *Republic*) that ethics is the central concern to which he always returns. The shackled prisoners can only be 'set free' when they let the light thrown out by knowledge of the good illuminate their mangy, miserable existence.

Psychology Psychologists offer four explanations for moral behaviour (as they put it): it is either to please (or to avoid shocking) other members of their social group. Or it may be as a result of the promptings of our conscience; or it may be because of a good upbringing, one that rewarded good behaviour and punished bad; or finally it may be because good behaviour is simply recognised by the (Socratic) rational individual as simply the best way to live in the world. Studies have found little difference between the stated moral beliefs of delinquents and non-delinquents – if anything, the delinquents may be more indignant and intolerant of what they consider to be 'bad' behaviour. (Some psychologists say that 'bad behaviour' is the result of too strong a conscience.) At its extreme, this dissonance can lead to a nervous breakdown, which is why Socrates was sorry for anyone who did anything wrong.

Pythagoras (570–470 BC) Pythagoras was born on the island of Samos. He not only made important contributions to music and astronomy, metaphysics, natural philosophy, politics and theology, he was the first person to bring the concepts of reincarnation, heaven and hell to the Western world, declaring that the doctrines were a personal revelation to himself from God. After the tyrant Polycrates declared him a subversive, he went to Italy, where he established a school of philosophy and a monastic order based on practising vegetarianism, poverty and chastity. Pythagorean meals consisted of honeycomb, millet or barley bread, and vegetables, and the philosopher himself would pay fishermen to throw their catch back into the sea, once even telling a ferocious bear to eat barley and acorns, and not to attack humans any more. Pythagoras not only showed respect for animals, but also for trees, which he insisted were not to be destroyed unless there was absolutely no alternative. Lesser plants too merited concern: on one occasion an ox was injuncted not to trample a bean field.

The famous 'Pythagorean theorem' was in use long before Pythagoras but what was significant about it was the method of deduction. Pythagoras showed (in the manner made famous by Plato in the Socratic dialogue with Meno) that the world could be investigated and explained using human reason, that the laws of nature could be deduced purely by thought alone. Pythagoreans believed that mathematics offered a glimpse of a perfect reality, a realm of the gods, of which our own world is but an imperfect reflection, and contrasted this pure, incorruptible and divine realm with the corruptible, earthly sphere. Sadly, it was in this sphere that the human soul was trapped, caught in the body as in 'a tomb'.

Refugees Since 1951, under the UN Refugee Convention, people fleeing persecution can apply for 'refuge' in any countries that are signatories. But they have to get there first. Which is why the signatories are busy setting up elaborate defences to stop these 'illegals' entering. Again, although many of the people involved are fleeing persecution, as the convention imagines, some are simply fleeing poverty or unemployment. The convention does not oblige countries to take so-called economic migrants, who can be deported to wherever they came from, so there has grown up a kind of migration game in which refugee status is both desirable and jealously protected.

Of 22 million refugees known as such to the UN in 2001, the vast majority were in relatively poor countries, such as Pakistan and Iran, which simply bordered the ones the refugees had fled from, such as Iraq and Afghanistan. The nine richest countries in the world offered in that year to prise open their doors a crack to allow in, between them, about 100,000 refugees.

Rights There are many kinds of rights these days: animal rights, human rights, women's rights, tree rights (see Dilemma 94). But none of them are really worth very much. No one seems to agree on them. Philosophers have spent millennia trying to pin down just what are the 'real' rights, but perhaps Thomas Hobbes came the nearest when he said that there is just one – the fundamental right to self-preservation. From that, to be sure, he derived some more rights, including the 'right to remain silent', and even the right to run away in battles, but that one on its own causes enough problems.

Slavery Today we find churches spearheading social change, calling for civil rights, the protection of unborn children, an end to human rights abuses in other countries, etc. This has not always been the case. On issues such as women's rights and human slavery, religion has impeded social progress. The church of the past never considered slavery to be a moral evil. The Protestant churches of Virginia, South Carolina, and other Southern states actually passed resolutions in favour of it. Human slavery was called 'by Divine Appointment', 'a Divine institution', 'not immoral' but 'founded in right'. Many New Testament verses call for

345

obedience and subservience on the part of slaves. Many of Jesus' parables refer to slaves whilst Paul's infamous epistle to Philemon concerns a runaway slave who he unambiguously states should be returned to his master. Other than Deuteronomy, in the Old Testament, which says 'You shall not surrender to his master a slave who has taken refuge with you', the abolitionist had to find non-Biblical sources to argue the immoral nature of slavery, a cautionary tale for those who take their lead from religion.

Actually, Europeans have not only been slave traders; perhaps a million of them were slaves too. During the medieval period, Islamic pirates in the Mediterranean used to raid the coasts of Italy and Greece in particular, capturing 'Christians' who were then sold as slaves in North Africa. Unlike the European version of slavery though, the slaves were considered as 'fully human' and it was both possible and intended that these prisoners might be freed after payment of a suitable sum to their new owners.

And slavery is by no means merely a historical phenomenon. For example, at the start of the new millenium in Niger alone, there were officially 43,000 slaves. They were descendants of prisoners taken during wars, and were obliged to wear bracelets indicating themselves as such. As well as of course working for their masters for nothing, they were often castrated or told whom they were to marry, and families were split up at the owners' whim. They ate only the 'leftovers'. Naturally their children became slaves too.

This practice had been prevalent in sub-Saharan Africa since the seventh century, and continues in Mauritania, Mali and Chad today – for example. Happily, in Niger, since 2004, the practice has been declared 'incompatible with Islam' and is now illegal under heavy penalties.

Adam Smith (1723–90) is a much more radical philosopher than he is usually given credit for. Where earlier philosophers, such as Plato and John Locke, saw society as needing to be based on altruism, or at least the suppression of selfishness (as in Niccolò Machiavelli and Thomas Hobbes), Smith allows society to be determined by an entirely greater, non-human force – economics. His two great works are the *Wealth of Nations* (1766), still a popular read with right-wing politicians, and the *Moral Sentiments*. This last ties his colours firmly to the mast erected by his friend and fellow Scot, **David Hume**, of ethics as social convention. Smith declares that moral identity, indeed all moral behaviour, depends on social interaction and originates in the observation of others. Yet '**Justice**' becomes the key task of governments, even as economic forces are allowed to let rip.

Utilitarianism is the doctrine that the correct course of action is the one which will produce the most happiness (or pleasure). It is usually ascribed to Jeremy **Bentham** in the eighteenth century, but in fact, in the Platonic dialogue the *Protagoras*, a suggestion is made that what is needed is the ability to weigh up pleasure against pain – an early kind of 'hedonic calculus'. (Hedone being Greek for pleasure – we have the word 'hedonist' for anyone who seems particularly motivated by it.) Speusippus, on the contrary, held that pleasure (and pain) were two sides of the same thing – and that thing was evil.

Voltaire (1694–1778) François-Marie Arouet Voltaire went through several stages in his philosophical life. At one point he followed Isaac Newton's lead and supposed that the world just might be divinely ordered to be the best of all possible worlds, as Dr Pangloss would put it. But as an older man, Voltaire became more pessimistic and instead reworked Newton's view of the universe as a kind of giant machine in which we are all doomed – a view sometimes known as 'pessimistic fatalism'. (Which it is.) Happily, this was a temporary phase, and towards the end of his life Voltaire discovered a chink of light, in that it might be possible for us to take certain small positive actions even in the face of a hostile and godless universe.

Notes and cuttings

Notes on quotes

Words attributed to philosophers in quotation marks or set as extracts are direct
quotations from published works, albeit, as in the Descartes 'lectures', they may
have been put in the context of the 'active voice'. Similarly, the use of italics and
even capitalisation is not usually as in the original, but *anywhere* I felt like.
Disgraceful. Anyway, here are some *essential* notes for tracking down quotations,
references and sources, as well as a few extra leads.

Forward!

More details on the first nuclear war are in: Robert Lifton and Greg Mitchell,
Hiroshima in America: Fifty Years of Denial (New York, 1995) and William Laurence,
Dawn Over Zero: The Story of the Atomic Bomb (New York, 1946).

1 and 2   The lifeboat

Garret Hardin's theory is set out in 'Living on a Lifeboat', published in
BioScience, 24 (1974, pp. 561–68), although in 'The Economics of Wilderness'
in (*Natural History*, 78 (1969), he also notes: 'Making great and spectacular
efforts to save the life of an individual makes sense only when there is a
shortage of people.'

3   The psychologists' tale

The song in the discussion of the dilemma is 'Strange fruit', the singing of which by
Billie Holiday was a significant moment in the growth of the Civil Rights movement
in America. The song starts: 'Southern trees bear a strange fruit / Blood on the
leaves and blood at the root / Black body swinging in the southern breeze /
Strange fruit hanging from the poplar trees'. The images – many of them
postcards! – were collected for the exhibition 'Without Sanctuary: Lynching

Photography in America' by James Allen and John Littlefield, two of the 'ordinary people' but set on 'doing the right thing'.

The Psychology of Moral Behaviour, by Derek Wright (Pelican, 1971) offers a brief summary of that sort of psycho-scientific thinking.

4 Custom is king

One of the most comprehensive collections of this sort of 'cultural relativism' stuff was made by William Graham Sumner, eccentric professor of Harvard University, at the end of the nineteenth century. His book, *Folkways* (first published 1906), packed with such stories, is a classic of the kind.

A recent account of 'cultural relativism' including discussion of the child-slaves is *The Culture Cult, Designer Tribalism and Other Essays*, by Roger Sandell (Westview, 2002). How much slavery is there now anyway? The ILO estimated there were 8.4 million child slaves in 2002.

5 and 6 The internet bargain and the toaster

Thomas Nagel's views on 'Moral Conflict and Political Legitimacy' are published in a paper for the journal *Philosophy and Public Affairs*, 16 (1987, pp. 215–40) as well as in his book *Mortal Questions* [*sic*] (Cambridge University Press, 1979). The issue that he raises of moral conflict is taken further by Judith Wagner de Cew in her paper, 'Moral Conflicts and Ethical Relativism' in *Ethics*, 101 (aptly!) (October 1990, pp. 27–41). The Mill quote on the 'ultimate standard' comes from the section 'The Resolution of Moral Conflicts' in *Utilitarianism*. Bertrand Russell's 'Sceptical Essay' was the 'Conquest of Happiness' (1930) with the other quotation from *Eastern and Western Ideals of Happiness* (1928). A lecture by Phillippa Foot on 'Moral Relativism' is collected in *Relativism Cognitive and Moral* (University of Notre Dame Press, 1982, pp. 152–66) whilst Bernard Williams's views can be read in *Proceedings of the Aristotelian Society*, 75 (1974–75, pp. 215–28).

The strategy of 'debunking' dilemmas can also be traced back to A. J. Ayer, whose *Language Truth and Logic*, published in 1936, marked the high point of the Vienna circle. Named after the city that hosted their meetings, and featuring Wittgenstein as a kind of adjunct member, the group liked nothing better than to discuss the futility of all philosophical discussions. The year 1936 was, however, also the year that its central figure, Moritz Schlick, was gunned down by a jealous student, and that another Austrian philosopher (never invited to join the hallowed circle), Karl Popper, demonstrated precisely the weakness and deficiencies of over-reliance on 'science'. And lastly, it was also the year that Moritz Schlick published a very interesting paper on what can and cannot be 'said', in the *The Philosopher* (see http://www.the philosopher.co.uk).

7 The liar

Maria's correspondence with Kant is collected in volume 11 of the edition of Kant's works published by the Prussian Academy of Sciences (Walter de Gruyter, Berlin, 1922).

11–14 Descartes

Descartes' quotes are taken directly from *Discourse on Method*, part V, 116–17. As to free will, an interesting paper on 'Determinism and the Illusion of Moral Responsibility', by Paul Ree, is on the internet at http://www.zeroaltitude.org

15–21 Some pretty ancient dilemmas

The cheerful Augustinian quotes are from *The Confessions*, Book VII, ch. xii. The woeful ones are from Book II, chs i, iv, vi and x. The Fragments are from Epicurus' books *On the End of Life* and *Ethics*. Seneca's uplifting story is related in a letter, Epistle 9, and Aristotle exempts evil at Book II, 1107 of the *Ethics*.

22–26 Against e-Ville

Bentham's greatest happiness is to be found in *The Commonplace Book* (*Works*, x. 142), Hutcheson's in the *Inquiry into the Original of our Ideas of Beauty and Virtue* (1725) Treatise II, Concerning Moral Good and Evil, section 3, 8. Chairman Mao, whose slogan 'Power comes out of the barrel of a gun' may have caught 'Mad

Dog's' eye, and has a more subtle philosophy of power set out in the numerous articles and speeches of the *Red Book*. For more on anarchism, see *Anarchism*, by George Woodcock (Penguin, 1962). Jean Rostand was writing in *Pensées d'un biologiste* (*Thoughts of a Biologist*, 1939). He goes on: 'Kill everyone – and you are a God'!

27 Breeding experiments

Plato's 'breeding programme' is outlined in the *Republic* in Book V, section 468. Dr Uri wrote in the *Medical Tribune* (24 August 1977) and calculated that if sterilisation was allowed to continue at that rate, all pure blood Indian races would be eliminated by about 2000. Happily, this is not so.

35–39 Notes to censors

The lady in the seashell is of course Botticelli's *Birth of Venus* (*c*.1480). 'The wit' was E. S. Turner, quoted on p. 61, *Youth, Popular Culture and Moral Panics*, by John Springhall, published in the USA by St Martin's Press in 1998. The interrogation is quoted in the same book by John Springhall, a historian with sociological leanings, from which fragrant pot pourri several of the other stories come too. See A. E. Waite's scholarly text *The Quest for Blood* (1997, private printing) for an overview of 'Penny Dreadfuls', a field, as he says, now

> replaced by a vast output of modern blither, in which the voice of vulgarity up to date has replaced the voice of the gutter. It is tares that flourish now and wilted stalks in place of the growths of old – rich hemlock and mandragore.

40–43 Business week

More on *The Blaring Radio* and 'cold bath' ethics is in J. D. Mabbott, *An Introduction to Ethics* (Hutchinson, London, 1966, p. 89). Some interesting UN and related papers on AIDS are at http://www.hivdev.org.uk whilst a conspiracy theory site arguing that AIDS is not communicable at all, other than by direct injection, is at http://www.duesberg.com. George Soros has written a whole book on the sceptical position outlined in *The Witness*. In *The Alchemy of Finance* (1987) he advances his 'anti-Smithomoney' thesis that money is not always good, and, in particular, that financial markets pursue ends contrary to human needs and values.

44 The Devil's chemists

More details in Joseph Borkin, *The Crime and Punishment of I. G. Farben* (Free Press, New York, 1978; Glover, 1977). IBM was also doing business as usual during the war, supplying and maintaining computer systems that recorded (amongst other things) the fate of concentration camp prisoners using six categories. The code for 'exterminated' was '6'.

45–49 A pentad of moral stories

Mill discussed debts in *Utilitarianism* (Everyman edn, ch. v, pp. 45–47). For those with a special interest in this, Kant distinguished between 'perfect' and 'imperfect' duties – repaying money you owe is one of the former, giving money to the poor is one of the latter. Wittgenstein's views on ethics were revealed in a lecture delivered to the philosophy department in Cambridge in November 1929, published in the *Philosophical Review*, 74/1 (January 1965). The debate between Socrates and Euthyphro is in the dialogue the *Last Days of Socrates*. Finally, the Islamic view mentioned can be seen in Usool-e Kafi, 'Anecdotes of the Pious Ones', section on 'The rights of neighbours'.

50 and 51 Monkey business

See also M. Bekoff and D. Jamieson's edited collection *Readings in Animal Cognition* (MIT Press, 1995), or even Theodore Barber on *The Human Nature of Birds* (1993).

52 and 53 Life's not fair and Infantile ethical egotism

An 'alternative' theory of child development by Jean-Jaques Rousseau is described in *Emile*. Rousseau influenced the likes of Jean Piaget and the 'progressive' educationalists by claiming that children are born all right, and are from then on simply influenced, for good or ill, by their environment.

55 The beauty trap

The discussion here follows up some of the points expressed by reviewers of Nancy Etcoff's book of that name, particularly Simon Ings.

60–63 The Panopticon

For example, see *The Panopticon Writings*, edited by Miran Bozovic (Verso, 1995).

64–68 Animals too: the vegetarian's dilemma

Plato's veggie heaven is described in the *Republic* at 372c. Bertolt Brecht (1898–1956) offers the thought in *Die Dreigroschenoper* ('The Threepenny Opera'), II, finale. Nietzsche is nodding *not* to support Nazism, of course, but to support the ideal of the hunter-killer, and I don't suppose Brecht would have either, although his character 'Mother Courage' offers pieces of dubious advice such as: 'Peace is nothing but slovenliness, only war creates order' and 'the finest plans are always ruined by the littleness of those who ought to carry them out'. Fred Brown was quoted in newspaper reports on 19 June 2002. And the dubious Paul's cautionary style of moral guidance can be found in the Bible at: Romans 1:29–30; Romans 13:13; Galatians 5:19–21; Ephesians 4:19; Ephesians 4:29–32; Colossians 3:13; I Timothy 6:6–11; II Timothy 3:2–4.

69–72 Fairy tales

'The Frog-King' and 'The Juniper Tree' are freely adapted from the 1812 version of *Household Tales* by Jacob and Wilhelm Grimm. J. R. R. Tolkein's views on *Faerie* come from *Tree and Leaf* (Allen and Unwin, 1964, pp. 15–16). See *The Philosopher*, vol. LXXXIX, no. 2 (http://www.the-philosopher.co.uk) for an interesting discussion of imagery in philosophical poems, by Chengde Chen, who says that 'the importance of an appropriate image to an abstract theory cannot be overestimated'. Charles Dickens's views are in an article entitled 'Frauds on the Fairies', for the New York journal *Household Works* (1854). Maria Tatar has documented all the social subtexts in her entertaining and erudite deconstructions of fairy tales, *Off With Their Heads* and *The Hard facts of the Grimms' Fairy Tales*.

'The Dreadful Story of Pauline and the Matches' has been adapted (very slightly) from *Struwwelpeter* by Heinrich Hoffmann. Similarly, the pictures here are a new interpretation of the traditional ones.

72   The Illegals

An Australian Senate inquiry heard in 2002 that one boat, codenamed 'SIEV X', epically enough, and carrying some 400 people, sank in October 2001 with the loss of 353 lives. This, despite it having been tracked by Australian Defence Forces since setting out from Indonesia. The inquiry was trying to find out *why* no attempt was made to rescue survivors until several days after the overcrowded boat had sunk. (The only survivors were picked up by Indonesian fishing boats.)

73–76   Stories of Relatavia

Cultural relativism is sometimes traced to the eighteenth-century German anthropologist Johann Gottfried von Herder, American anthropologist Franz Boas and English philosopher Isaiah Berlin. (Well, that's three cultures in agreement then.)

77–82   War ethics

The unpleasant story of bombing in general is told by Sven Linqvist in *A Brief History of Bombing* (Granta, 2002). The 'justice' of wars is discussed in *War and the Liberal Conscience*, Michael Howard (Oxford, 1978). The views of Einstein and Brodie on 'the bomb' are described in *Dilemmas of Nuclear Strategy*, edited by Roman Kolkowicz, a US political philosophy professor (Cassell, 1987). The Brodie essay referred to is 'War in the Atomic Age', collected in *The Absolute Weapon, Atomic Power and the World Order*.

83–86   Environmental ethics

Darwin's comments are from Chapter 2 of *The Origin of Species*. Harvard's own Edward Wilson has warned in *The Future of Life* (2002) that half of all species may disappear by the end of this century. Philosophers refer to the problem of where to draw the line, be it killing dodos or making piles of sand (grain by grain) as the 'Problem of the Heap', or more formally the 'Sorites' paradox. 'Killing the wolf' quotes are from Aldo Leopold, *A Sand County Almanac: Sketches Here and There* (1948) (Oxford University Press, New York, 1987, pp. 129–32) and *Round River* (Oxford University Press, New York, 1993, p. 153). The quote in support of pain is from 'Human Duties and Animal Rights', by Joel Feinberg, in *Rights, Justice and the Bounds of Liberty* (Princeton University Press, 1980). Feinberg argues that if a toothache is bad in itself, not just in its 'consequences', then it must be as bad for a man to have one as a woman, as a lion as a . . . ?

87–88   Money matters

The first two quotes are from Smith's *Theory of Moral Sentiments*, Book I, iii, then from TMS III ii, as well as from Aristotle's *Nicomachean Ethics* Book IV, *c.*1120–35. Then there is a quote from the *Wealth of Nations*, Book IV, ii, before finally back again to the *Moral Sentiments*. For the context of the quotes in 'More money', see *The Theory of Moral Sentiments*, especially sections I, iii and III, ii and the *Wealth of Nations*. For Aristotle's view, it's back to the *Nicomachean Ethics*, Book IV, *c.*1120–35.

The story of the salt tax in India as mentioned in *Death and Taxes*, is told fully in Roy Moxham's bizarre but fascinating book *The Great Hedge of India* (Constable, 2001).

89   Rough justice

The grisly picture of Spiggott is one of many 'improving' images from the nineteenth-century *Newgate Calendar*, published in London and named after the notorious prison there (Volume I, 1824, 13–133). The *Calendar* was one of those books, along with a Bible and the *Pilgrim's Progress*, to be found in any decent English home through most of the nineteenth century. The tales of punishments meted out to highwaymen and other felons were intended to instil the principles of right living in children. One version even featured (as a frontispiece) a picture of a devoted mother giving a copy to her infant son while indicating out of the window at a body swinging eerily on a gibbet.

The reader can find out more about the celebrated Clarence Darrow, including some dandyish pictures of him (and maybe read transcripts of the cases too), on the internet at: http://www.crimelibrary.com

94–96   Sanctuary Island

The legal status of the environment is discussed in academic terms in *Law, Language and Ethics: An Introduction to Law and Legal Method* edited by William Bishin and Christopher Stone (1972, Mineola, NY: Foundation Press) and *Where the Law Ends: The Social Control of Corporate Behaviour* by Stone himself (1975, New York, Evanston, San Francisco, and London: Harper & Row). Tree rights including Stone's 1974 essay 'Should Trees Have Standing?' are frozen forever in *Thinking About the Environment: Readings on Politics, Property and the Physical World*, edited by Matthew Alan Cahn and Rory O'Brien (1996, Armonk, NY: M. E. Sharpe).

Other Sanctuary Island quotes are from John Rawls, *A Theory of Justice* (1972, Oxford, p. 512); from the paper 'Animal Rights: A Triangular Affair' (first printed in *Environmental Ethics*, 2, 1980, pp. 311–38) reprinted in *Environmental Ethics*, ed. Robert Elliot (Oxford University Press, 1995, p. 75) and for Aldo Leopold's view see also the *Sand Country Almanac* mentioned above.

97 and 98   Film notes

Quotes are from: Zev Barbu and Thomas Elsaesser on 'Screen Violence'. Both being essays from *Approaches to Popular Culture*, edited by C. W. E. Bigsby (Edward Arnold, 1976). Then there's more in *Man in the Modern Age*, translated by Eden and Cedar Paul (1951), and Matthew Arnold, *Culture and Anarchy* (1882). Karl Jaspers was writing in *General Psychopathology* (1928).

99   100 Person Village

David Hume's famous epithet can be tracked to the *Treatise of Human Nature*, Book II, Part iii, Section iii. Susan George's unduly controversial, tendentious and partisan account of world poverty, *How the Other Half Dies: The Real Reasons for*

World Hunger, was published by Penguin Books in 1976, and has been reprinted many times since. As to Wat Tyler, an interesting new book on the parallel and more recent 'mystery' of what happened to Congo's first people's leader – Lumumba – is *The Assassination of Lumumba* by Flemish historian Ludo de Witte (2000), detailing the role played by the Belgian commercial as well as political establishment, including the King of Belgium.

100 and 101

The C. S. Lewis quotes are from 'Vivisection', *God in the Dock*, edited by Walter Hooper (Grand Rapids, MI: William B. Eerdmans, 1970, pp. 224, 225, 228) and *The Abolition of Man* (New York: Macmillan, 1947, pp. 81, 82). It's all a bit like Bertrand Russell's swarm of flies which are to be found in just one more of his 'Sceptical Essays': 'Dreams and Facts' (1928).

Further reading

One of the strange things about ethics is that of the wide range of books it has spawned, there are few that have really raised their nose above the crowd. Without doubt, there are many gems of ethics lying undisturbed in the publishers' warehouses, or the basement shelves of libraries. The reader is therefore unable to tap the collective wisdom of 'popular opinion' to find a few books to start with in any area; rather, they must rely either on serendipitous chance (what's in the bookshop or library) or – worse no doubt – some official reading list. I say 'worse' having checked many reading lists in the course of preparing this guide and finding that the 'recommended reads' are really just those of a decade or three ago being reheated and topped with this year's literary cherry. Meanwhile, as it were, all around, the great sea of ethics literature lies unexplored. But here are a few ideas.

Introductions to ethics

Brenda Almond's *Exploring Ethics* (Blackwell, 1998) is an engaging overview of the main ethical theories and perspectives, presented as the discoveries of an explorer coming upon a lost tribe, a literary device if not wholly unexpected, at least more engaging than no literary device.

Peter Singer's *How are We to Live?* is a nice clear essay on ethics as a guide to living, which is the approach I take here too, so why not recommend it. Singer seems to like editing volumes of recycled papers, such as the collection of papers for Oxford University Press, *Applied Ethics* (1986), which includes Thomas Nagel on 'Death', David Hume on suicide, James Rachels on euthanasia, Judith Jarvis Thomson on abortion and John Stuart Mill on capital punishment. There are additional papers on 'Games Theory' and nuclear war, and population ethics, as well as the editor himself on 'All Animals Are Equal'.

Today's Moral Problems (second edition, Macmillan, 1979), edited by Richard Wasserstrom, is another useful tome including the famous *Roe versus Wade* court case, sections on privacy and on 'sexual morality', including pornography, and John Rawls' widely reprinted article 'Two Concepts of Rules'. This last is supposed to explain the difference between justifying a practice like punishment and justifying a particular punishment. (It must be a good point, but I could not follow it, but perhaps it will serve others better.)

Another wide-ranging compendium is James White's *Contemporary Moral Problems*, which ranges from war to welfare and AIDS to animals by way of suicide, capital punishment and euthanasia. Not necessarily, as they say, in that order. But it is *Ethics in Practice*, edited by Hugh LaFollette, that wins the prize for most articles and papers including 'What Do Grown Children Owe Their Parents' by Jane English, and 'The Rights of Alan Bakke' by Ronald Dworkin. Alan, it turns out, was a white would-be student who came up against an affirmative action programme in California and did not like it much.

Ethical theory

Moral Relativism: A Reader, edited by Paul Moser and Thomas Carson (Oxford, 2001) provides a useful summary of academic discourse on that vexed topic. Particularly interesting is Martha Nussbaum's paper with the unlikely title of 'Non-Relative Virtues', which gives a sympathetic account of Aristotle's approach to ethics and the role of virtue theory in deciding the right action – one virtue for each type of decision. There is also a paper on 'Female Circumcision/Genital Mutilation and Ethical Relativism' by Loretta Kopelman, setting out arguments for saying that it 'violates justifiable and universal human rights' and that we should 'promote international moral support for advocates working to stop the practice'.

Five Moral Pieces, by Umberto Eco (Secker & Warburg, 2001) in which Eco discusses vexed moral issues including war ('worse than crime') and media management.

Human nature

Perhaps still on the vexed subject of dying, but really rather more on the vexed subject of social life and human society, is Emile Durkheim's celebrated study *Suicide*, in which Durkheim famously offers a demonstration through collective statistics of that very individual phenomenon. Durkheim's other writings, too, may provide some unexpected ethical insights.

Mary Midgley's *Beast and Man: The Roots of Human Nature* (Methuen, 1978) is an attempt to re-evaluate humanity from the point of view of animals, or rather animal behaviour. Midgley accuses conventional philosophy of misunderstanding and distorting the rest of nature, driven by their own dogmatism and ignorance. A fault, she traces through to the present with the latest crop of 'socio-biological' theories.

Bruce Chatwin's *The Songlines* (Vintage, 1998) contains many subtle and occasionally profound observations on human nature, the environment, racism and war. Vikram Seth's recent illustrated reworking of some traditional tales (*Beastly Tales for Here to There*, Orion Books, 2001) likewise contains many insights and a particularly thought-provoking comparison of the 'Eagle and the Beetle', in which the arrogant eagle comes to rue its wanton and cruel treatment of the beetle's friend, the rabbit. The moral being: even the mighty eagle is not above the revenge of those it contemptuously mistreats. And the relevance to today? Ah, well, that I leave to the reader to decide.

Social justice

As well as Susan George's book, mentioned earlier, there is *Faces of Hunger: An Essay on Poverty, Justice and Development* by Onora O'Neill (Allen & Unwin, 1986); and the Club of Rome's study *The Limits to Growth* (Meadows *et al.*, Pan, 1972) 'on the effects and limits of continued worldwide growth'. Since then, of course, there is now a wide range of popular works decrying trade policy and cultural imperialism, such as John Pilger's 'black armband' book *The New Rulers of the World* (Verso, 2002), but whatever their other claims and merits, they are less philosophical than evangelical.

In my own 'alternative travel' guide, *No Holiday* (Disinformation Company, 2006) I offer additional 'geo-political' stories on Che, human rights and much else beside. The companion book to this, *101 Philosophy Problems* (3rd edn, Routledge, 2007) offers several ethical scenarios including one on 'The Lost Kingdom of Marjons', which is a role-playing look at John Rawls's theory of justice.

Another take on social justice is offered by Adam Smith and his theory of the pre-eminent virtue of money (Dilemmas 87 and 88). Smith's *Wealth of Nations* is not as dull as many might imagine. Indeed, it was once considered quite a rabble rouser. The most important parts are really all in Books I and II, even though the work as a whole is ten times longer. Any edition which includes these two books is enough for a basic grasp of Smith's style, method and main lines of argument. However, the edition edited by Kathryn Sutherland, *An Inquiry into the Nature and Causes of the*

Wealth of Nations: A Selected Edition (Oxford World's Classics) has a very substantial overview of the work too. Those who become obsessed with the dour Scot may like to read more about his life and times in, for example, *Adam Smith*, by R. H. Campbell and A. S. Skinner (Croom Helm, 1982). This is not to mention all the essays on Smith and his contribution to theory in the various specialist journals – an example, the short essay, 'A Note on the Pure Theory of Consumer's Behaviour', which appeared in *Economica* in 1938, by Paul Samuelson – just one part of a great debate started by Smith's *Wealth of Nations*.

Some other historically important works which certainly influenced Smith include *Tableau Economique*, by François Quesnay (1758, but see, for example, the edition by Kuczynski and Meek, published by Macmillan, 1972); the *Discourse on Inequality*, by Jean-Jacques Rousseau (1782); *An Inquiry Concerning Human Understanding* (1748), and *Treatise of Human Nature* (1740) both by Smith's old friend, David Hume.

Works that were in turn influenced by him include *Capital*, by Karl Marx (1867); and *Some Unsettled Questions of Political Economy*, by John Stuart Mill (1844).

Having developed a specialised taste for social science then, the reader may find some leads in *Smith, Marx and After*, by Ronald Meek (Chapman and Hall, 1977), *Capitalism and Modern Social Theory* by Anthony Giddens (Cambridge University Press, 1971) or even *The Political Theory of Possessive Individualism*, by C. B. Macpherson (Cambridge University Press, 1962). On a slightly sourer note *Anarchy, State and Utopia* by Robert Nozick (Basic Books, 1957) and *The Rich Get Richer and the Poor Get Prison* by Jeffrey Reimann (Wiley, 1984) put the opposite case.

For a general discussion of political philosophy, which sets Smith and the other great philosophical figures into context, the reader should make it a categorical imperative to obtain my own *Political Philosophy: From Plato to Chairman Mao* (Pluto Press, 2001).

Sexual politics

Feminism existed in Ancient Greece, and indeed before that too, in China, India and Africa, but the records of it are sparse. So the discussion of gender and sexual politics requires rather more contemporary sources than classical ones. John Stuart Mill's (with Harriet Taylor Mill) definitive text, *The Subjection of Women*, is one, though. Alice Roosi's collection *Essays on Sex Equality* (University of Chicago Press, 1970) contains the key writings of both. Another 'classic' perhaps is Bertrand Russell's *Marriage and Morals* (1929) in which Russell discusses 'the place of love in family life', amongst other things. More recently, *In a Different Voice: Psychological Theory and Women's Development* (Harvard, 1982) by Carol Gilligan suggests that 'a consciousness of the dynamics of human relationships' is 'central to moral understanding'.

Kate Millett's well-known *Sexual Politics* (Virago, 1979) is an entertaining account of sexual politics divided into three sections: the theory, the historical background, and the literary casebook. This last involves dissecting the works of D. H. Lawrence, Henry Miller, Jean Genet and Norman Mailer – all well-known misogynists of course.

Janet Radcliffe Richards's *The Sceptical Feminist: A Philosophical Enquiry* (Routledge, 1980) offers an avowedly 'analytic' interpretation of women and society, saying, for example, that current attitudes towards abortion are part of a male attempt to punish women's sexual activity, that 'women's work' is 'rightly' not valued and that prostitution, self-adornment and even logic are 'okay'.

Genetics

The Blind Watchmaker (Penguin, 1986), by Richard Dawkins, is an example of the new 'popular science' type book, in this case offering a restatement of the power of natural selection to explain evolution and, the author 'controversially' goes on, 'the meaning of life' itself. In similar vein is *The Selfish Gene* (1976).

A more conventional survey of *Our Genetic Future* (Oxford University Press, 1992) is offered by the British Medical Association (subtitle: *The Science and Ethics of Genetic Technology*) in a paperback offering a workmanlike overview of both the main areas of research and the arguments prevailing 'for and against'. Screening, copyright issues, genetic modification of animals are all included. Bryan Appleyard's *Brave New Worlds: Genetics and the Human Experience* is a more palatable introduction to the subject, containing the usual journalistic blend of 'quotes from philosophers' and case studies.

Legal issues

The Ethics of Homicide (Cornell University Press, 1978), by Philip Devine, is 'a timely and challenging commentary on all forms of killing, including abortion, capital punishment, euthanasia, suicide, murder and war', comprehensive rather than enlightening, and its great merit is only in firm assertions such as 'one ought not for instance place a bomb on an airplane in which other people are going to travel'. Perhaps *Political Violence*, by Ted Honderich (Cornell, 1977), which deals with the kind of issues raised by our would-be e-Ville doers, is a more worthwhile read – Honderich does at least allow for occasional acts of violence in 'the cause of democracy' as it is put there. Or there is Jonathan Glover's little paperback, *Causing Death and Saving Lives* (Penguin, 1977), in which he too considers issues such as when to switch off life-support machines, execute prisoners or abort babies. Glover too takes up the issue of state authority to cause death (*vide* bombing Dresden or crushing Messrs Spiggot), quoting with disapproval G. E. M. Anscombe who once said that states ('rulers') had the right to kill as the threat of violent coercion was 'essential to the existence of human societies'. More recently, in *Five Moral Pieces* (Secker & Warburg, 2001), Umberto Eco discusses various vexed moral issues including war ('worse than crime') and 'media management'.

Honderich and Glover are pursuing the right to kill people who are very much alive. More specifically on the question of killing people who may not 'really' be alive is *Life's Dominion* (HarperCollins, 1995) by Ronald Dworkin, concerned with the ethical issues governing the acceptability (or otherwise) of abortion and euthanasia. Dworkin approaches the subject from the perspective of the lawyer, and much of the book is spent discussing various celebrated cases, such as *Roe versus Wade* (access to abortion) and *Griswold versus Connecticut* (access to contraception).

In the same sort of area are John Harris's book *The Value of Life* (Routledge, 1985), and for those who like their medical ethics packaged as 'dilemmas', *Moral Dilemmas in Modern Medicine*, edited by Michael Lockwood, offers a collection with a 'case study' flavour, including many of medical ethics' favourite philosophers: Warnock, Raanan Gillon, even Michael Lockwood. Not to mention *Pornography: Marxism, Feminism and the Future of Sexuality*, by Alan Soble (Yale, 1986), which is a comprehensive introduction that should provide leads for approaches too.

Lying

Lying, as we have seen, was a great concern of Kant's but it has its more recent followers too. Sissela Bok's *Lying: Moral Choice in Public and Private Life* (Harvester Press, 1978) makes the issue the starting point for a discussion of professional ethics, and includes a useful selection of the writings on the topic of St Augustine, Thomas Aquinas, Francis Bacon and so on. Her later book, *Secrets: Concealment and Revelation* (Oxford, 1982) takes us into business ethics and issues like 'whistle-blowing'.

Animal rights

Peter Singer is one of the loudest voices in defence of the animal kingdom, and has written several influential and accessible works including *Practical Ethics* (second edition, Cambridge, 1993) – ostensibly an introduction to the whole field of course! – and an edited summary *In Defence of Animals* (Blackwell, 1985) which includes papers by Tom Regan, Stephen Clark and Mary Midgley, as well as some on 'activists and their strategies', by Alex Pacheco, Donald Barnes and Philip Windeatt, amongst others. Another less readable but more 'classroom-oriented' collection is *Ethics, Humans and Other Animals*, introduced by Rosalind Hursthouse, which includes various study exercises and summaries, for example: 'Midgley on Speciesism', 'Singer on Killing'.

Environmental ethics

Gaia: A New Look at Life on Earth (Oxford, 1979), by the scientist James Lovelock, is certainly a gentle way to start thinking about our obligations to Planet Earth, if rather less useful for those looking to establish philosophical theories of tree rights. Better for that is probably Christopher Stones's *Earth and Other Ethics: The Case for Moral Pluralism* (Harper & Row, 1987), or Richard Sylvan and David Bennett's *The Greening of Ethics* (White Horse Press, 1994).

Index

F

G

surveillance 264–7; vivisection and non-moral 333

V

vivisection 333–4; and Descartes' experiments 16–17; in drug tests 220–1; Fontaine and Shaw's views of 179; Voltaire's view of 177–8

W